DECIDING WHAT TO TEACH

title entry

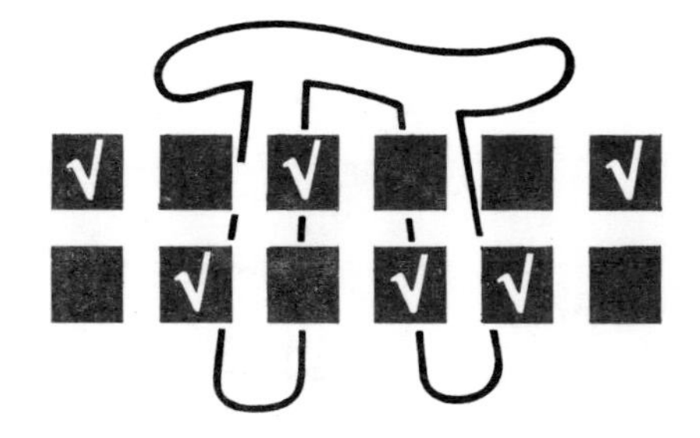

Project on the Instructional Program of the Public Schools ■ National Education Association ■ 1201 Sixteenth Street, N.W., Washington, D.C. 20036

DOROTHY M. FRASER is the writer of this report. She is professor of education, Hunter College, City University of New York.

First Printing, October 1963
Second Printing, February 1964

 ■ Library of Congress Catalog No. 63-22608

Single copy: cloth, $3.25; paper, $2.25. Discounts on quantity orders: 2-9 copies, 10 percent; 10 or more copies, 20 percent. All orders not accompanied by payment will be billed with shipping and handling charges added. Orders amounting to $2 or less must be accompanied by payment. Order from and make checks payable to the National Education Association, 1201 Sixteenth Street, N.W., Washington, D.C. 20036. ■ Other major reports of the Project on Instruction are the following–Published by NEA: *Education in a Changing Society,* cloth, $2.75; paper, $1.75. *Planning and Organizing for Teaching,* cloth, $3.00; paper, $2.00. Published by McGraw-Hill Book Co.: *Schools for the Sixties.* ■ Information concerning other Project publications may be found on page 262.

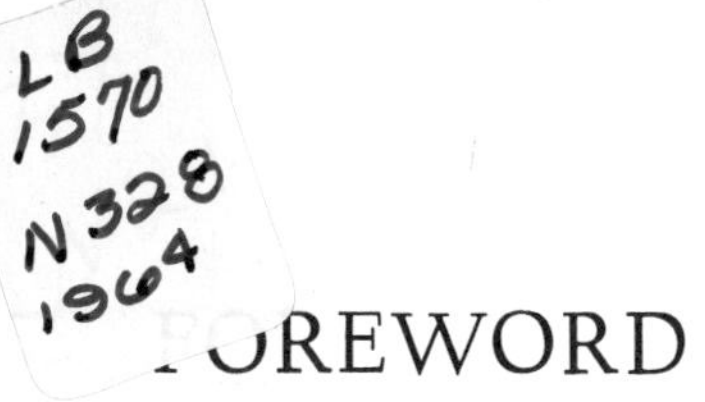

FOREWORD

Beginning with the gathering of 43 educators in Philadelphia in August 1857, the organized profession has given high priority to curriculum and instruction. The Project on Instruction is one of several major efforts sponsored by the National Education Association in this century to upgrade the quality of American education and to give it direction. These have included the 1918 statement of the "Seven Cardinal Principles" of education by the NEA's Commission on the Reorganization of Secondary Education and the 1938 and 1961 Educational Policies Commission statements on *The Purposes of Education in American Democracy* and *The Central Purpose of American Education.*

Authorized in 1959, the National Committee of the NEA Project on Instruction was commissioned as a means of providing guidance in a time of rapid change for schools. Many people have joined in this effort: elementary and secondary school teachers, school administrators, scholars in the academic disciplines, university professors of education, and distinguished laymen. Their interest and willing cooperation have been impressive testimony to a shared concern for improvements in learning.

The NEA is grateful for this valuable contribution and for the wise guidance given to the Project by the National Committee, its director, and staff. Special recognition is due Dorothy M. Fraser, whose special competence in the area covered by this report has been of great help. The Committee has been most fortunate in having its deliberations so ably expressed.

William G. Carr
Executive Secretary, NEA

Melvin W. Barnes, Chairman
National Committee
Project on Instruction

CONTENTS

PREFACE

The facts of our twentieth century life—a rapidly changing society, a mounting store of knowledge, and new understandings about people and about learning—create some basic problems relating to the instructional program of the schools. There is no shortage of ideas about what these problems are and how they should be solved. There is, in fact, a constant babble of voices as millions of people with many and often conflicting ideas speak out about education.

Some of the voices call for a return to the "solid subjects." Some prescribe the same program for all pupils, regardless of individual differences. Some ignore what is known about the ways children learn. Some express concern only for more and more attention to their particular subject.

Some of the voices come from outside the profession. Some come from within the profession at the university level of academic and professional scholarship, and many come from leaders in elementary and secondary education.

All of these voices have a right to be heard. One voice that should speak out clearly indeed is the voice of the teaching profession itself. With this firm belief, the National Education Association established in 1959 the Project on the Instructional Program of the Public Schools (Project on Instruction). To this Project it gave a major task: Make thoughtful and creative recommendations to serve as a guide to the profession and the public in their combined efforts to study and improve the quality of the instructional program in the schools.

A fourteen-member National Committee and a headquarters staff were appointed to carry on the work of the Project. The National Committee was composed of classroom teachers, public school administrators, and university professors. From time to time, distinguished citizens and scholars in the academic disciplines served in special advisory capacities.

Early in its deliberations, the Committee examined its role as a spokesman for the organized teaching profession. The members agreed unanimously that the Committee's function was not to respond to the "critics," nor to enunciate a "national curriculum," nor to recommend specific content. Rather, the Committee decided it could make the most significant contribution by identifying critical concerns in American education and formulating recommendations about them.

Inevitably, limits had to be set for the scope of the Project. These limits were set in terms of the timeliness of the issues, the feasibility of their resolution, and the desire not to duplicate significant work already completed or now in progress by other groups. In addition, it was determined that an analysis of a few crucial decision areas was more in keeping with the Project's goals than a generalized approach would be. Therefore, issues related to pupil or staff evaluation, teacher education, and matters dealing directly with the teaching act were not given major attention.

Three major tasks, then, gave structure to the Project: (a) identification and clarification of instructional issues or questions, (b) development of recommendations about the issues, and (c) explanation of the reasoning used to arrive at the recommendations. In the identification process, two categories—"Deciding What To Teach" and "Planning and Organizing for Teaching"—emerged to become the focus of intensive study. For analysis of these issues, Project participants used three sources of data: (a) the academic disciplines; (b) social forces and trends, including the status of present instructional practices in the schools; and (c) the research in human growth and development and the psychology of learning. Twelve specific decision areas were identified; twelve questions were asked about the instructional program. The Committee is on record that, within the limits set by the Project, these are the important questions about which decisions must be made. They are—

Decision Area I
DECISION MAKING
Who should make what decisions about education?

Decision Area II

RESEARCH, EXPERIMENTATION, AND INNOVATION

How can an extensive program of educational research, experimentation, and innovation be developed?

Decision Area III

EDUCATING ALL CHILDREN AND YOUTH

How can the instructional program of the school be designed to develop the individual potentialities of all members of the school population within the framework of a society that values both unity and diversity?

Decision Area IV

ESTABLISHING PRIORITIES FOR THE SCHOOL

What are the distinctive responsibilities of the school in contrast to those that are distinctive to the family, the church, industry, and various youth-serving agencies?

What responsibilities should the school share with other institutions and with other youth-serving agencies?

What, then, should be included in the school program?

What should be excluded from it?

Decision Area V

THE SCHOOL'S ROLE IN DEALING WITH NATIONAL PROBLEMS RELATED TO YOUTH

What is the school's role in dealing with serious national problems such as youth unemployment and juvenile delinquency?

Decision Area VI

TEACHING ABOUT CONTROVERSIAL ISSUES AND ABOUT COMMUNISM

What is the school's role in teaching about controversial issues and about communism and other ideologies?

Decision Area VII

A BALANCED PROGRAM

How can the school provide a balanced program for the individual and maintain it amidst various pressures for specialization?

Decision Area VIII
SELECTING CONTENT
How can schools make wise selections of content from the ever-growing body of available knowledge?

Decision Area IX
ORGANIZING CONTENT
How should the content of the curriculum be organized?

Decision Area X
ORGANIZING THE CURRICULUM
How should the curriculum of the school be organized to give appropriate direction to the instructional process?

Decision Area XI
ORGANIZING THE SCHOOL AND THE CLASSROOM
How should the school and the classroom be organized to make the most effective use of the time and talents of students and teachers?

Decision Area XII
INSTRUCTIONAL MATERIALS, TECHNOLOGY, SPACE
How can the quality of instructional materials be improved?
How can the products of modern technology be used effectively?
How can space be designed and used to support the instructional program?

These twelve questions and thirty-three recommendations are outlined and discussed briefly in *Schools for the Sixties,* which is the official report of the National Committee of the NEA Project on Instruction, published by McGraw-Hill Book Company. They are taken up separately and in greater depth in the three supporting volumes published by the National Education Association, of which this, *Deciding What To Teach,* is one. The others are *Education in a Changing Society* and *Planning and Organizing for Teaching.*

Decisions on what to teach encompass many factors. Those dealt with in this volume are learning and the structure of knowledge, the development of a curriculum for all members of the school population, problems of what content to include and what to exclude, the establishment of balance and priorities, and the treatment of controversial issues in the classroom. Central to all of these decisions is the decision-making process itself, an area in which there is less clarity among those involved than one might suppose. This issue is explored in some detail here.

No one on the National Committee anticipates or particularly desires complete agreement with all of the recommendations discussed in this volume. If some recommendations are at odds with beliefs firmly held by other equally conscientious educators, what must be resolved is not the integrity of the individuals who agree or disagree but the validity of the beliefs themselves. An objective search for reliable answers to basic questions in education is a continuing need. Such a search should be conducted with the certain but not discouraging knowledge that some of the answers will be validated, some will be disproved, and some will be supplanted by others.

The Project reports will make a difference in the decision making of America's schools only if they are used as a guide for self-study, not if they are adopted without careful thought.

Ole Sand, Director
Richard I. Miller, Associate Director

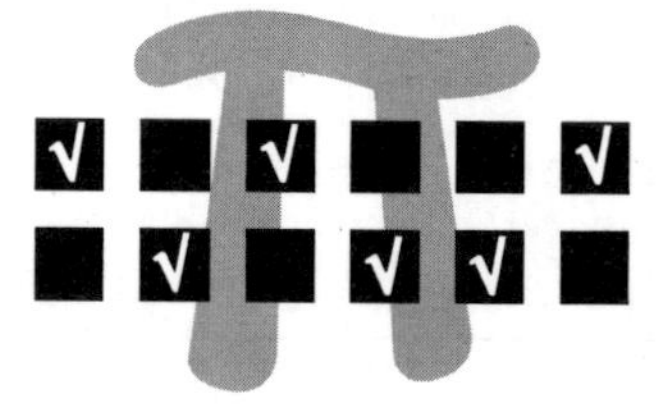

CHAPTER ONE
CURRICULUM PROBLEMS IN PERSPECTIVE

Two Generations of Curriculum Change
Re-Evaluating the School Curriculum
Needed: Guiding Principles

A perennial question is "What shall the schools teach?" This question, which has been answered many times but never finally, must always be dealt with according to the nature of society and the changing needs of each generation. It has been answered in different ways at different times in our own history. For example, the classical curriculum of the colonial Latin grammar school eventually gave way to the broader offering of the nineteenth century secondary school. In turn, during the twentieth century the high school has become an instrument of education for all youth instead of a single-purpose, college preparatory school. Today the question of what the schools shall teach continues to be debated, with different answers from different people.

TWO GENERATIONS OF CURRICULUM CHANGE

During the past three fourths of a century educators in the United States have given conscious, systematic, and continuous attention to selecting desirable content for the public school curriculum. From about 1890 to 1920, major influence on the school curriculum was exerted by recommendations from national committees. Some of them were set up by the National Education Association, some by such organizations of academic scholars as the American Historical Association and the American Classical League. Some were cosponsored by the National Education Association and the academic group representing the field of knowledge concerned. Most of these early committees made specific recommendations as to blocks of subject matter which should be taught and the grade placement of this content. Certain of their recommendations made enormous impact on the schools; indeed, some aspects of the elementary and especially the secondary school curriculum reflect their influence even today.

During the period from about 1920 to about 1950, a number of national committes studied the curriculum of various subject fields. In most cases the resulting recommendations were not so specific as to content and grade placement, nor were they so directly influential as those of some of the early committees. Schools placed more emphasis on local curriculum planning than they had in previous periods, and academic scholars took less part in the planning process.

The Impact of the Behavioral Sciences

The rapid growth during the first half of the twentieth century of the behavioral sciences as fields of systematic research brought new dimensions to curriculum planning. As a result of studies in human growth and development, educational psychology, educational sociology, and philosophy, curriculum planners were no longer satisfied to proceed by assigning blocks of subject matter to particular school grades. Such problems as the role of direct experience in learning, individual differences among pupils, and the relation of maturation to readiness for particular learnings were investigated. The findings suggested that additional factors should be considered along with logical sequence of content in planning the school program. The concept of the activity curriculum was developed. Content did not become less important, but the basis for its selection was changed.

Studies of the relation of content traditionally presented in various subjects, such as mathematics or spelling, to the situations adults met in daily life suggested that much of the information taught in school had little application to daily life in twentieth century America. These studies also suggested that considerable information needed for everyday living in the increasingly complex, urbanized society was not presented in the typical school curriculum.

Other studies were focused on the learning process, for teaching is effective only when students learn. Although much remains to be discovered about how people learn, some general conclusions have emerged. Content that is presented as isolated bits of information may be learned through memorization. While some materials may be memorized after they are understood, memorization alone does not help students to understand and apply the information, nor is it likely to affect skills or attitudes.

A person develops and makes effective use of skills such as writing complete and correctly punctuated sentences by repeatedly applying rules he himself has formulated or comprehended through another approach rather than by memorizing rules. The individual's attitudes and values are shaped by many forces of which school experience is only one but an important one. *How* he studies about democracy or conservation and *how* he is taught science or literature affect the attitudes he develops toward these ideas or fields of knowledge. Conclusions about how people learn suggest that deciding *how* to teach is an integral part of deciding *what* to teach.

The results of research in the behavioral sciences indicated that curriculum planning should take into account the following factors: the nature and needs of the individual learner at successive stages of maturation, the nature of the learning process, the nature of contemporary society and democratic values, and the roles individuals must perform in their society. Educational leaders gave attention to stating the school's objectives in a specific form with attention to the learner's needs.[1] They included as objectives of instruction the development of skills and attitudes in connection with the mastery of knowledge. They urged that content and ways of presenting it be selected to achieve the stated objectives. Pointing out that each subject field contained far more information than could be taught to elementary or secondary school students, they urged that content be selected which would have most meaning for the particular pupils involved and would, at the same time, help to achieve the full range of the school's objectives. Recognizing that some objectives were not being approached directly through existing classroom instruction, educational leaders urged that they be achieved through a school activities program which came to be called the extracurricular or activity program. Cocurricular activities are, in spite of the label, a part of the curriculum of the modern school.

Curriculum planning at the local level became a deliberate, systematic process. It became standard practice to involve teachers in curriculum development in order to fit the school program to the immediate situation. This procedure was seen to have the additional advantage of encouraging the teacher's growth through curriculum study, thereby increasing his effectiveness in working with pupils.

These developments have resulted in a more flexible selection of content and instructional method from one school to another and in presentation of a much wider range of content in every school. Traditional subjects did not disappear from the school curriculum except in a few cases, such as Greek. But in most subjects there were efforts to organize the content psychologically, to promote better learning by pupils, instead of logically, according to the form of scholarly fields of knowledge. Also the specific content presented in many subjects was changed. Thus lists of spelling words were revised on the basis of studies of usage. Some words that were frequently used in current newspapers and in communication about everyday affairs were added, while others that were infrequently used were dropped. New subjects, often of a practical nature, were introduced. For example, hygiene or health was added to the elementary school curriculum. In the secondary school a variety of courses such as typing, business English, home economics, and shop were introduced to serve particular groups of students.

Common Elements But Diversity

It is easy to overestimate the degree of variation from one school to another in what is taught today, since a high proportion of common elements are present in all school systems. Nevertheless, the United States is a nation of diversity in its educational system as in its other institutions. There is variation in specific content taught, in the grade placement of the content, in the relative richness or poverty of the curriculum, and in the way instruction is carried on. Somewhere in the United States an example can be found to illustrate almost any conclusion, favorable or unfavorable, a person may wish to draw about the school curriculum, just as examples can be found to illustrate conflicting opinions about the courts, principles of business operation, or other aspects of national life. This fact must be kept in mind in evaluating current comments about what is being taught in our schools.

RE-EVALUATING THE SCHOOL CURRICULUM

Today a variety of forces converge to create a demand for reassessment of the school curriculum. The continuing revolution in science and technology, changing patterns of economic life, the expanding role of government in an increasingly interdependent society, and sharpening conflicts concerning values all have brought dramatic changes and new tensions in American life and culture. The tremendous growth of world population, the upward surge of former colonial peoples toward independence and economic development, and the conflict of ideologies between democratic and communist nations have brought increasingly complicated problems of international relations which must be ameliorated if modern cultures are to avoid disruption.* A higher level of political, economic, and cultural understanding and performance than has yet been attained by any people in the world's history must be reached by the citizens of the United States if they are to select wise leaders and support them in appropriate, effective policies. Our society looks to the school, as its specialized agency for education, to carry major responsibility for this task.

Thus, it is not surprising that many of the current concerns about the public schools of our nation are focused on what is taught or is not taught. These concerns range over a broad diversity of questions, criticisms, and proposed solutions, most of which relate to the central problem of achieving excellence in individual and national life. Most of these concerns are new only in the way they are expressed; they have received recurring

* For discussion of these forces, see the following: National Education Association, Project on the Instructional Program of the Public Schools. *Education in a Changing Society*. Washington, D.C.: the Association, 1963. 166 pp.

attention from philosophers and practical schoolmen since the days of Plato and Aristotle.

Today some critics are charging that "soft" subjects dominate the curriculum of American schools and are calling for a return to solid subjects, usually meaning the subjects that dominated the college preparatory curriculum of nineteenth century schools. Others find the major curriculum problem to be a serious lag between what is known, i.e., recent discoveries and interpretations of scholars in the various fields of knowledge, and what is taught in school.

Some commentators hold that the school is providing instruction that should be the responsibility of other social institutions, such as the family and the church. In doing so, they say, the school neglects its responsibility for the intellectual development of children and youth. Others reply that many of youth's needs are not in fact taken care of by other social institutions, no matter how desirable it is that they should be. They insist that the school can make little progress in encouraging the student's intellectual development without helping him solve his problems of emotional and social adjustment.

Opinions also vary as to the priorities that should be established among the subjects the school could teach. Shall increased emphasis and time in the school program be given to the sciences and to advanced mathematics? Shall English no longer be a required subject each year in the secondary school, or shall the time devoted to English be expanded? Shall foreign language study begin in the elementary school for all children of normal and superior ability? If so, which languages shall be stressed? How much time should be given to social studies subjects, and which of these fields of knowledge should be emphasized? What is the place of the practical subjects, the applied sciences and arts, in the education of youth?

In short, to restate Spencer's classic question, exactly what knowledge is of most worth for American youth in the latter twentieth century? What are the unique responsibilities of the public school in the United States?

Within various groups of Americans—educators, academic scholars, parents, civic leaders, and the lay public in general—different responses are made to these questions and issues. On one point, however, there should be unanimous agreement. Wise decisions about what the schools shall teach in order to carry out their responsibilities in the years ahead will be decisions arrived at through rational deliberation in the light of the best available evidence.

NEEDED: GUIDING PRINCIPLES

Most local school systems have recognized the need to reassess their instructional program periodically. Indeed, in many schools the work of re-evaluating and revising aspects of the curriculum is continual. The current discussion of educational problems is stimulating a more rapid rate of curriculum change across the nation. To the extent that revisions are made thoughtfully, with consideration of all pertinent facts, this acceleration is desirable. There is danger, however, that sweeping revisions will be made hastily in response to much-publicized experiments or demands from pressure groups without adequate consideration of the student's total education. Elements may be introduced which are inappropriate for the particular student body or which have not been adequately tested. The urgent need to improve the curriculum can best be achieved by making haste thoughtfully and safeguarding that which is effective in existing programs.

Early in its deliberations the National Committee of the NEA Project on the Instructional Program of the Public Schools examined its role as a representative of the organized teaching profession with regard to decisions about what the schools should teach. There was unanimous agreement among members that the Committee's function was not to describe a national curriculum nor to recommend specific content to be taught in the various school subjects. Rather, the Committee has undertaken to identify principles that can be used in local and state school systems to reach wise curriculum decisions.

The recommendations and the data presented in this report deal with major curriculum problems and issues as determined by recent surveys, including those conducted by the staff of the Project. The problems and issues have been analyzed in the light of the data sources indicated in the Preface—social forces, human development, psychology of learning, the academic disciplines, and existing school situations. On the basis of this analysis a position or, in some cases, alternative positions regarding the outstanding issues are stated, and methods of arriving at sound curriculum decisions are proposed. In some cases, action programs designed to test alternative positions or to implement recommendations are suggested.

As those responsible for curriculum planning in local school districts and state education departments reassess and revise present instructional programs, the issues and factors discussed in this volume should be found relevant. The recommendations and suggestions of the Project on Instruction can be applied in a manner appropriate to the individual situation.

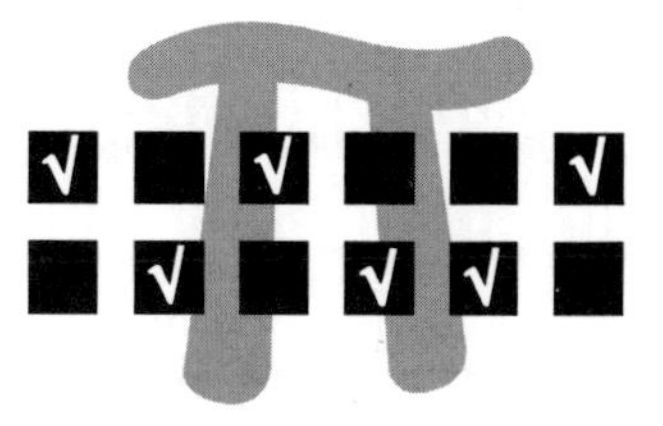

CHAPTER TWO

LEARNING, THE DISCIPLINES, AND THE SCHOOL PROGRAM

A Swinging Pendulum
The Problem of Communication
The Nature of the Disciplines
Learning and the Structure of Knowledge
Recommendations of the National Committee

Much current discussion of the school curriculum is focused on the relation of the academic disciplines, the organized fields of scholarly knowledge, to the school program. Two generations ago this question was little debated. It was generally assumed that the school program should be patterned on the academic disciplines, with each of these presented as a separate subject. Developments in educational research and practice during the past half century have caused this assumption to be examined and modified. Today the question of the proper relation between the academic disciplines and the school program has become a central issue as the school curriculum is studied critically.

A SWINGING PENDULUM

Three factors—the learner and how he learns, social forces and influences upon the schools, and the knowledge that is available to be taught—have traditionally affected, implicitly or explicitly, decisions as to what the schools should teach. Until the twentieth century, however, social goals and the traditionally organized bodies of knowledge were the emphasized factors.

With the rise of the systematic study of human development and the psychology of learning, the emphasis shifted in curriculum planning. The nature and learning processes of the pupil and society's goals for the school became screens for the selection of content to be taught. The answer to "What knowledge is of most worth?" for a pupil at a given stage of development was determined to a considerable extent by applying these screens. For various reasons the social and emotional growth of young people came into the purview of the school along with or as part of their intellectual development. Systematically organized bodies of knowledge were viewed as reservoirs from which pertinent materials were to be selected and arranged in a curriculum designed to meet not only the needs of society but also the newly recognized, more broadly viewed needs of the learner. For example, a review of professional writings published between 1925 and 1955 shows that teaching literature as a means of citizenship education was favored over treating it, at the high school level, as a humanistic discipline.[1]

The trend away from a curriculum structured on the disciplines was not a "retreat from content," as some have charged, for twentieth century schools present a broader range of content than did earlier schools. Nor did the trend deny the necessity for learning in an organized fashion. It represented a drastic change in the basis on which content was selected and organized for study. Systematic study of the various branches of human knowledge—the disciplines*—was not a primary consideration in planning much of the school curriculum, although in some fields, such as mathematics, it was assumed that certain steps must come before others. After the early years of the century, as academic scholars took less part in planning the school curriculum, as the study of critical problems of society was introduced in the school, and as the mental health of the pupil was considered along with and as a part of his intellectual growth, the nature and structure of the traditional disciplines as a factor in planning the school program was given less and less attention.

In recent years the pendulum has apparently begun to swing back. With the rapid expansion of many fields of knowledge in recent decades, there is a demand that school programs carry pupils further into the various fields of knowledge than ever before. The longer period of preparation needed to prepare a scientist, doctor, or specialist in any field has led colleges and universities to urge that students be ready to undertake a higher level of study at the onset of their college education. In addition, many people recognize the necessity for all citizens to work from a broader and deeper base of knowledge if they are to be able to understand the complicated issues confronting voters and taxpayers today.

* It is interesting and perhaps significant that this meaning of the term discipline, which is widely accepted today, was considered archaic a generation ago. See the second edition of *Webster's New International Dictionary of the English Language* (unabridged).

The concept of readiness for learning which was widely accepted in the period before World War II has also been reexamined in recent years. Earlier, readiness for learning many things, such as reading, chronology, or aspects of mathematics, was believed to be closely tied in with biological growth. Recent studies have led some psychologists to modify this concept of readiness, to place less emphasis on biological and more on environmental factors. Many now suggest that by providing the learner with a rich background of appropriate experiences his readiness for learning many things can be developed at an earlier age than was formerly believed possible.

As the need for closer cooperation between leaders in education and those in the academic disciplines has been recognized, the academicians have renewed their interest in the schools. Within the academic disciplines themselves during recent decades, specialists have given increased attention to examining the nature, structure, and method of inquiry in their respective fields of knowledge.

As a result of these various developments, educators and academicians are reconsidering whether the structure and method of the disciplines should again become a major consideration (though not the only one) in organizing school subjects. For example, scientists, psychologists, and educators met together at Woods Hole, Massachusetts, in 1959, under the auspices of the National Academy of Sciences, to consider this question. The results of their deliberations furnished the basis for the stimulating book, *The Process of Education.*[2] A disciplines seminar sponsored by the National Education Association in June 1961 brought together educators and specialists from the major academic fields to discuss the nature of these disciplines and their relation to the school program.* Academic scholars and educators are cooperating in a number of special studies which have been de-

* For a report of this seminar see the following: National Education Association, Project on the Instructional Program of the Public Schools. *The Scholars Look at the Schools: A Report of the Disciplines Seminar.* Washington, D.C.: the Association, 1962. 64 pp.

scribed in another publication of the Project on Instruction* and in a recent report of the Association for Supervision and Curriculum Development, *Using Current Curriculum Developments*.[3] These studies may bring considerable changes in the curriculum of elementary and secondary schools during the decade ahead.

THE PROBLEM OF COMMUNICATION

Communication between academic scholars and educators regarding the proper relation of the school curriculum to the disciplines has been and continues to be faulty. Gaps in communication always occur when groups with different backgrounds approach a common problem. The difficulty in this case is intensified by the relative lack in recent decades of joint efforts by academic scholars and curriculum planners. It is also intensified by the disparate goals that are given priority by the groups involved.

Difference of Objectives

It is natural for the academic scholar, whose commanding interest is his field of knowledge, to view his discipline as having an "elegant" structure which others should understand and appreciate. Sometimes this overriding interest in the importance of scholarship causes him to expect school graduates to be ready to pursue specialized study in his field of knowledge. The teacher in the school, on the other hand, usually has not pursued a single discipline to the advanced level of the university professor. The teacher of children and youth is likely to believe that social and intellectual development go hand in hand. He has studied child development and educational psychology. He probably has a firsthand knowledge of the range of abilities and interests in

* National Education Association, Project on the Instructional Program of the Public Schools. *Current Curriculum Studies in Academic Subjects.* (Prepared by Dorothy M. Fraser.) Washington, D.C.: the Association, 1962. 102 pp.

the school population. Teachers, especially those who work with elementary school children, are likely to be critical of suggestions that seem to be subject matter centered without regard to the learner's nature and needs as understood by teachers. Leaders in early childhood and elementary education, particularly, remember the efforts that were required to raise the elementary school program above the level of memoriter learning.

Semantical Problems

Terminology is often another barrier to communication. People, including educators and academicians, frequently are not precise in expression. A word or phrase may carry multiple meanings and be understood differently by different persons, depending on their background or experience. For example, when the mathematician suggests that algebra be introduced in the primary grades, the elementary teacher may assume (and many have done so) that the traditional algebra of the ninth grade is intended. The mathematician, however, may only mean to give first graders opportunities for learning experiences with algebra at a level comparable to that at which they are taught to read maps. This is often described as a readiness level, although basic concepts of map interpretation are being introduced.

Academic scholars, even those within a given field, often disagree upon the proper relation of the academic disciplines to the school curriculum. Indeed, they may disagree as to the nature of their own discipline. In current discussions such expressions as the structure of the discipline, the style of thought in the field, and the method of the discipline are often used without clear definition. These terms carry different meanings for different persons. The word *discipline* itself, although it is usually understood to refer to a field of knowledge, lacks a universally accepted definition. A first task, therefore, is to clarify the meanings of such terms and the concepts they represent. It is a task that academicians and educators must undertake cooperatively.

Improved communication among all groups concerned with school curriculum decisions is essential if wise decisions are to be made. All who take part in curriculum planning have an obligation to state their own purposes clearly and definitely as well as to seek out the meaning of and reasons for suggestions that come to them. Even after the barriers to understanding have been overcome, differences of judgment may remain. But only then, after the atmosphere of misunderstanding and misinterpretation has been dispelled, can properly considered decisions be reached.

THE NATURE OF THE DISCIPLINES

Discipline, as we have seen, is generally accepted today to denote a branch or field of knowledge. The term has been defined more precisely as "a collection of parts of systematized knowledge arbitrarily selected and bound together in a manner suitable for learning, mental training, and preparation for more advanced study and research."[4] Not all academic scholars will accept this definition, however. Some reject it because it suggests that the traditional organization of knowledge, stemming from Aristotle, is but one of several possible organizations and not necessarily the most effective one, at that. This definition stresses the ordering of knowledge to make it learnable and usable. Under it the number of identifiable disciplines may be expanded enormously to include fields of study which draw content from several of the traditional disciplines, as in the case of such fields as conservation, communications, and education, for examples.

The definition cited above is useful for two reasons in considering the relation between the academic disciplines and the school curriculum. It suggests a number of characteristics of a discipline that, as evidenced by recent publications and discussions, seem to be widely accepted. It also raises some points of disagreement about the nature of the disciplines.

A discipline is more than a collection of information; it is a body of knowledge organized around basic concepts. These basic concepts form the *structure* of the discipline. That is, they provide a structure or perhaps several complementary structures within which the relationships of specific facts can be established and the meaning of the facts understood. Each discipline has its particular approaches, tools, and methods for discovering and ordering information. These constitute the *method of inquiry* of the discipline.

Disciplines Evolve

A discipline is not static. It changes with the addition of new information, as when physicists found the basis for creating a chain reaction, when the Dead Sea scrolls were added to the historian's reservoir of sources, or when evidence from new excavations becomes available to archeologists.

More fundamental than the addition of information per se are the changes that come in the basic concepts and structure of a discipline when new facts appear or old ones are reinterpreted. Then it becomes necessary to invent new theories to explain the data. Frequently new problems are raised by the solution of old ones. Examples of such changes may be seen in the development of atomic physics. Not only may the structure and method of a particular discipline be revolutionized by such revisions but also its relationships to other fields of knowledge may be altered and an intermediary discipline—biochemistry, for example—may be created.

A discipline changes when the level of inquiry or the organization of materials is changed. For example, it changes when the questions to be studied are limited and pursued within a clearly established structure of concepts or when they are broadened in a way that requires the creation of a new conceptual structure. Thus the historian's investigation of the causes of the American Civil War will proceed with limited questions while he works within the context of an economic interpretation of history. His level of inquiry or organization of data becomes broader when, by making the economic interpretation one of several elements to be considered, he broadens the conceptual framework or structure within which he organizes his findings.

At a given time the rate of change in certain disciplines may be more rapid than in others. In recent years changes in the natural sciences, mathematics, and certain of the behavioral sciences have dramatically illustrated this fact. It has been estimated, for example, that the length of the cycle of revision in a scientific field is about fifteen years.[5] But all of the disciplines are susceptible to revision and are, in fact, undergoing some degree of change as long as they remain fields of study.

Components of a Discipline

Each discipline has a content, structure (or structures), and method (or methods), but none of the three components can be fully understood in isolation from the other two. Specific data take on different meaning as the basic concepts of the discipline are revised or as the methods and levels of inquiry shift. The "what" of the discipline—its content and conceptual structure—can be interpreted only in the light of the "how," the method and level of inquiry. The latter, in turn, must be appropriate to the content and concepts under investigation. When we take this view of the disciplines, we emphasize the method of inquiry as an integral part of a field of knowledge.

Some scholars reject the possibility of developing a single scientific method. They contend that the specific methods of inquiry cannot be separated from the content and structure of a particular discipline. They believe that there are methods of inquiry peculiar to each discipline and that the selection of methods and tools must be determined in the light of the conceptual structure of the field. Other scholars, while agreeing that each discipline has its distinctive techniques and tools, follow Dewey's argument that there is a rational method of determining and relating facts and drawing conclusions from them.[6] This broad method, they say, applies with variations to each of the disciplines.

Classifying the Disciplines

The variety of conceptions of the nature of individual disciplines is indicated by the different classifications that have been suggested for the fields of academic knowledge. In the typical college and university organization, the academic fields may be divided into the natural sciences and mathematics, the social sciences, and the humanities, each with its subdivisions. This traditional view of the disciplines has been reflected in the school curriculum in the recent past. Disagreements with this classification appear, however, when certain fields are considered. Is history a social science or one of the humanities? Is geography properly a natural science or a social science? How is psychology to be classified?

In another classification the fields of knowledge are grouped according to function: those that are primarily investigative, like the natural sciences; those that are chiefly appreciative, as the humanities; and those that are for the most part concerned with decision making, as the social sciences.[7] Here again, the association of particular fields of knowledge with one or the other of these types may be debated.

A third analysis, proposed by an English educator, identifies four "modes of human experience": the logical, exemplified by mathematics and languages; the empirical, based largely on the natural sciences; the moral, to be pursued through literature, history, and religion; and the aesthetic, to which literature, music, and the "plastic arts" make greatest contribution.[8]

Other proposed schemes could be cited, but the foregoing examples are sufficient to indicate the variety of approaches that are currently used or suggested for classifying man's knowledge into broad fields or groups of disciplines. They also suggest some of the different views of the nature of the disciplines.

LEARNING AND THE STRUCTURE OF KNOWLEDGE

What is the relation between effective learning and the learner's grasp of the structure of a subject? This practical question is raised by the current examination of the relation of academic disciplines to the school program. Some have given an implicit answer to the question by advancing the view that the structures of the disciplines should be taught to the pupil as early as possible in his school career. An examination of this proposal is warranted.

Structure, Comprehension, and Retention of Knowledge

Does early presentation of the structure of a field make specific content of the subject more comprehensible to the learner, as has been suggested? Does it enable him either to retain specifics longer or to relearn them more quickly and easily?

Learning in Context. Principles of learning which have been generally accepted by educational psychologists and professional educators indicate the importance of organization or structure for meaningful learning, whether the learner is six or sixty. For example, nonsense syllables that the learner is unable to fit into a meaningful structure are learned more slowly and forgotten more quickly than meaningful words or phrases. A rule of grammar, if memorized as an isolated specific, does not carry the same meaning as when learned as part of a broader context, nor will it be retained as long. A forgotten fact will be relearned more quickly if it has been initially understood and learned within a conceptual structure. A conclusion or interpretation that has been forgotten may be reconstructed if the learner remembers the organization of ideas to which it is related.

Modern school programs take these principles into account when content is presented in "wholes" of a size and level that the learner can comprehend. Effective teachers help the pupil to understand drill material by putting it into context before the drill occurs. They help him see relationships between new information and the previous knowledge of a subject he has already acquired. They do not attempt to teach isolated bits of knowledge.

Just as facts and ideas are better understood and have more meaning when related to structure, so must a meaningful structure be related to and develop from facts and ideas. Generalizations, theories, or principles that are memorized in isolation from their supporting specifics pay the same limited learning dividends that accrue from the memorization of isolated facts. Even if it is understood by the pupil in a general way, the principle or theory may have little significance to him until he has obtained enough related information to understand its importance. The theory may, in fact, actually mislead the learner because he does not have sufficient specific information to interpret or apply it correctly. Thus, while some fundamental structures or concepts may be fairly easily taught at a younger age than that at which they are usually presented, they may add little or nothing to the pupil's comprehension of the subject.

From Concrete to Abstract. Within each field of knowledge there are structures of varying degrees of concreteness and complexity. Structures that are readily absorbed at an early age may have little resemblance to those envisaged by many who advocate the early teaching of general principles. A structure or frame of reference that is easily comprehended by the high school student may be only confusing to a child in the primary grades and may actually interfere with his learning. The fact that "when you add one it's always the next number" may intrigue a child in grade 2. The statement represents some grasp of the structure of number, but it is far from elegant or inclusive. Often structures that take the form of working rules are more easily comprehended than those that are more abstract and inclusive. A student may early be convinced that "you should change the sign when you transpose, and there is a good reason for doing so"; but he may need far more experience to attain a convincing appreciation of the addition or subtraction of equals from equals. In physical science, the student probably can use the thumb-and-finger rule concerning an electromagnet and its polarity long before he can grasp the more fundamental framework of physical laws from which this relationship emerges.

Some studies have shown that emphasis on the organized structure of the material yielded no discernible advantage in the learning achieved by students.[9] The probable explanation in these cases is that the conceptual structure presented was not one that the learners could grasp readily or completely. As a result, the structure emphasized by the teacher may have been merely an additional burden to pupils instead of an aid to learning.

Studies of concept formation support the conclusion that structures comprehensible for children are much simpler than those that function for adolescents and that the latter are likely to be of a lower degree of generality and complexity than those used by the scholar.[10] These studies suggest that the course of development is from the immediate, concrete, and simple to the more remote, generalized, and complex. It seems likely that the structure or frame of reference from which the child can best view his social or physical world develops in a corresponding fashion.

The Role of Readiness and Development in Learning. Studies of readiness for learning indicate that the desirable progression in schooling moves from the concrete to the generalized, from the simple to the complex. Three factors are believed to affect readiness:[11] physical and mental maturation, emotional factors such as anxiety or self-confidence, and previous background of learning or experience. Some specialists in child development and educational psychology continue to lay greatest stress on the maturation and emotional factors, an emphasis that was generally accepted in recent decades. They warn that an attempt to hasten school progress by forced learning may be not only useless but dangerous to the child's intellectual and emotional development. Others, while recognizing the negative effects of forced learning, believe today that it is wasteful to wait for readiness. Instead, according to this school of thought, much can be done to develop readiness without harm to the learner by providing experiences suitable to the stage of his development. Psychologists of this group suggest that accepted age norms for learning particular subjects merely show how children react to existing school programs. If the programs were revised, readiness for study of many topics might be achieved earlier.

More than a generation ago, Alfred North Whitehead addressed himself to the problem of fitting the content and method of instruction to the individual pupil's development. He described the "rhythm of education," identifying three stages of mental growth. At the level of *romance,* the learner encounters a range of facts and ideas and perceives relationships among them imaginatively and incompletely. At the stage of *precision,* he develops a way of analyzing and ordering facts and ideas and acquires new ones in a systematic fashion. In the phase of *generalization,* the learner combines the freshness of approach of the romantic stage with the use of classified ideas and techniques for ordering the newly discovered facts and ideas. Whitehead urged that education "should consist in a continual repetition of such cycles. Each lesson in its minor way should form an eddy cycle issuing in its own subordinate process. Longer periods should issue in definite attainments, which then form the starting-grounds for fresh cycles. We should banish the idea of a mythical, far-off end of education. The pupils must be continually enjoying some fruition and starting afresh. . . ."[12]

More recently we have heard the hypothesis that the young child can be helped, through concrete experiences, to perceive intuitively concepts and generalizations that he will later learn to handle at the abstract level of logical thought. Those who take this position have been influenced largely by the work of Piaget and his associates. They suggest that "any subject can be taught effectively in some intellectually honest form to any child at any stage of development" as long as the way the child views his world is understood and respected.[13] According to this position, the broad structures of the fields of knowledge should be introduced at the intuitive level in the early school years. They can then be developed through a "spiral curriculum" in which the learner achieves an increasingly expanded and refined development of the concepts. His readiness for learning at each stage, it is suggested, will be increased by his earlier, simpler experiences with the concepts or structures.

The Role of Application in Learning. The general principles of learning suggest that the principles, theories, or generalizations over which a pupil will gain and retain control will be those that he frequently applies with success. Studies of concept development indicate that a learner may quickly lose a concept he has once understood if he has no further occasion to use it. That is, the permanence and breadth of the child's grasp of a concept are affected by the amount of reinforcement the concept receives through application.[14]

How many separate structures can the learner at a given stage of maturity handle successfully at the same time? Attempting to teach many discrete structures may result in none being developed fully enough or applied frequently enough to be retained by pupils. Whether the learner who is presented with many separate subject structures will have difficulty in relating specifics to the correct structure is a cognate consideration. The effort to teach too many structures may cause one of them to interfere with another so that none is useful to the pupil for organizing his learning.

Progression in Learning. The foregoing discussion does not deny the importance of structure for enhancing learning. Nor does it deny the urgency of introducing generalizations, theories, and principles as early in the pupil's career as is feasible. As the child develops concepts and generalizations, he gains powerful tools for learning and thinking. He can use the concepts and generalizations he has abstracted from his experience to identify and categorize new objects, ideas, and events that he encounters. His conceptual structure for a topic or a broad field of knowledge enables him to select, relate, and organize pertinent materials. As one psychologist has put it, "conceptualizing makes possible rational behavior—exploring, ordering, solving, creating, and predicting."[15]

Indeed, as John Dewey pointed out more than two decades ago, the essence of the educative process is the "progressive organization of knowledge." Recognizing that experience is basic to learning, he reminded his readers that "no experience is truly educative that does not tend both to knowledge of more facts and entertaining of more ideas and to a better, a more orderly, arrangement of them." A structure or conceptual framework that becomes an integral part of a child's thought will strengthen his intellectual activity throughout life.[16]

Grasp of the organized subject matter and structures of the disciplines constitutes one of the goals toward which the learner should move. However, the structures of the disciplines are not the starting point. The level of the structure taught at any stage should be related to the experience, background, and maturity of the learner. The structures or concepts that function most vividly in the minds of children are likely to have little resemblance to the complex and powerful models in the mind of the scholar. Even if scholars in a given discipline could agree on the basic structure of their field, which does not seem to be the case in most or perhaps all of the disciplines, the transfer of this structure bodily into the school curriculum might lead only to confusion of the learner. Hence the assumption that curriculum problems can be solved by inviting scholars to lay out the structure of their disciplines is hardly tenable.

Avoiding an Atomized Curriculum. The number of discrete structures which can be taught effectively at the same time must be considered in relation to the total curriculum. Two alternatives present themselves. One is to study the various groups of disciplines to determine (a) what simple unifying structures within each of the broad groupings the young child can develop and (b) how the intermediate and advanced structures, those suitable for older students and which lead into study of separate disciplines, can be evolved from the simpler structures. Within recent decades this alternative has been generally adopted. If, as some academic specialists maintain, it is impossible to find simple structures that are suitable means of introducing the young child to broad fields such as mathematics, the natural sciences, the social sciences, or the humanities, then the second alternative is to select a limited number of discrete disciplines to be introduced in the elementary school and a somewhat larger number to be studied by pupils in the secondary school.

Those who prefer the first alternative point out that if only one or two disciplines from each of the broad groupings were selected for study by elementary school children and a few more for secondary school students, young people would be given a view of the world which would be narrow indeed. It is doubtful that society's need for an educated citizenry could be met through such a program. Those who support the second alternative suggest that a thorough comprehension of a few subjects may give the learner a set toward substantial mastery of some other subjects. That is, through a full experience with a few subjects, perhaps pupils may develop a set to high standards of competence which would motivate them toward excellence, later, in other fields of study.

Whichever alternative is selected, if the pupil's school experience is to result in meaningful learning it cannot be atomized into so many separate subjects that he has no opportunity to comprehend any of them or to retain what has once been understood. Those who urge the early teaching of the structure of discrete disciplines must face this practical consideration. It is impossible to teach all or even a large proportion of the disciplines as separate subjects, even if it is proved that the structure of each discipline can be presented so that elementary school children can grasp it. The subjects to be studied by a pupil, even at the senior high school level, must be limited to the number he can pursue to a useful level of competence within the available school time.

Much research is needed to determine the characteristics of appropriate structures for children of different ages, abilities, and experience. The relation between the simple frames of reference which will serve the young child, those of intermediate level which should be evolved by older pupils, and the complex structures of the scholars must also be studied. The danger of premature closure must be avoided. That is, the use of structures of various levels must be managed so that one leads into the next, avoiding a situation in which the child clings to his earliest frame of reference for an area. As the learner becomes capable of handling a more advanced conceptual framework, he must be helped to realize the need to refine his generalizations and principles and to actually achieve this growth.

Effects of Structure on Interest and Motivation

Does early teaching of the structure of the subject enhance the student's interest and motivation for learning in the subject and encourage continued study of it after formal schooling is completed?

Scientific investigation of motivation in the educational process is still in an early state, according to educational psychologists.[17] Nevertheless, the enormous importance of the learner's interest and an active will to learn is widely recognized by teachers and psychologists alike. Many factors seem to be involved in motivation, and since true motivation is something that the learner develops internally, these factors must often be inferred and are impossible to measure with precision. A number of generally accepted principles concerning motivation have been formulated, however, some of which can be applied to the question at hand.

It is believed that whetting the appetite is a first step in arousing interest. For this reason, modern schools introduce the study of a topic or a block of work by having pupils examine colorful pictures or models or listen to an exciting account, by demonstrating the importance or usefulness of the study, or by arranging some other vivid experience at a level appropriate to the maturity of the learners. Another form of whetting the appetite may consist of relating the new study to something in which the pupil already has developed an interest and gained insight. Here the importance of an early understanding of the structure of the field could be significant, if the structure has been grasped by the pupil clearly enough for him to comprehend readily the relationship the teacher intends.

The adult's appetite for pursuit of a field of knowledge is likely to be whetted more easily if he has had enough previous contact with the field to have evolved his own structure of ideas about it. With such background, he can relate new information to generalizations or impressions with which he is already acquainted. This phenomenon applies to incidental exposure to new information as well as to systematic study. For example, suppose a newspaper reports that evidence was recently discovered that man has lived in organized communities almost twice as long as was formerly believed and describes the manner in which the evidence was obtained. The news item will be of interest to the adult who can use this information to revise the conception of the prehistoric period which he formed during school studies. He may be moved to obtain and read a recent book about the beginnings of man so that he can better understand the implications of the new evidence. The news item is likely to have limited interest and meaning, however, for the person who has no conceptual structure regarding prehistory.

Interest and motivation for study are likely to be enhanced by progress in understanding and applying what is learned and by reinforcement through continuing success. Initial discouragement caused by failure in learning tasks may have negative effects on interest, motivation, and general attitude toward the field of study concerned. Children (and adults) often try to escape learning tasks that they consider beyond their abilities. On the other hand, they are likely to work beyond the requirement on those in which they perceive a chance of success. With a successful beginning, the learner is more likely to handle later setbacks without loss of interest. This principle of motivation through successful progress underlines again the necessity of teaching the structure at a level and in a manner that permits the pupil to grasp it. It is the learner's command of the conceptual frame which counts—not the structure that is in the mind of the teacher.

How the pupil is encouraged to approach his learning tasks in a subject will, it seems likely, have considerable effect on his motivation for continuing pursuit of it.[18] The quality and permanence of his learning will also be affected. If he is presented with situations and encouraged to discover and test his own answers (rules, generalizations, or principles), the pupil is more likely to become interested in the subject than if the teacher or textbook presents the rules or principles, however clearly. Some have suggested that the learner is likely to develop positive attitudes toward the field of knowledge if the structure of the subject is taught through the discovery approach, which is discussed more fully below, and that these attitudes will contribute to a continuing interest after his formal schooling is completed.

It is probable that, if the basic concepts of the subject are presented at a level that the pupil can comprehend and if he is allowed to participate actively in developing the pertinent rules and principles, the learner's interest and motivation for further study will be stimulated. On the other hand, if the presentation of structure is inappropriate in level and method, the pupil is likely to learn dislike for the subject even though he develops some degree of competence in it. This conclusion emphasizes the need to consider not only the nature of the disciplines but the nature of the learner and the learning process as well.

Effects of Structure on Transfer of Learning

Is transfer of learning facilitated by teaching of the structure of the subject?

Effective schooling must help the pupil to transfer his learning —that is, to place meanings, interpretations, skills, and attitudes into new contexts—for the school cannot hope to prepare students specifically for every situation they will meet. As societal change brings innumerable new situations to be dealt with and as the expansion of knowledge opens new doors at a rate that is almost beyond comprehension, the need for transfer of learning becomes increasingly urgent. Means of improving transfer become invaluable tools for the educator.

According to educational psychologists, transfer of learning is likely to take place when two conditions exist: The subject is aware that transfer is possible, and he recognizes in a new situation elements similar to those in a previous situation for which he has already developed satisfactory responses.

These satisfactory responses may be of different types. They may be skills that can be applied, such as locating a book through the use of the card catalogue. They may be facts that are recognized as relevant, such as a number fact that is pertinent to the solution of various problems. The responses may take the form of generalizations such as "some kinds of plants are easily propagated from cuttings while others are best raised from seed" or "most events in human affairs result from a combination of causative factors." A transferable response may be a procedure for analyzing a new situation, such as examining a political candidate's proposal or planning the steps for a scientific research project. It may be an attitude toward a new situation or toward his own ability to handle it which will determine the person's approach—interest or boredom, liking or antipathy, self-confidence or its lack.

Successful (appropriate) transfer depends on recognition or understanding of relationships between old and new situations. It has already been suggested that grasp of a conceptual structure can be an important aid to identifying relationships, generalizing from specifics, and maintaining interest.

Early teaching of structures, or the overarching principles of a discipline, may reasonably be expected to facilitate transfer of learning *to the extent that they become a part of the learner's working equipment.* Probably there will be more transfer from a limited structure vividly grasped than from an elaborate one that is potentially more useful but not adequately comprehended by the learner. In one study of the teaching of addition to second grade children, for example, more identifiable transfer resulted from encouraging them to keep the numbers in columns than from teaching the principle that units must be added to units and tens to tens.[19] The simpler structure, the rule, had apparently been understood and could be applied, whereas the broader principle was not. The older pupil who attempted to locate a magazine article by checking the library card catalogue was attempting to apply or transfer a method of locating information which he did not fully understand.

In short, teaching the structure of the subject is seen as a means of facilitating transfer of learning as well as of helping pupils understand and retain information. But to attain this benefit the structure must be presented at the level of simplicity or complexity that can be readily grasped and used by the pupil at his stage of development.

Flexible Structures and Creativity

How can learners be helped to evolve flexible structures for the various fields of knowledge? Can creative thinking be encouraged by helping learners evolve flexible structures for the subjects they study?

Two factors make it essential that learners consider generalizations—conceptual structures—as tentative in nature, susceptible of revision, and capable of application in differing but appropriate situations. One is the pupil's own need to refine his conceptual framework for a field as he gains broader and deeper knowledge of it and as he grows in ability to handle generalized and complicated ideas. This need has been discussed above. The other factor is found in the discipline itself, since new discoveries and interpretations modify the concepts and methods of inquiry in the field of knowledge. Science and mathematics curriculums are undergoing drastic revisions today to incorporate more recently developed concepts that had been neglected. At the rate research is progressing in these fields, some of the content that is now being introduced may become obsolete before it is fully incorporated into curriculum plans and teaching materials. Comparable changes are being made in other school subjects, and the same problem of the lag between research findings and curriculum content exists.

The learner must understand that some of the specifics, principles, and generalizations he studies will be modified or even revolutionized within a few years, certainly within his lifetime. Even as he organizes his learning into appropriate concepts or structures, he should view them as the best that he can achieve at the moment but subject to future revision. He should be helped to see a subject not as a fixed, immutable body of information but rather as the best picture man has been able to evolve, to date, of this aspect of human experience.

Students who gain some understanding of the methods of inquiry employed in a given field probably will be less likely to view its conclusions or content as final and complete. If the learner discovers something of how the scientist has developed his theory and how the methods of science have been evolved, for example, he will be prepared for new theories or revised interpretations. If he revises his own conceptual structures as he gains additional information and insights, he may see the need for holding them as tentative. A new dimension of understanding is thus added to the pupil's grasp of his studies and to his ability to apply the principles and generalizations he has evolved.

The Discovery Approach. Learning through discovery offers a means of stimulating interest in a subject and developing favorable attitudes toward it. The discovery approach also offers opportunities for the teacher to introduce the pupil to methods of inquiry. It should not be confused with the activity curriculum, since discovery may be applied in a curriculum that is organized around traditional subjects and includes a high proportion of preselected content.

Some examples may clarify what is meant by the discovery approach. Children can discover and state their own generalizations about the number system by manipulating concrete materials, verbalizing their conclusions at their own level of understanding, and applying these conclusions in a variety of situations. Older children can study a physical map of an unfamiliar region to formulate hypotheses about climates, distribution of population, probable locations for cities, and types of economic activity. They can then check their hypotheses to discover why their incorrect hunches were wrong and to affirm those that were right. Students can experiment with styles of written expression by writing about an event for assumed different audiences or from the viewpoint of different persons involved or to stress different aspects of it. Rules of grammar can be induced from examination and comparison of many examples, instead of being learned and then illustrated by the same examples. Science experiments can be conducted so that pupils come to their own conclusions, instead of being told in advance what results to expect. Even though the answers are "known" in many of these situations, the pupil can still "discover" them for himself.

The discovery approach may help pupils to gain a better understanding of the principles they have formulated. It may also help them learn how to arrive at generalizations and how to see relationships among data, if these processes are made explicit to the learners. The generalizations that children can formulate in mathematics or geography or language can probably help them gain an impression of how the mathematician, geographer, or linguist goes about his work.

The values of learning through discovery have long been recognized by educational psychologists. Elementary and secondary school teachers have employed this approach in the classroom to some degree, perhaps under another name such as the problem method. The essential elements are the active participation of the pupil in confronting a problem to which he is not given a solution and his use of induction to formulate principles, draw conclusions, and establish relationships among data.

This classroom procedure has been used deliberately to help students gain insight into methods of inquiry employed in a given subject. The junior high school students who investigated a local history problem probably learned a great deal about certain kinds of sources and how to evaluate and use them, if their teacher was alert and effective in guiding them. The high school students who studied survey methods in order to survey a particular aspect of their community probably gained some understanding of one of the methods of inquiry a behavioral scientist may use.

Cautions Concerning the Discovery Approach. Recent proposals emphasizing learning through discovery and having children learn to think like mathematicians or scientists or historians can give constructive impetus to the school program when correctly understood and applied. However, certain cautions should be observed.

The level of mathematical thinking, historical method, or economic analysis, for examples, which pupils in elementary schools or high schools can employ is relatively limited. Its relation to the scholar's methods of inquiry is about the same as the relation simple structures of knowledge which young learners can develop bear to the refined and complex structures of the professional. Those who expect otherwise will only delude both themselves and the learners. To permit pupils to believe that they are indeed performing like scholars will scarcely develop in them an appreciation and desire for the excellence in learning toward which the school must guide them.

Learning through discovery must not be understood to mean that the pupil can investigate, without background, an idea of which he is ignorant. Rather it means that the pupil, like the scholar, uses information available to him as the basis for a conclusion, principle, or theory that he himself formulates at his own level. The richer the background of information he can bring to the discovery situation, the more refined and successful his effort is likely to be. Thus the hypotheses that the sixth grader can formulate by studying a physical map of an unfamiliar region, as suggested earlier, will probably be less detailed and complete than those that a high school senior should be able to develop and certainly much simpler than those of the geographer.

The teacher's role in encouraging learning through discovery is crucial. He must guide the selection of discovery situations to ensure that they are potentially within reach of his pupils. As the work proceeds the teacher may need to assist the learner in overcoming obstacles, perhaps by asking questions that will help the pupil analyze his difficulty or remind him of aspects he needs to consider. The teacher must be alert to see that any generalization, principle, or theory formulated by the pupil is not in error or to help him discover and correct the error.

Only a small part of the school curriculum or of a single subject can be treated through the discovery approach. Limits of time, inaccessibility of certain kinds of materials and experiences, and restrictions of the pupil's own ability and research techniques make it impossible that he rediscover all that he needs to know of science, history, or any other field. Nor can he learn through direct experience all that he can usefully comprehend about methods of inquiry in the various fields.

Fortunately, the benefits of learning through discovery probably can be gained through relatively occasional use of this approach. Discovery situations placed at intervals in the sequence of each subject field can be used to maintain interest and illuminate meaningful presentations of other kinds—information and explanations provided by the teacher, reading materials, or films, for example.

Developing Creativity. How can the school help young people grow in creative thinking or creative imagination? This question has received continuing and increasing attention in recent years.[20] It is related to questions that have been raised concerning the need for flexibility in the individual's structures of knowledge and the implications of learning through discovery. Recent studies have suggested that creative thinking, as judged by the variety, novelty, and number of responses or associations for a stimulus, can be encouraged by appropriate classroom procedures.[21]

Creative thinking begins with "openness," a tendency or willingness to bring together a wide range of ideas, facts, and hypotheses and to consider their relationships without being bound by preconceived or conventional conclusions. It proceeds through questioning, testing, hypothesizing, and experimenting in a search for conclusions or products that are satisfying and acceptable to the individual. In this process the learner must be able to set aside, at least temporarily, the principles, generalizations, and other structural elements he has learned; only then can he conceive and test a variety of new and original ideas.

The product of creative thinking is original in the sense that it is developed by the individual himself; it is not necessarily a novel or unique outcome. It must eventually be evaluated against criteria appropriate to the discipline involved.

To think creatively the thinker must draw on his store of experience, information, and concepts, as well as on his ability to use these resources flexibly. The scientist who develops a theory to account for recently discovered data must select from the vast range of previously known data and from his experience in handling the data in order to cast, test, and modify hypotheses. At a different level and in a different field, experiments have shown that intermediate grade children improve in the originality of their story writing when presented with a variety of multisensory experiences through still pictures and films, recordings of music, and stories, for example, before they begin a creative writing assignment. To think creatively, the thinker needs raw materials; the more he has, the richer his imaginative thought can be, provided he is not bound by his material.

Torrance has urged that "children can be taught in such a way that their creative thinking abilities can be used in acquiring even the traditional educational skills."[22] He concludes, however, along with others who are studying the development of creativity,[23] that the school discourages creative thinking when it consistently presents pupils with answers to be learned instead of providing strategic opportunities for the learner to discover his own answers.

The results of efforts to identify and teach the elements of creative thinking suggest that learning through discovery, as here described, can help students develop the ability to think imaginatively and creatively. The need for openness at the beginning of the creative thinking process is related to the need to teach pupils that the concepts, principles, and generalizations they develop are subject to modification.

Bases for Organizing Knowledge

Do the academic disciplines provide the only useful organization of knowledge, or should the schools introduce young people to other bases for organizing information, in addition to the conventional disciplines?

The academic disciplines have proved their value over the centuries as useful vehicles for synthesizing and ordering man's accumulation of knowledge. Their systematic organization, or structure, facilitates both the preservation of knowledge already gained and the continuing research that expands the horizons of mankind. If handled appropriately, the conventional disciplines can assist the learner to comprehend many aspects of the world he lives in. That point has been the burden of much of this chapter.

If knowledge is to be applied in many situations, however, it must be organized around concepts and principles usually not derived from a single discipline. Many problems of the modern world, whether of individuals or nations, can be considered rationally only through a multidisciplinary approach. That is, knowledge pertinent to resolving such a problem must be drawn from several of the conventional disciplines. Interrelationships among the data from the various subject fields must be recognized. The information thus assembled must be so organized and applied that it illuminates the problem and reveals courses of action for dealing with it.

Thus the handling of a health problem at either the personal or public level may require information from the fields of sociology and psychology as well as from several of the physical and natural sciences. Efforts to solve the critical problem of juvenile delinquency have been based on data from several of the conventional disciplines including political science, sociology, and psychology. Putting an astronaut into space would have been impossible except through the synthesis of pertinent knowledge from a variety of conventional disciplines.

The individual tends to relate facts within a structure or organization he is accustomed to and understands. If his school studies were organized entirely or chiefly on the basis of the traditional disciplines treated as separate subjects, an adult is likely to have difficulty in seeing interrelationships among the fields. If, on the other hand, the learner has experience with study of data selected from several disciplines and organized to apply to practical problems and areas of living as well as experience with the conventional disciplines, he can be helped to develop alternative structures for the handling of information. If he himself has experience in selecting data from more than one subject field and organizing them around a topic or problem he is investigating, he can gain some understanding of the nature and processes of the multidisciplinary approach.

Thus it is suggested that the school curriculum should include both such conventional academic disciplines as biology, physics, and chemistry and such applied subjects as health education and home economics. It should also provide for studies organized around topics and problems that cut across disciplinary lines, like those presented in problems of democracy, general science, and core curriculum classes.[24]

RECOMMENDATIONS OF THE NATIONAL COMMITTEE

Only the first steps have been taken in restudying the relation of the academic disciplines to the school program. Children must continue to learn, and schools must continue to help them learn while the re-examination proceeds. Therefore, the recommendations of the National Committee of the Project on Instruction concerning the relation of the disciplines to the school curriculum contain two elements. One has to do with policies the schools should follow in the light of evidence now available. The other consists of suggestions for a continuing inquiry concerning this relationship.

BASES FOR ORGANIZING CONTENT

RECOMMENDATION: *The content of the curriculum should be organized in such ways that students may progress, from early to later school years, toward an increasingly mature utilization and organization of their knowledge. Helping learners see interrelationships and achieve unity from the diversity of knowledge is basic to any organization of content.*

School staffs should experiment with a variety of ways of organizing content. The nature, meaning, and structure of the discipline and differences in the ways students learn should be taken into account in selecting a particular plan of organization and evaluating its effectiveness.

The content of the curriculum selected for study by young children should be organized into broad fields of knowledge such as science, social studies, the arts, and the language arts and into units of study using content appropriate to the maturity of the learner. Older children and youth should build on this interdisciplinary foundation to move toward a more closely focused study of separate subjects in the senior high school, but they should also have opportunities for an interdisciplinary approach to the study of the contemporary world and its problems. In this way, students will grow from early to later school years toward an increasingly mature and differentiated organization of their knowledge.

CURRICULAR SEQUENCE

RECOMMENDATION: *In each curricular area, the vertical organization of subject matter should take account of (a) the logical structure of the subject; (b) the difficulty of material as related to the student's intellectual maturity; (c) the relation of the field to other fields.*

*Procedures and instruments for evaluating pupil progress must be specifically geared to the school's educational goals and to the curricular sequence in use in the school.**

To help students achieve an increasingly mature organization of knowledge, the school program should provide for continuity and increasing breadth and depth of content from one school year to the next. The principles and generalizations selected for development should be sufficiently limited in number so that the learners have many opportunities to reinforce understandings and apply them. The simpler principles to be developed with young children should be so formulated as to provide a basis for, be in harmony with, and lead naturally into the more highly differentiated and elaborated structures that can be developed by

* This recommendation is discussed more fully in *Planning and Organizing for Teaching,* another volume of the Project report.

senior high school students. Learners, whatever their age, should be helped to relate facts and knowledge to concepts or organizing principles so that they continually expand their conceptual frames of reference for each field of study.

If some of the current demands for teaching the structures of separate disciplines are satisfied, there is danger that the instructional program will consist of a series of compartmentalized, noncontinuous experiences for pupils. This danger is especially strong regarding the elementary school, in which two generations of effort have been required to replace rigid time schedules and multiple separate subjects with a more unified treatment of content. Academic scholars and professional educators have a responsibility to resist proposals resulting in a fragmented school program.

Classroom procedures that encourage learning through discovery are one potential means of encouraging creative thinking, of stimulating interest and insight, and of helping pupils develop conceptual frameworks for the subjects they study. It seems likely, also, that the experimental approach can help learners recognize the tentative nature of the concepts and generalizations they form. The discovery approach must, however, be employed as one of a variety of procedures.

WHEN TO TEACH WHAT

RECOMMENDATION: *The fact that very young children* can *learn relatively difficult aspects of science, mathematics, and other subjects is at best an incomplete answer to the question of whether they* should *learn them at this particular stage of their development. Decisions about* when to teach what *should be based on both the learner's ability to understand and the relative importance of alternative ways of using the learner's time at any given point in his school experience.*

Recent experimentation provides rewarding glimpses into the relative ease with which the very young learn aspects of physics, mathematics, and foreign languages, but the fact that they *can* learn these subject matters is at best an incomplete answer to the question of whether or not they *should.*

Teachers, curriculum workers and administrators, scholars in the academic disciplines, and scholars in professional education should cooperate in the study of this problem, each group contributing according to its special competence. Teachers and administrators have firsthand knowledge of their pupils, the school and community in which they work, and the educational goals they are trying to achieve. Specialists in the academic disciplines can contribute a knowledge of the structure, method, and content of their field. Scholars in the educational disciplines can apply the latest research in learning, human development, school-society relationships, and factors involved in decision making.

Members of each group should recognize and perform in the roles for which they have special competence. For example, the scholar without experience in teaching children should refrain from dicta about how to teach his subject to third graders or ninth graders and should also refrain from specifying what should be taught to children at a given age, just as the teacher should recognize his need for assistance from the scholar in selecting pertinent up-to-date content and concepts to be taught.

In summary, the question of when to teach a particular problem or phase of a subject should be explored and answered in the light of our developing knowledge about the learning ability of boys and girls. Experimental evidence, not tradition or untested hunches, should be the guide. Ease of learning, usefulness, and pleasure in learning are principles to be applied. A great deal of specific material can be left to be learned when it is needed. Final decisions about what to teach at each school level, however, should take into account the range of educational purposes that the school should serve for all pupils.

REGIONAL CURRICULUM AND INSTRUCTION CENTERS

RECOMMENDATION: *Adequately staffed and supported regional curriculum and instruction centers should be encouraged. These centers, located mainly in universities, should work in partnership with local schools to initiate innovation and conduct experimentation and research to improve the instructional program of the public schools.*

This recommendation is discussed more fully in another volume of the Project report,* but it has specific application here. It is the view of the Committee that in the period ahead there should be extensive experimentation sponsored by schools, state education departments, and university research centers in order to cast new light on the nature of the structures of knowledge that can be learned effectively by students of various abilities and stages of maturity.

The structures of the various disciplines need to be clearly identified and described in language that the nonspecialist can comprehend. While the academic specialist must be a central figure in this process, he will need the help of nonspecialists. One of the problems to be faced in this connection is that scholars within a given discipline frequently have different views as to what are the major components of its structure so there are differences to be resolved within the disciplines themselves.

With regard to the disciplines in the school curriculum, questions such as the following need to be investigated: What sequence of experiences can be developed in the different subject fields to help learners move from simple to complex structures? How can the dangers of premature closure of structures be avoided? What kinds of curriculum materials are needed at different stages in these sequences? What experiences can be used in the various subject fields to provide for learning through discovery? Does introducing the broad structures of a subject to the young child through the intuitive approach, as suggested by the work of Piaget and his associates, enable the learner to grasp it more easily and completely at the logical level in later school years? If so, is the difference in quality of later learning sufficient to justify the time and resources used in the early instruction? Answers to many of these questions are being proposed without substantiating evidence. There is need to test such hypotheses through experimentation before accepting them as a basis for curriculum planning.

* See *Planning and Organizing for Teaching.*

KEEPING CONTENT UP TO DATE

RECOMMENDATION: *Each curriculum area should be under continuous study and evaluation and should be reviewed periodically. One purpose of such reviews is to determine whether recent findings in the academic disciplines are or should be reflected in the instructional program. These reviews should utilize the knowledge and skills of the teacher, the school administrator, the scholar in the academic disciplines, the scholar in the profession of teaching, and the lay citizen, each contributing his special competence to the total task.*

The rapid expansion of knowledge and the continuing revision of interpretations in most disciplines, particularly in the natural and social sciences, have been noted above. It is essential that the school curriculum include the most recent findings of scholarship and that content that is outmoded or unrelated to the current scene be eliminated. Each of the groups mentioned in the recommendation should participate in the task of updating the school curriculum, as no one of them is competent to do the job alone.

BASES FOR SELECTING CONTENT

RECOMMENDATION: *The objectives of the school, with a clear statement of priorities, should give direction to all curriculum planning. This applies to adding content, eliminating content, or changing the emphases on various topics and fields of study.*

Procedures and instruments for evaluating pupil progress must be specifically geared to the school's educational goals and to the curricular sequence in use in the school.

Underlying this recommendation, as all of the others that have been formulated by the National Committee, is the Committee's commitment to the broad purposes of American education. These purposes include but are not limited to the development of the intellectual powers of children and youth so that each shall gain, to the fullest extent possible, an understanding of his world, a command of basic concepts and generalizations based on knowledge, and the attitudes and skills needed for rational inquiry. The purposes of American education also include the achievement by youth of competence in human relationships, civic life, and economic activities as well as the development of standards of values and appreciation in the arts, literature, ethics, and other aspects of our culture.

This recommendation applies to all curriculum revision and experimentation, of course, but it deserves emphasis here. Some recent efforts to update aspects of the school curriculum, such as some of the curriculum projects concerned with the academic subjects, have been evaluated by measures that tested the student's retention of information concerning the discipline—and little more. The evaluation of each revision program should give attention to the range of objectives the school seeks to help pupils attain.

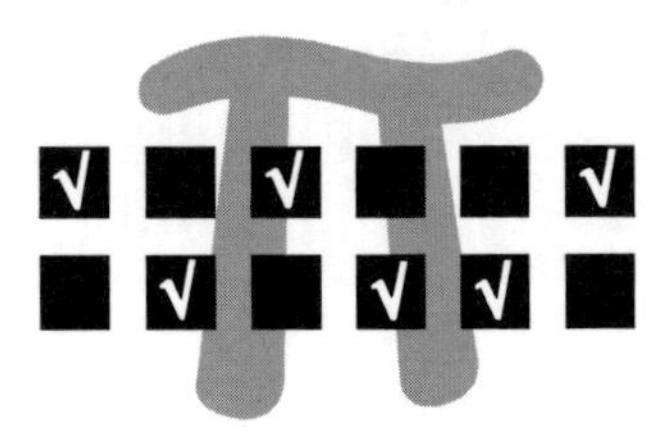

CHAPTER THREE
INSTRUCTION FOR ALL CHILDREN AND YOUTH

For Whom Must the Schools Provide?
The Complexity of Individual Differences
Differentiation for Special Groups
Providing for Differences Among Students
Recommendations of the National Committee

Public education in the United States is based on the democratic conviction that every child has a right to be helped, through elementary and secondary education, to develop his potentialities to the maximum. The national welfare demands that every child have such an opportunity. The vigor of our democratic institutions depends on the actions of citizens who apply their full range of abilities and talents to both private affairs and civic responsibilities. This conviction is vividly expressed in a statement recently developed by five departments of the National Education Association—"It is not in the might of the military, the productivity of industry, or the efficiency of transportation and communication that the true greatness of America lies. Rather, it is in the high esteem accorded the individual personality. Here, indeed, is our greatest contribution to men everywhere, and here is America's greatest secret weapon. Our philosophy of government from its very beginning, our deepest convictions, and our highest ideals have sought to clothe the individual with a sense of dignity, to recognize his potentialities, to unloose his creative powers, and to stimulate his initiative. It was on this platform that Jefferson, Adams, Lincoln, and Wilson rose to greatness."[1]

It is within this frame of reference that the National Committee of the NEA Project on Instruction has considered the problem of developing the curriculum for all members of the school population.

FOR WHOM MUST THE SCHOOLS PROVIDE?

The public schools serve over forty million individuals, each with his own pattern of potentialities and problems. These individuals range in age from the five-year-old kindergartener to the late adolescent in the secondary school.

The students in our schools come from a variety of backgrounds. They come from families of all sizes and of varying degrees of stability; from homes with high, middle, or low incomes; and from rural, urban, or suburban environments. They come from cultural subgroups in which educational achievement is variously valued—ranging from those in which such achievement is given high priority to those in which it is viewed with suspicion.

The forty million come to school with varying levels and kinds of abilities. Some learn quickly in certain fields but more slowly in others, while some are rapid, average, or slow learners in most fields of study. Some pupils develop a wide range of interests and aptitudes; others conform more or less effectively to the school's minimum requirements. They come with different self-concepts and personality traits. Some are self-confident and self-sufficient; others distrust their own abilities and lean heavily on peers or adults for reassurance and direction. Most fall between these extremes. Some are outgoing and self-possessed in social relationships; others are retiring and shy. Some have clear-cut realistic standards and goals toward which they strive effectively; in contrast, others have set their standards and goals unrealistically high or at a comfortable minimum or are drifting without definite aims.

The forty million come to school with varying physical conditions. Some are healthy and vigorous; others suffer from generally handicapping conditions such as malnutrition or specific physical handicaps. Some mature more rapidly than others of their chronological age group, some at about the same rate as most of their peers, and some more slowly.

The students in our schools have differing expectations about how extended their formal education will be. At one extreme are those who are waiting for the birthday that legally frees them from school; at the other are those who look forward to attending college and achieving a professional education.

In short, students in the public schools represent a cross section of the human abilities and aspirations of the nation. The school must provide programs of study which will both enable these children and youth to develop their unique potentialities and challenge them to do so.

THE COMPLEXITY OF INDIVIDUAL DIFFERENCES

Differences among individuals have long been recognized. Plato, in *The Republic,* proposed a social organization and an educational system based on the fact of individual differences. Only in relatively recent years, however, have psychologists, specialists in human development, anthropologists, and other scholars gathered data to describe individual differences in specific terms. This recent period has witnessed the first systematic efforts to identify the range and nature of characteristics in which individuals differ, to determine how individual characteristics can be modified, and to understand patterns of individual differences.

Although individual differences have been much studied, only a beginning has been made toward learning through research how the school should provide for them. Teachers working with pupils in classrooms cannot wait for definitive answers. As the students come, the school must take the best possible care of each, ferreting out applications of available pertinent knowledge of differences—and much of this is available.[2]

Many recent innovations in curriculum, content, and methods of instruction have been intended to provide for differences among students. Promotion plans emphasizing continuous progress instead of fixed standards and the demand for variety instead of uniformity in instructional materials and methods, for example, attempt the individualization of instruction. Other arrangements such as ability grouping, curriculum tracks, and special classes for atypical pupils have been based partly on the assumption that the range of differences within a class can be greatly reduced and perhaps eliminated by careful grouping of students.

Various groupings of students have been utilized in addition to grouping by chronological age. Children with severe physical handicaps constitute one such group. Differences in rate and depth of academic learning have been the basis for identifying academically gifted, average, and slow learners as well as mentally retarded children and youth. In recent years increasing attention has been given to the culturally handicapped, the potential dropout, and "alienated" youth. Some effort has been made to identify underachievers. Children and youth with great potential for creativity, as distinguished from academic giftedness, are the subject of considerable discussion today.

The complexity of individual differences is emphasized by the fact that no child fits exactly into one or another of these groups. Instead, each pupil possesses characteristics that cut across group identifications. For example, many culturally handicapped children are viewed as slow learners, potential dropouts, and candidates for the alienated-youth group, yet they are potentially gifted academically. Increasing evidence suggests that creative pupils may be only average learners in the academic sense, although many are found among the academically gifted as that group is customarily defined. Underachievers are found in every group.

From the outset it is clear that the educational needs of all youth cannot be met by a single, uniform program of instruction. Equal educational opportunity does not mean identical opportunity. Rather, it means that the curriculum must be differentiated for human variations if all pupils are to have equal opportunity to develop their potentialities. In planning the needed curriculum differentiations, it is helpful to recognize two levels of differences and needs among students. There are broad differences from one to another of the special groupings of pupils which have been identified—the culturally deprived, the academically talented, and so on. At a more subtle but equally significant level, unique differences, including intraindividual differences, exist between one student and another. Curriculum differentiation may be sought at each of these levels.[3]

DIFFERENTIATION FOR SPECIAL GROUPS

Three of the broad groups frequently identified in the school population have been selected for discussion here: the culturally deprived, the potential dropouts, and the talented. Each of these groups includes a sizable sector of the student population. Each cuts across other groupings that might be identified. It is urgent, from the viewpoint both of society's material well-being and its democratic values, to develop curriculums that will serve children of these groups more effectively. Nor is there any less urgency for serving other students—the slow learners, the so-called average pupils, and handicapped children—equally well. The discussion here is simply illustrative of the kinds of curriculum development which may serve type differences among groups of students.

The Culturally Deprived

Cultural deprivation is closely, though not uniformly, associated with low socioeconomic status. Culturally deprived children and youth are found in rural areas, in towns and small cities, and especially in the great metropolitan centers. Population studies indicate that in 1960 one third of the school age population in the nation's 14 largest cities was culturally deprived and that this proportion probably will reach one half in 1970. Curriculum adaptation for the culturally deprived student is therefore especially urgent in urban schools, although it is needed to some extent (and with equal urgency for the children involved) in most communities.

Culturally deprived children are found in all ethnic groups represented in American society, with the largest concentrations among such minority groups as the Negro, Puerto Rican, Mexican-American, and Indian. Not all children from minority groups are culturally disadvantaged; indeed, like other sectors of the population, these groups display a wide range of socioeconomic and cultural status. The situation simply reflects the educational and occupational disadvantages that minority groups in general face in American society.

Home Backgrounds of the Culturally Deprived. The parents of culturally deprived children often have limited education and are marginally employed. In many cases the family has moved frequently in search of employment or for other reasons, and its narrow environment moves with it. The family diet is likely to be inadequate and health practices poor. The children's acquaintance with music and other creative arts is limited. Books, magazines, and other materials to enlarge horizons are virtually nonexistent in the home. The children probably have little or no contact with such institutions as libraries or museums that might broaden their cultural experience. The frequent transfers from school to school are a further handicap to the children.

Often the pattern of the child's family life is unstable or disrupted, lacking the economic and emotional security that is characteristic of many middle class homes. School achievement is usually not highly valued in this environment, nor are the school's usual standards of speech, cleanliness, and social behavior. The picture varies from home to home, and there are positive as well as negative elements present, but the conditions described exist much too widely among those considered as culturally deprived.

The Nature of Cultural Deprivation. The effects of cultural deprivation are reflected in the inferior self-concept and limited aspirations exhibited by many culturally deprived children. They are reflected, too, in the measured intelligence quotients of these children and in the learning difficulties they encounter in school.[4] It is difficult for these children to relate conventional school studies to the real world in which they live; hence their motivation for school learning is likely to be low. In a school geared to children from more favored backgrounds—and most of our public schools are so geared—retardation for the culturally deprived youngster is likely to begin early and contribute to a mounting sense of failure and frustration.

In recent years, the nature and significance of cultural deprivation for school learning have received increasing attention from sociologists and psychologists.[5] Experimental programs to improve education for culturally deprived children and youth are being developed in a number of large cities.[6] Although the need for more research is recognized, a number of clues for enhancing the learning of culturally disadvantaged pupils have emerged. Among the major suggestions are these:

1. Provide a wide range of experiences of the kind that more favored children usually have.

2. Emphasize the teaching of reading, using a variety of materials and approaches and giving special attention to speech patterns.

3. Stress health and family living in a realistic manner related to the children's backgrounds.

4. Include study of the leaders and the contributions of minority groups to the national heritage.

5. Provide for study of the many ways of earning a living in the modern world and give older youth specific help in choosing and preparing for an occupation.

Such measures as these help the culturally deprived child form a more adequate self-concept, set higher objectives, and develop positive attitudes and behavior. Recent experimental programs emphasize closer, more cooperative relationships between school and parents than have existed in many schools in culturally deprived areas. They also emphasize cooperation with other social agencies with whom parents and children come in contact.

Providing Enriching Experiences. Various approaches are being tried to enrich the backgrounds of cuturally deprived pupils. In Racine, Wisconsin, for example, an all-day kindergarten is provided for a pilot group of 20 children identified as culturally deprived. They follow a typical school program in the mornings, with the afternoons devoted to hearing stories, examining pictures and books, watching selected films and television programs, and taking frequent field trips to parks, stores, museums, farms, and factories. These activities are "aimed at building a background of experience and understanding which can later lend meaning and motivation to learning to read."[7]

The Higher Horizons program in New York City emphasizes similar enriching experiences.[8] For third grade children, a wealth of films, pictures, charts, exhibits, and books for classroom use are available, and many trips are made to museums, parks, libraries, railroad stations, and so on; attendance at special children's concerts and theater programs has also been arranged. Junior high school pupils have attended plays, ballet performances, concerts, and the opera and visited college campuses, in addition to making field trips closely tied into their class studies. Questionnaire evaluations of this aspect of the Higher Horizons program show that teachers and parents believe the systematic efforts at cultural enrichment have contributed enormously to improved student morale and interest in school, as well as to statistically demonstrated gains in reading abilities and regular school attendance.

Emphasis on Reading. Because reading is a major key to school progress and because the culturally deprived pupil often finds learning to read a difficult task, high priority should be given to a special program of reading instruction.[9] Beginning in the kindergarten and primary grades, the program should move from appropriate informal methods to increasingly systematic instruction and be geared from the beginning to the special needs of the culturally deprived child. The number of children who will require remedial instruction in later school years probably can be substantially reduced by such a program.

Even in the beginning stages of reading, many enriching experiences are essential to give the children a background for interpreting written symbols. Reading materials related to the daily life of the children should be used. Special attention should be given to speech; the youngster who says "Ah's g'win hawm" has difficulty in learning to read "I am going home." Instruction in small class groups gives the teacher a chance to work intensively with each child.

Continued attention to reading is required in all subject areas through the middle grades and the secondary school, together with remedial instruction for those who need it. Like any other child, as the culturally deprived youngster masters the basic skill of reading he will be more successful in all of his school studies. With a major difficulty removed and conditioning for failure replaced by a realistic hope for success, the child can develop an improved self-concept, higher aspirations, and greater motivation for school learning.

Health Education. Emphasis on health education is particularly important in a curriculum for the culturally deprived child. To be effective this instruction, too, must be realistic for the child's situation. For example, standard menus based on foods that are foreign to them may mean little to Puerto Rican youngsters. The way to an improved diet may be through discussion of balanced meals based on nutritious foods that are familiar to them. Furthermore, health instruction in the school frequently must be supported by a program of parent education. Since economic deprivation is a major factor in the health problems of the culturally disadvantaged, special services the school can help to mobilize from other community agencies should also be considered.

Other Approaches for Releasing Potential. The value of study about leaders and contributions of minority groups has been well stated by the Educational Policies Commission: "Special attention to the history, culture, and contributions of Negroes and of Spanish-speaking peoples in the United States can foster self-respect, mutual respect, and a sense of identification with the school and the nation among children who are now largely ignored in school materials. Moreover, learning about progress in Puerto Rico or about contributions of American Indians and Negroes is appropriate for children of all backgrounds. And children who have lived in other places can often teach the class something about their earlier homes."[10]

Every learner needs long-range as well as immediate goals toward which he can orient his efforts. One of the emphases in experimental programs for the culturally deprived youth is on helping him establish constructive and realistic life goals. For some, this involves creating an awareness that college study is both desirable and possible. For others it may require more specific job orientation and preparation in the secondary school. Programs of part-time work combined with part-time study are being developed in a number of cities and states as a means of attacking the dropout problem (see page 62). As noted by the Educational Policies Commission again, an effective program of vocational education, in whatever form, promises multiple values for many youth from culturally deprived backgrounds. "Opportunities to learn job skills are relatively easy for the pupil to value. They can increase his interest in school. They can help him to consider himself a useful and respected person. They can develop the initiative and sense of responsibility that are basic to preparation for college as well as for new jobs. And they can be designed to introduce or incorporate lessons in science, economics, or other subjects."[11]

It should be remembered, however, that a specific vocational emphasis is appropriate only for *some* of this group. The school must recognize and serve the heterogeneity of talent and interests among the culturally deprived, or it will not meet its obligation to the student and to society.

An attitude of genuine respect for the personalities of culturally deprived children, accompanied by overt recognition that there are positive as well as negative factors in their backgrounds, is basic to success of the school's efforts to serve them. The communication that is needed with parents as well as children, if the school is to succeed in releasing the potential of culturally deprived youth, depends on such an attitude.[12]

The Potential Dropout

About 40 percent of the nation's children do not complete high school. They are the dropouts who leave school as soon as they become old enough to do so legally or soon thereafter. Grade 10 is the point at which many leave school. From the dropouts, who include a much higher proportion of boys than girls,[13] come a majority of juvenile delinquents and a high percentage of the girls who marry before or at the age of 17.

A larger proportion of school age youth finish high school today than ever before, but the sizable number who still drop out each year constitutes a critical social problem.[14] Increasingly, the youth who does not complete his high school education is unemployable. A high school education or better is becoming a requirement for employment. The unskilled jobs available to the dropouts of earlier generations are rapidly disappearing. It is urgent to solve the dropout problem, both for society and for the potential dropouts themselves.

The dropout group cuts across ethnic, social class, and geographic lines, although the largest numbers are from lower class families and many are members of minority groups. The problem is most serious in rural areas and very large cities and has been intensified in the metropolitan centers by in-migration from rural areas, especially from the South and from Puerto Rico.

Identifying the Potential Dropout. A number of studies indicate that the dropout group includes children from a wide range of intelligence. While a large proportion may be classified as slow learners, a nationwide study by the Department of Labor showed that 70 percent had measured IQ's above 90. A recent study in New York State revealed that 13 percent of the dropouts over a six-year period were above 110 in measured IQ. The average dropout is at least two years retarded in reading by the time he leaves school, and 9 of 10 have repeated at least one grade. Emotional immaturity, personality disturbances, and unstable home situations frequently attended the dropouts.[15] The most obvious characteristic of those who leave school early, however, is a record of difficulty and failure in school.

Havighurst and Stiles describe the dropouts as "alienated youth," young people who "are somehow alien to the larger society in which they live. Such youth have been unsuccessful in meeting the standards set by the society for them—standards of behavior, of learning in school, of performance on a job. By the time they reach adolescence these boys and girls are visible as the misfits in school. Either they are hostile and unruly, or passive and apathetic. They have quit learning and have dropped out of school psychologically two or three years before they can drop out physically."[16]

It is generally accepted that potential dropouts can be identified long before they reach school-leaving age, many as early as the elementary school years. Some schools have made progress in doing so. Such symptoms as reading retardation, school failures, poor study habits, recurrent tardiness and truancy, persistent lack of interest in school work, nonparticipation in extraclass activities, and apparent emotional disturbance are all signals. The school can recognize these signals and take action, either directly or by referral to other agencies or both. Early identification and appropriate handling of the pupil's problems as he grows up are therefore urged as preventive measures.[17] The Phi Delta Kappa Commission on the Prevention of Juvenile Delinquency has estimated that the numbers of teen-age alienated youth might be cut in half if all schools developed preventive programs, beginning in the kindergarten and primary grades.[18]

Work-Study Programs. To reduce dropouts and delinquency among teen-age students, work-study programs are recommended. Programs of this general type have been carried on in some schools for many years as part of vocational education. Recently, special adaptations of the work-study principle have proved effective in reducing dropout rates. For example, in New York City, a Work-Experience Program for potential school leavers was begun in 1955 with a pilot study in one vocational and one academic high school.[19] On the basis of promising results from the pilot study, the program has been expanded to 10 senior high schools, some vocational and some academic. The students spend the mornings in school and report for work in private industry in the afternoon, holding such jobs as errand boy, stock boy, or clerical worker. The classes are small (15 to 20) and the teacher-coordinator gives part of the school instruction and supervises the work on the job.

In this program, the school instruction emphasizes improvement in basic skills. Reading, job orientation, guidance, enrichment opportunities, and articulation between school and out-of-school environment are stressed. Many visual materials are used. A recently published bulletin gives materials for 13 special units of study from which teachers of these groups make selections and adaptations for their particular group.[20]

Most of the students enrolled in this Work-Experience Program have improved in school attendance, achievement, and attitudes toward school. Of those enrolled in the school year 1959-60, more than 30 percent returned to regular school programs, 30 percent continued in the Work-Experience Program, and 24 percent became fully employed or entered the armed services. The benefits to students and to society from such a program seem clear.

Pilot projects to develop various patterns of work-study programs for potential dropouts are presently under way in a number of cities and states. In Kansas City, Missouri, for example, a group of eighth grade boys (13 or 14 years old) considered to be potential dropouts and delinquents are enrolled in an experimental six-year work-study program, now in its second year, while a control group follows the regular school program.[21] St. Louis, Missouri, one of the cities in the Gray Areas Program, is experimenting with a work-study program enrolling 300 pupils who have encountered serious school difficulties.[22] Seven cities in New York are participating in the School to Employment Program (STEP) sponsored by the state education department. STEP is a work-study program for 15-year-olds identified as potential early school leavers. Pupils must spend at least two hours each day in school and work in public agencies, being paid from state funds and supervised by the school.[23] In Lane County, Oregon, a program to carry the potential dropout boy through the summer and back to school in the fall has taken the form of a summer work camp in which 16-year-olds work at cleaning up and maintaining state parks.[24]

A comprehensive plan for a work-study program for alienated youth has been proposed by the Phi Delta Kappa Commission on Prevention of Juvenile Delinquency. Boys from 13 or 14 to 18 years of age who are identified as potential school leavers would be included. Three stages are outlined: The younger boys would work in groups, under the school's supervision, in jobs that would be outside the regular labor market. These might include "sheltered workshop" situations in the school or work that would contribute to community well-being—cleaning up and maintaining parks, school grounds, beaches, and alleys, for example. From such group work the boys would move into part-time jobs in business or industry, still under school supervision. In the third stage the boy, now approaching full responsibility for himself, would work full time in a regular job with some guidance and supervision by the school or other employment service personnel. Such a work-study program under the school's direction should, in the opinion of the Commission, be supplemented by other community agencies that would provide opportunities for recreational and social activities. The cost would be much less, however, than the bill society pays each year for youth who are unemployable because of inadequate attitudes and skills and for youth who become delinquent.

The current emphasis on work-study programs to ameliorate the problems of school dropout and delinquency reflects an emergency situation. The long-range solution must lie in discovering the potential school leaver as early as possible and providing a school program to help him grow into a self-reliant, constructive citizen able to make the most of his abilities, small or great. This solution is within our grasp, if school budgets can be increased adequately.

The Talented

For at least two generations, concern for the education of the gifted or academically talented children and youth has been reflected in an accumulation of research studies.[25] The number of conferences, publications, and special school programs dealing with talented pupils indicates how this concern has accelerated in the past decade.[26]

Identifying the Talented. The student group given this attention varies in definition from study to study and from program to program. Chief attention, however, has been paid the upper 15 to 20 percent of the total school population of the nation, as identified by IQ's and scores on achievement tests. The emphasis has therefore been on academic aptitude and performance and on the college preparatory student.

Studies of academically talented learners have indicated that certain characteristics in addition to high IQ seem to be associated with giftedness. These include early physical and mental development, broad interests, alertness in observation, early and continuing interest in books, ability to stay with an interest over a period of time, ability to concentrate, easy and rapid learning—particularly in reading and arithmetic in early years—ease in handling abstractions, and a tendency toward leadership and acceptance of responsibility.[27]

The limitations of the IQ as a measure of various aspects of talent have been increasingly recognized in recent years. Attempts are now under way to identify pupils who are gifted in creativity. Although over the whole IQ range there is a fairly high correlation between measures of creativity and IQ, some evidence suggests that highly creative persons are not necessarily persons of extremely high intelligence as measured by current intelligence tests. For example, Getzels and Jackson compared a group of highly creative adolescents with a group of high IQ students from the same school population, one that was considerably above average in academic ability.[28] They found the average IQ of the high creatives to be 127, which was 23 points below that of the high IQ group. In spite of this differential the two groups were about equally superior in scholastic achievement, but they differed in significant ways: "The high IQ's tend to converge on stereotyped meanings, to perceive personal success by conventional standards, to move toward the model provided by teachers, to seek out careers that conform to what is expected of them. The high creatives tend to diverge from stereotyped meanings, to move away from the model provided by teachers, to seek out careers that do not conform to what is expected of them."[29]

Other studies also have indicated the close relation that seems to exist between creativity and divergent, unconventional thinking as compared with convergent, conforming thinking that is characteristic of many highly intelligent persons identified by high IQ's. It seems likely that many highly creative children will be missed if schools rely on intelligence tests as the major means of identifying gifted students.[30] Much more research is needed, however, before definite conclusions can be drawn about the relation of creativity and other aspects of intelligence.

Undeveloped Talent. Another group of potentially gifted students who have been largely neglected are those whose talents have been masked or actually suppressed by limited cultural backgrounds. The dramatic results of such programs as the Demonstration Guidance Project in New York City have indicated that an enriched, experience-based curriculum combined with emphasis on guidance tends to find such children and help them develop their abilities.*

In the Demonstration Guidance Project, for example, a group of 147 children selected from the upper half of their school population went from a median reading retardation of 1.4 years in grade 7 to 0.3 years above grade level at the end of the ninth grade. The median pupil in the group made a gain of 4.3 in reading score during 2.6 school years. One fifth of the group gained 11 points or more in IQ, as measured by the Otis Beta Intelligence Test, and the average gain was 4 points. The special school program was continued through the senior high school. Follow-up studies of the first group of Project pupils, who had completed only six months of the special junior high school program, showed that by the eleventh grade 13 of the boys had recorded IQ increases of 21 to 40 points. Among this first Project class, as compared with previous groups from the same junior high school, over one third more pupils than before finished high school, more than twice as many completed the academic course of study, and over three times as many entered some form of collegiate education.[31]

Studies of the educational records of adolescents identified as academically talented have led to widespread concern for the talented underachiever. These studies have revealed that perhaps 40 percent of the pupils in the upper third of the IQ range, certainly students who have the potential for advanced study, do not enter college. Reviews of the grades earned by students of high academic potential, as indicated by IQ, have shown that

* This Project was later expanded into the Higher Horizons program which includes pupils at all levels of ability. See pages 57-58 of this volume.

from 15 to 25 percent or even more of these pupils are falling below the achievement level that might have been anticipated.[32]

Clinical studies and experimental remedial programs have indicated that the causes of underachievement are extremely complex and differ from child to child. No decisive variable has been discovered which can account for differences between achievers and underachievers, and no single or simple approach that can be used to deal successfully with problems of underachievement has been found. One major conclusion has been reached, however. Since underachievement begins early and becomes part of the pupil's "life style,"[33] early identification and help for the potential underachiever will produce more results than remedial work in the senior high school.

Searching for the Talented. Efforts to identify talented students of various types should begin as early as possible in their school careers and continue throughout the secondary school, since evidence of superior ability may appear at any point in the child's development. Early identification is important for two purposes. As children grow up they can be helped to develop a realistic conception of their own abilities and set appropriate standards and goals for themselves. Equally important, school experience can be planned to develop the potential abilities of each child. Anderson has emphasized the relation of development and talent in these words: "It is a mistake to assume that talent will reveal itself in the absence of stimulation and concern; talents manifest themselves through activities which demand skill components. . . . The developmental principle involved is very clear. If a child learns to swim [for example] at the age of six years, rather than at the age of twenty, he will have many more opportunities to swim and will get a much greater amount of practice than the older person, and generally he will reach a higher level of final performance."[34]

Adequate identification procedures include observations of children by teachers and parents and examination of their achievement in class and extraclass activities as well as study of their scores on intelligence and achievement tests. Both group and individual intelligence tests should be used. If the school does not have the resources to administer individual tests, consistent scores on group tests administered over a period of years will usually be indicative. In either case, mental ability tests should be given periodically through the child's school career. Measures of creativity now can and should be included as one part of the identification process.[35]

Teaching the Gifted. There is no single prescription for a school program that will help talented children and youth develop their potential ability, but there is widespread agreement on the general characteristics of such a program. Some of these characteristics apply to both elementary and secondary schools, while some are particularly applicable to one level or the other.[36]

In both elementary and secondary school, talented children profit from an enriched program that carries them more deeply or more broadly into the subjects they study. Enrichment does not consist of additional exercises or assignments of the same type already completed but of the introduction of materials and learning activities requiring a more mature level of study and performance. When second graders are learning to tell time, for example, gifted children who have mastered this skill may "devise ways of telling the passage of time other than looking at a clock or sundial. For example, one may count his pulse, or the number of breaths he takes; variations of the hour glass principle may be used; water dropping from a narrow-necked funnel is another possibility. Study the history of clocks and discover the ingenious ways man has devised in the past to tell the passage of time."[37]

In the study of history, gifted high school students may use college level readings and collections of source materials, in addition to or in place of high school level materials. At every grade level, enrichment should involve the use of a wide range of appropriate materials, including various kinds of nontext and reference books, magazines, audiovisual materials, and community resources. Enrichment for gifted pupils may also include additional subjects beyond the basic curriculum. In the elementary school talented youngsters may be the first to begin foreign language study, for example. Adolescents of superior ability may include additional electives in their school program.

Provisions for differences among individuals, suggested in the next section of this chapter, can be applied in planning the program of study for gifted students. Thus talented pupils of all ages need many opportunities for guided individual study at a level appropriate to their maturity. Even in the primary grades talented children, with guidance, can pursue individual study of a special interest and gain the thrill of "finding out for themselves."

Flexible class procedures and assignments for the gifted stress open-ended assignments and activities that encourage divergent, original thinking and demand the use of problem-solving and critical-thinking skills. While he must learn to hold himself to painstaking work and sufficient repetitive practice, the talented student should be encouraged to move beyond drill assignments as soon as he has reached a satisfactory level of achievement. Throughout his school career, the gifted child needs to meet standards sufficiently high to demand his best efforts yet not so high as to be impossible of attainment.

In the elementary school good programs for gifted children build a strong foundation of basic study skills and habits and of constructive attitudes toward themselves and others. The talented youngster needs to learn to be precise where precision is important. He must discipline himself to the repetitive practice required to gain control of important skills, even though he can jump ahead to the "big idea" long before he has command of the steps leading to it. His elementary school studies should help the child of superior ability explore a range of subjects even though he has already developed a strongly specialized interest that he may prefer to pursue to the neglect of other areas. His elementary school experiences can help the talented child learn to accept himself as a person who can and should do many things well, often better than others can do them. At the same time, he should learn here to work easily with others and respect them as deserving the same consideration he desires for himself.

In his secondary school program the gifted youth should have opportunity for specialized studies in the fields of his particular interest, with a view to pursuing these fields in college and beyond. Thus an adequate high school program includes a range of electives in the various curriculum areas. Some of these may be advanced placement courses which may be substituted for the standard courses in the same subjects, but others besides advanced placement offerings are needed. A program of studies in high school which stresses academic subjects but is not limited to them facilitates the college progress of the academically superior student.

A range of extraclass and summer activities from which the superior student may select broadens his civic, social, and intellectual horizons.[38] These activities may include, in addition to those customarily found in high schools, special noncredit seminars and subject matter clubs worked out in cooperation with nearby colleges or drawing on the services of adults in the community. Association with adult specialists in his field of interest can help to provide the talented youth with the models he needs to set goals and build a pattern for his own development.

Curriculum Differentiation for Other Special Groups

The foregoing discussion of three broad groupings of children and youth indicates important factors in adapting the curriculum to the common learning needs of special groups of students. These same factors should be considered in planning for physically handicapped children, slow learners, or other groups that may be identified.

PROVIDING FOR DIFFERENCES AMONG STUDENTS

Differentiating the curriculum to serve individuals necessitates modification of the traditional lock step of uniform assignments carried out through identical study materials and standard procedures for all. Pupils should be helped to move toward common learning goals in areas of common educational needs but be provided appropriate alternative routes to the goals. The strengths and weaknesses of the individual have to be considered and ways found to develop the strengths and remedy the weaknesses.

Differentiating the curriculum means providing opportunities for the individual pupil to go as deeply and broadly as he is able into the fields of knowledge of his special interest. It involves helping each learner set his ladder of individual goals high enough so that he must extend himself to reach the top rung instead of stopping at the bottom. Further, it requires the usc of a variety of materials and classroom procedures, since both method and content contribute to individualization of instruction.

Use of Varied Materials

One key to curriculum adaptation is the use in every class, whether elementary or secondary and whether homogeneously or heterogeneously grouped, of a range of learning materials. Not all students will study from a great number of sources, although the more able probably will. When a variety of study materials is readily available, the teacher can help each pupil find those most useful to him. Reliance on a single textbook for study of a subject is both fallacious and undesirable.

Textbooks and reference books written at different reading levels should be available. Nontext reading materials of various degrees of reading difficulty dealing with various aspects of the topic under study are needed. A full range of audiovisual materials—films, filmstrips, recordings, models, and graphic materials of all sorts—should be on hand. Lists of community resources, including people to be consulted and places to be visited, are also useful. The growing body of programed materials and the developing tool of educational television must take their place alongside the more conventional learning materials now at the command of teachers and students.

In the case of both educational television* and programed materials, some enthusiastic supporters would have the new media

*For a discussion of educational television, see *Education in a Changing Society* and *Planning and Organizing for Teaching.*

simply replace the conventional textbook as the sole or the dominant source of study material. The result could well be less curriculum differentiation than now exists. The teaching profession must be alert, however, to see that these media find their appropriate role among the many kinds of learning materials that can be used to develop flexible programs of study.

Providing Continuity for the Learner

Although trite, the phrase "begin where the learner is" expresses a valid idea. To help pupils learn effectively, teachers must know where each pupil stands in his grasp of the material he is to study.

In a well-planned curriculum, important skills, ideas, and generalizations are introduced as early as they are appropriate and given deeper and broader elaboration in each successive school division. Hoped-for ranges of pupil achievement can and should be identified in general terms for the primary, intermediate, junior, and senior high school years, since teachers recognize that there will be enormous variations from one pupil to another in the level of achievement actually attained in each school year.

The pupil learns by building on previously gained knowledge, understanding, and skills. The materials he uses and the assignments he completes should help him advance with continuity. He should not be forced into wasteful repetition on the one hand or, on the other, be plunged into work that is beyond his depth.

To provide for continuity in learning, effective teachers systematically assess the level of achievement each pupil has attained and plan the class work so that he can proceed from that point. Standardized tests administered annually, biannually, or triannually do not provide the needed information for planning during the school year. More informal assessments are needed frequently, for example, at the beginning of each block or unit of study in a subject. These assessments should be focused specifically on the topics, understandings, and skills to be emphasized. On the basis of such pretests and diagnostic exercises and through analyses of pupil performance on preceding assignments, the teacher can direct some students to more challenging study materials and others to more elementary readings and activities. In some cases, independent work on a particular topic or skill may be indicated. When the analysis shows that several students share a common need or a specialized interest, flexible grouping within the class may be the best procedure. Thus pupils who need longer experience with a particular skill or concept, such as a better understanding of compound sentences or how to interpret scale in reading a map, can work together. Those who are ready for more advanced study can form other short-term groups. Whether the need is for simpler or more advanced work, flexible grouping can serve the specific purpose.[39]

Independent Study

Combined appropriately with group activities, independent study can be used to adapt the curriculum to each pupil's needs. Indeed, some of the most important past efforts to individualize instruction at both the elementary and the secondary levels have emphasized independent study procedures.

Laboratory methods that were developed a generation ago, such as the Winnetka and the Dalton plans, emphasized the independent study approach as a means of permitting students to move through a predetermined program, each at his own rate. Experiments with these laboratory plans indicated that they were effective in reducing retardation and in speeding up the rate of student learning.[40] They were never adopted as widely as their demonstrated results seemed to justify, however. Possibly one reason was that effective use of the laboratory plan was demanding of teacher time and required competencies that many teachers had not acquired. Elaborate sets of materials, including diagnostic tests, study guides, practice materials, record forms, and achievement tests, had to be developed to fit the curriculum of the particular school. The success of the plan also depended on a pupil-teacher ratio small enough to allow the teacher to give each pupil adequate individual guidance. Overcrowded schools and classrooms of the past two decades strengthened the hold of more traditional methods of instruction.

Current experimentation with such instructional media as programed materials and language laboratories involves some of the same elements of individualizing instruction as were present in the laboratory plans of a generation ago. However, the new media also involve other elements that make direct comparison with the older plans impossible. Now each student can work at his own pace, using materials pitched at the level of difficulty appropriate for his stage of development and in a laboratory situation permitting a tutorial relationship between teacher and pupil.

Independent study should be given another dimension, the opportunity to pursue individual projects students have selected and adapted from those suggested by the teacher or which they themselves design. Through such projects each pupil can explore and expand his specialized interests, refine his work-study skills, and strengthen his capability for self-direction and self-reliance.

For successful use of independent study to adapt the curriculum for individual pupils, a number of conditions should be observed.[41] The study needs teacher guidance that is appropriate in degree and kind to the maturity and abilities of the student. Reasonable checkpoints for the student must be set when the independent study project is planned, the nature and frequency of these points to be suitable for the particular pupil. Adequate materials and facilities for individual work are required. The independent study should be viewed by both student and teacher as a regular and integral part of school work, not as a make-up assignment or as extracredit work. Independent study is a part of every normal pupil's experience; it is not to be reserved for the academically superior students.

Some recent proposals for emphasis on independent study are parts of broader plans for drastic reorganization of the school program. Greater use of independent study may be encouraged by but need not await revolutionary changes in the organization of the school. Students can be given individual study opportunities within a conventional curriculum framework—indeed, some schools offer these opportunities today.

Alternative Specialized Courses in Secondary Schools

Perhaps the most commonly used device for adapting the secondary school curriculum to individual students has been the provision of alternative specialized courses among which students may select. As the secondary school population grew to include a wider range of abilities and interests, multiple curriculum tracks—college preparatory, vocational, business or commercial, and general, for example—were developed in the larger comprehensive high schools. In many schools the student was enrolled in one of these curriculum tracks from entrance to exit. Under this circumstance, the multiple tracks provided for type differences among groups rather than for individual differences.

Some of the student's individual needs may be met by a flexible administration of the multiple-track plan, however. The school offers a range of elective subjects, some clearly college preparatory and others clearly vocational, commercial, or general in nature. An individual high school program is worked out for each student, with the selection of courses made in terms of his interests, abilities, and long-range goals. This program then is reviewed each year in consultations between the student, his parents, and a guidance counselor, so that changes in the student's purposes and levels of achievement may be accommodated.[42]

Such a plan of individual programming, which has been in use in some high schools for many years, enables the college-bound student to elect individual courses regardless of their track as he sees need for or is interested in them. For example, he may wish to take commercial typing and shorthand in order to support himself during advanced studies as well as for the personal value of these skills. The student who does not plan to attend college may wish to elect academic courses in which he has a strong interest and for which he has adequate background and ability. This flexible plan also facilitates a change from a program of study which is oriented toward academic, vocational, or general studies toward one with another orientation, if the student's purposes and demonstrated levels of achievement change.

Individual programming for elective courses has the further advantage that students are not identified by the label of a specific group, such as academic, vocational, or general. Freedom from such labels encourages more realistic choices by many students since, as Conant pointed out, "a feeling of prestige is apt to be attached to those who are enrolled in an academic program if the school is rigidly divided into groups with different programs; and there will be pressure from ambitious parents to have their children, irrespective of ability, enrolled in the college preparatory track. Such pressures are often difficult to resist and may lead many students to attempt advanced mathematics, physics, and foreign language courses which they cannot handle."[43]

Elective courses are assigned to a particular grade in some schools—biology to grade 10 or economics to grade 12, for example. There are strong arguments for opening elective courses in the senior high school to any qualified student, regardless of his grade level. Students in any high school year vary in their maturity, their background for particular fields of study, and their performance in different areas of skill, as well as in general academic ability. Some ninth or tenth graders may be as well equipped as most twelfth graders to handle economics or an advanced literature course. By opening electives to qualified students of any grade and perhaps scheduling certain ones for alternate years, many schools can support a wider range of courses and thus enlarge the opportunities for specialized study by all students.

In smaller high schools, placing electives on a mixed-grade basis can be especially helpful for enriching a frequently impoverished elective offering. Other expedients have also proved valuable in these schools. Individual students may study appropriate correspondence courses under the supervision of a qualified member of the school staff. In some regions televised courses can be studied by small groups of students or by individuals. Courses on film and programed texts are available for a few subjects. In some instances regional planning has been carried on to enlarge the range of courses available in small schools. Circuit teachers, such as specialists in industrial arts, visit the cooperating schools on a regular schedule to teach classes that otherwise could not be offered. Language laboratories supplied with taped course materials, used in combination with the services of a circuit teacher of foreign language, permit expansion of the modern language program.[44]

Considerable curriculum flexibility for individual students can be achieved by providing a range of alternate courses and by having an individualized program of studies for each student. To truly individualize instruction, however, teachers must utilize the range of materials and procedures that are discussed above.

Extraclass Activities

In most secondary schools many extraclass activities are conducted to provide for special interests of students. Music and speech activities such as chorus, orchestra, band, dramatics, and debate sometimes give students who cannot schedule a class in these subjects opportunities for enriching experiences. Intramural sports supplement the regular classes in physical education. Special interest clubs or discussion groups in such areas as foreign language, current events, science, creative writing, photography, and home economics expand the range of choices available to many students. Voluntary seminars are increasingly conducted as a means of introducing students to fields of knowledge that cannot be explored in scheduled classes.

The enrichment values of extraclass or cocurricular activities for the individual student have been recognized for more than a generation. A recent sampling survey asked principals of 831 secondary schools to list all cocurricular activities that had been dropped or added between 1956 and 1961.* In schools of all

* National Education Association, Project on the Instructional Program of the Public Schools. *The Principals Look at the Schools: A Status Study of Selected Instructional Practices.* Washington, D.C.: the Association, 1962. pp. 7-8.

sizes—small, medium, and large—five times as many clubs had been added as had been dropped. The greatest addition was in athletic clubs (139), chiefly in small and medium-sized schools that may not previously have had these extraclass activities. Also added were specialty clubs such as speech, drama, music, and art (105); science clubs (77); and preprofessional clubs (70). This listing of added extraclass groups and clubs suggests that such voluntary activities continue to hold their popularity among efforts to meet the varied individual needs of students in secondary schools.

RECOMMENDATIONS OF THE NATIONAL COMMITTEE

Two leading educational issues of the sixties are related to the problem of developing the curriculum to serve all members of the school population. How should the schools serve various types of children and youth? What should the schools do about the overriding domestic problems of youth in contemporary society?

The National Committee of the Project on Instruction has responded to these questions with the following major recommendations.

THE INDIVIDUAL AND THE NATION

RECOMMENDATION: *The instructional program should provide (a) opportunities for developing the individual potentialities represented in the wide range of differences among people; (b) a common fund of knowledge, values, and skills vital to the welfare of the individual and the nation.*

To achieve these objectives, the instructional program cannot be the same for all. Provision for individual differences should be made by qualified teaching personnel through diagnosis of learning needs and through appropriate variety of content, resources for learning, and instructional methods.

Developing a curriculum adapted to individual pupils is a matter of enabling teachers and pupils to differentiate the school program so that each pupil can learn as rapidly, as broadly, and as deeply as his own abilities permit. As the variety, nature, and range of individual differences among learners have been more fully comprehended, it has become clear that a uniform program of study planned for a mythical normal child or a mythical group constricts rather than encourages the development of the abilities of individual pupils. Studies that have been made of various groups in the school population and curriculum proposals for them stress the heterogeneity that exists among pupils in each group that is identified.

Some curriculum differentiation may be achieved through programs designed for groups of students who are identified by types of differences in their backgrounds, abilities, or other outstanding characteristics. When the range of differences among pupils within a class is reduced by such grouping, both the common and the individual needs of students may be met more effectively. If, however, the "myth of the group" blinds the teacher to the heterogeneity that inevitably exists among his pupils, no matter how striking their common characteristics may be, he is encouraged to offer a uniform program for all. Then the advantages that can be gained by narrowing the range of differences are lost. To develop the unique potential of each pupil and to enable him to overcome his particular pattern of learning problems, there should be regular use of diagnostic measures, varied learning materials, and independent study, as well as flexible grouping arrangements.

Early identification of children's special abilities and particular learning problems is essential if the school is to provide a curriculum to meet their individual needs. Potential talents may be lost or minimized unless the child has opportunity to begin their development at an early age. Learning problems are better dealt with through preventive measures than through remedial programs to correct difficulties that have become fixed. The number of youth for whom remedial teaching is necessary can be reduced through school programs in which their learning difficulties are recognized and handled as they emerge.

Schools that serve areas where many of the families are culturally and economically underprivileged should make up as far as possible for the handicaps of the children. They should give particular emphasis to enriching the children's experience in the kindergarten and first grade and should continue this enrichment in the elementary and secondary school as it is needed. Because learning to read often presents special problems for culturally deprived youngsters and because this ability is a key to much of school learning, the school should provide reading instruction that is especially designed to help these children overcome their difficulties in gaining command of this basic learning tool. Because cultural deprivation masks potential abilities and limits the aspirations children can hold for themselves, schools that serve deprived areas should provide special guidance and other helps to overcome these problems.

Continued research, experimentation, and analysis are needed to invent new approaches, procedures, and materials for curriculum differentiation and to refine old ones. But some useful ways of breaking the barrier of a uniform, stereotyped curriculum have been discovered and demonstrated. Evidence of this is the fact that the approaches and procedures cited in this chapter are now being used in the schools of the nation, to various extents, in many places.

YOUTH UNEMPLOYMENT AND JUVENILE DELINQUENCY

RECOMMENDATION: *The schools can help to combat such serious national problems as youth unemployment and juvenile delinquency by (a) evaluating the intellectual and creative potential of all children and youth in the schools; (b) identifying early the potential dropout and delinquent; (c) developing positive programs to challenge these young people to educational endeavor; (d) participating in cooperative programs with parents and with community groups and organizations—business and industry, labor, service groups, government agencies, and the many youth-serving agencies.*

A school staff that faces its instructional problems realistically will find much valuable help in the growing body of information about children and youth in today's society—particularly about urban children and youth. Current studies in sociology, psychology, and education yield information about factors that frequently deter learning and about ways in which schools can cope with these factors.

The studies challenge some of the assumptions and point out some of the misconceptions that have stood in the way of greater progress in educating children who are economically and culturally deprived. The assumption, for example, that these children are not interested in education rests heavily but precariously on the fact that many culturally deprived young people are discontented with school. They *are* discontented with school, but they are not necessarily disinterested in education; in their experience and in their vocabulary, school and education have not been synonymous. The values they attach to education are not adequately reflected in the school's instructional program, as they see it. The school places a high value on education for its own sake and for the contribution it can make to self-fulfillment, broadly interpreted. These values are not impressive to many culturally deprived young people. What they want from education is help in making a living and in being more secure economically. They also want a workable knowledge of reading, mathematics, and science and oral and written communication so that they can find their own way through the intricacies of modern living without being "taken in" and without being overly dependent on others for protection against ignorance.

Schools should devote special efforts to early identification of potential dropouts, beginning in the early elementary years. They should develop school programs that will help these children avoid the social maladjustment and the learning problems that encourage them to drop out before they have completed their high school education. The school should help children and youth utilize the service of other community groups and organizations that conduct recreational, health, or other youth-serving programs.

To meet the immediate crisis faced by adolescents who are potential dropouts and delinquents, there should be further development of work-study programs for youth who have done poorly in school. Enough evidence that such programs are effective, although they do not solve all problems, has accumulated to justify extending them to the large group of students identified as potential dropouts and delinquents. If Congress passes legislation to support youth employment programs, the schools should work closely with such programs.

Nine recommendations dealing with school organization, which are developed in the last volume of the Project report, have important implications for the problems involved in developing the curriculum for all members of the school population. They are presented here in summary form. The reader may consult *Planning and Organizing for Teaching* for an elaboration of them.

NONGRADING, MULTI-GRADING, GRADING

RECOMMENDATION: *The vertical organization of the school should provide for the continuous, unbroken, upward progression of all learners, with due recognition of the wide variability among learners in every aspect of their development. The school organization should, therefore, provide for differentiated rates and means of progression toward achievement of educational goals.*

Nongrading and multigrading are promising alternatives to the traditional graded school and should be given careful consideration in seeking to provide flexible progress plans geared to human variability.

BASES FOR ABILITY GROUPING

RECOMMENDATION: *The assignment of pupils to classroom groups should be based on knowledge about students and teachers and on understanding of goals to be achieved.*

Efforts to set up groups in terms of ability and/or achievement do little to reduce the over-all range of pupil variability with which teachers must deal. However, selective grouping and regrouping by achievement sometimes is useful, particularly at the secondary school level.

TEAM TEACHING

RECOMMENDATION: *In order to provide individually planned programs for learners, taking into account the specific objectives to be achieved, the horizontal organization of the school should permit flexibility in assigning pupils to instructional groups that may range in size from one pupil to as many as a hundred or more. Well-planned cooperative efforts among teachers—efforts such as team teaching, for example—should be encouraged and tested.*

SELF-CONTAINED CLASSROOM

RECOMMENDATION: *The school should be organized in such a way that it provides opportunity for each student to (a) experience continuity and relatedness in his learning, and (b) have a close counseling relationship with competent teachers who know him well. Various forms of organization should be explored to determine their effectiveness for these purposes.*

The contributions of specialized personnel should be used as students progress through the elementary and secondary school. At whatever point specialized personnel are brought into the instructional program, their work should be coordinated with and related to the total program.

CLASSROOM GROUPING

RECOMMENDATION: *In schools where the classroom is the unit of organization, teachers should organize learners frequently into smaller groups of varying types and sizes. Decisions as to size and membership of such groups should be based on knowledge about learners and on the specific educational purposes to be served at a given time for each learner.*

INSTRUCTIONAL MATERIALS CENTERS

RECOMMENDATION: *In each school system, there should be one or more well-planned instructional materials and resources centers, consisting of at least a library and an audiovisual center. In each school building, there should also be an instructional resources facility.*

These centers should be staffed by persons who are adequately prepared in curriculum and instruction, in library service, and in audiovisual education.

ETV AND RADIO

RECOMMENDATION: *The use of educational television (ETV) and radio to broaden and deepen learning should be encouraged. Such use should be accompanied by a vigorous program of research and experimentation.*

PROGRAMED INSTRUCTION

RECOMMENDATION: *Schools should make use, with proper supervision, of self-instructional materials and devices (programed instruction) that facilitate varied learning opportunities and continuous progress for learners of widely divergent abilities. The use of programed instruction should be accompanied by a vigorous program of research and experimentation.*

INSTRUCTIONAL MEDIA

RECOMMENDATION: *A comprehensive study and action program is needed to improve the quality and use of printed teaching materials and other instructional media. Such a study and action program requires the participation of both the producers and the consumers of these instructional materials and media.*

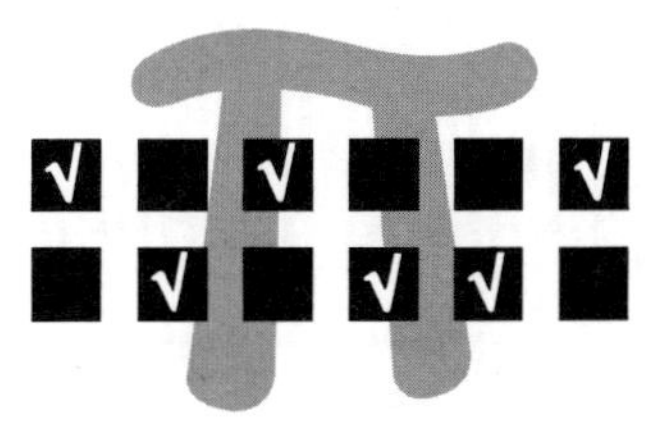

CHAPTER FOUR

WHAT SHALL BE INCLUDED IN THE CURRICULUM?

A Continuum of Opinion
The Expansion of the School Program
Broadened Goals and the School Program
The School and Youth-Serving Agencies
Responsibilities of American Schools
Social Trends As Curriculum Content
Recommendations of the National Committee

The question "What shall the schools teach?" and its counterpart "What shall the schools *not* teach?" constitute a central issue in many recent attempts to appraise American education. Individuals and groups have made widely varying recommendations as to the content and emphases that should be given major treatment, receive only peripheral attention, or be excluded from the school program altogether. Some favor an expanded school program that includes a broad range of subjects and activities, both practical and academic in nature. Others propose a restricted program focused sharply on academic subjects. Between these two positions we find recommendations that reflect many shades of opinion about the proper role of the school in American society as well as different views of the learning process.

A CONTINUUM OF OPINION

There is agreement among educators and laymen alike that one function of the school is to induct youth into the culture of their society. This induction, it is agreed, involves transmitting our heritage to the new generation. But this heritage includes much more than can be taught in the school, and selections must be made. What elements should be chosen and on what basis? Is social utility of particular knowledge a leading criterion? Is the survival of certain elements over the ages a chief basis of selection? Are priorities to be given materials that have inherent, immediate interest for today's students? Should elements of the heritage which introduce students to the academic disciplines, or the fields of knowledge as traditionally organized, be given priority? Should the relevance of particular content to critical problems of society today be a criterion for selection? How much emphasis should be placed on the problems themselves?

In a relatively static society there is likely to be a high degree of consensus in answers to these basic questions. But American society has experienced rapid transformation in recent decades, and the rate of social change is expected to continue to accelerate.

Therefore disagreements arise as to how youth can most effectively be inducted into a changing culture. Divergences among philosophies of education become more apparent. Conflicting elements in various theories of learning are highlighted. The effective development of intellectual competence or the power of rational thought, is given high priority by all schools of educational philosophy; yet how best to achieve it is a subject of fundamental disagreement. Thus the question of what shall or shall not be included in the school program is a central issue.[1]

The range of opinions concerning the school's function may be illustrated by citing three possible positions on a continuum. The first position, at one extreme, limits the school's responsibility to the intellectual training of children and restricts the curriculum almost exclusively to academic subjects.[2] The second, a middle position, prescribes a somewhat broader program, one that takes into account the child's total development. While reflecting due regard for emotional, social, physical, and vocational aspects of his growth, this position emphasizes the pupil's intellectual development as the basic function of the school and calls on other social institutions and agencies to share responsibility for the child's other needs.[3] According to the third view, at the other extreme, the school would accept full responsibility for the entire range of intellectual, social, physical, and vocational needs of youth served by the particular school and provide an expanded program of instruction and services to meet these needs.[4]

Comparison of these divergent positions does more than highlight their disagreement as to the purposes of education. It also shows that even people who agree on broad educational purposes may disagree about the school's proper role in achieving these purposes. The education of a child and his experience in school are not synonymous. Family, church, mass media, nonschool recreational facilities, and social agencies in the community are powerful educational forces in the lives of children and youth. The schooling of young people needs to be studied in relation to these nonschool educational forces. Moreover, this relationship should be re-examined as changes occur in the schools, in the nonschool agencies, and in the total society.

THE EXPANSION OF THE SCHOOL PROGRAM

The current controversy over what the schools shall and shall not teach has roots reaching far into the nation's past. Certainly it dates back to the time when Benjamin Franklin, a practical man, proposed a secondary school program that would include applied as well as academic subjects. The demands for a broader, more functional program of studies in both the elementary and secondary school grew through the nineteenth century. Before the century ended, the common school curriculum gradually came to include, in addition to the three R's, some aspects of such subjects as history, geography, government, natural science, physical training, drawing (chiefly as a practical subject), manual training, cooking, sewing, and music. A similar trend brought into the secondary school a greater number of subjects, including "practical" studies.

This expansion of the school curriculum was heartily criticized by some who spoke in colorful language of the need to get rid of "fads and frills," return to a school program consisting of "essentials," and eliminate the tendency to make learning too easy and too entertaining. One critic, writing in 1900, presented these arguments and concluded, "The mental nourishment we spoon-feed our children is not only minced but peptonized so that their brains digest it without effort and without benefit and the result is the anaemic intelligence of the average American schoolchild."[5]

The continued expansion of the school curriculum during the first half of the twentieth century is well known. In introducing additional subjects and services, the schools were responding to a variety of pressures and developments discussed more fully in another volume of this Project report.*

* See *Education in a Changing Society.*

The school's response to an increasingly complex technology was not a case of empire building by educators, as some current comments would imply, but a response to pressures from various sectors of society. Demands for commercial and vocational education suited to the needs of the new technology, for example, came from employer, labor, and agricultural organizations and led to the introduction of full programs of courses in these fields soon after the turn of the century. Driver education is a more recent example of an addition made to many school programs in response to demands from organized groups, including the Automobile Association of America, the National Safety Council, insurance companies, and organizations such as those represented on the President's Committee on Traffic Safety. These groups, impressed by the enormous toll of highway deaths and injuries, called on the school to help solve this problem caused by the new technology. Current pressures for physical fitness programs in the schools, spearheaded by the President's Committee on Physical Fitness, provide a third example. Induction of the young into their culture has been regarded as including direct preparation to live under the conditions created by an industrialized, urbanized society.

Pressures were exerted on the schools to prepare children in many areas heretofore considered the responsibility of home, church, and other segments of the community. These pressures arose partly because changing patterns of family and community life diminished the amount of informal, out-of-school education in such areas as health, homemaking, recreation, and vocational preparation. They arose also because conditions of urban living made it increasingly imperative, both for society and for the individual, that all children learn ways of living safely and healthfully, making wise consumer choices, using leisure time positively, and practicing constructive citizenship. The need for greater personal competence for living in the complex society of twentieth century America was recognized by such varied groups and movements as the Better Business Bureau, the National Association for Mental Health, and the periodic White House Conferences on Children and Youth.

Such pressures were reinforced by realization that a body of scientific or technical knowledge bearing on these areas was being built up that was not available to many parents and other adults. This knowledge could be transmitted to young people more effectively, it was believed, through systematic school instruction than through informal contacts with parents and others in the community.

Factors within the school itself also contributed to the expansion of the school program and to a broadening of educational purposes. The changing nature of the growing school population has been noted in earlier chapters. The wider range of abilities and vocational goals represented in this new school population, particularly in the secondary school, reinforced demands that a broader range of subjects and services be offered by the school. The induction of youth into the culture called for differentiated school programs for pupils of different levels of ability, cultural backgrounds, and vocational objectives.*

Investigations in the behavioral sciences suggested the close relation between the child's intellectual growth and his physical, emotional, and social development. Evidence accumulated that a pupil preoccupied with emotional problems or suffering from poor physical health is handicapped in his intellectual endeavors. This evidence suggested that, for the school to fulfill effectively its traditional responsibility for intellectual training, it must care for these other aspects of the pupil's development.

The school should provide for these needs of children and youth, it was urged, not only to facilitate intellectual training but because the needs were important in themselves. As a result, more explicit attention to character education, civic training, mental health, physical fitness, social development, and occupational guidance was given in many schools. These areas were provided for through the program of studies, extraclass activities, and special services such as guidance counseling and health examinations.

* See Chapter Three.

BROADENED GOALS AND THE SCHOOL PROGRAM

The teaching profession's acceptance of the school's responsibility for the social, emotional, and physical development and the specific vocational goals of pupils as well as for intellectual training was made explicit by two famous statements of educational objectives. They were the "Seven Cardinal Principles of Education" (1918) and *The Purposes of Education in American Democracy* (1938). Both statements also stressed the school's obligation to acquaint young people with critical social trends.

Nevertheless, transmission of the cultural heritage and intellectual training of the young remained basic educational purposes. The curriculum of every school continued to include the fundamentals along with the new emphases and subjects. The addition of health education or home economics did not mean that students no longer studied English or science, for example. Study of society's problems did not replace history. Change in the school program was a matter of adding new responsibilities rather than eliminating its older ones and of seeking more effective ways of inducting the young into their society.

During the period since World War II the broadened conception of educational goals expressed in the "Seven Cardinal Principles" and *The Purposes of Education in American Democracy* has become more and more a part of the American culture. Today, acceptance of broad goals for the schools pervades the thinking of many lay citizens as well as that of most professional educators. The development of a national community and the increased mobility of the population have reinforced the idea that mental and physical health, civic training, and social development of the young are proper responsibilities of the schools. So has the interest of the general public in psychology and personality development, as indicated by the many popularized articles and books dealing with these areas. A segment of tradition has begun to build up in support of school programs that serve emotional, social, and physical needs of youth.*

* See Chapter Seven for a discussion of these and other broad forces affecting curriculum decisions.

Programs and activities of such lay organizations as the National Congress of Parents and Teachers, the National School Boards Association, and various citizens committees for the schools are evidence of public acceptance of broad educational goals for the school. The recommendations of the 1960 White House Conference on Children and Youth concerning education also revealed that there was a widespread agreement among the delegates that the schools, in addition to providing intellectual training, should prepare children and youth to meet the civic, vocational, and personal-social responsibilities that confront citizens in modern America. [6] Even many persons who have charged the schools with placing undue emphasis on nonacademic aspects of their programs do not deny that formal education should take social, physical, and vocational needs of the learner into account. [7]

It is the view of the National Committee of the Project on Instruction that identification of the essential objectives of the school program must be premised on a recognition that education is a process of changing behavior and that a changing society requires that its members acquire the capacity for self-teaching and self-adaptation. Therefore, priorities in educational objectives need to be placed upon such ends as (a) learning how to learn, how to attack new problems, how to acquire new knowledge; (b) using rational processes and developing an abiding interest in learning; (c) exploring values in new experiences; (d) understanding concepts and generalizations; (e) competence in basic skills.

The Committee recommends these objectives for schools in every community in every part of the United States. They might be considered the national objectives of the schools. *How* they are to be achieved in the school program will vary from one community to another, as will the degree of emphasis on social, physical, and vocational needs of learners. These objectives constitute general criteria for deciding what shall be included and excluded in planning the school program. They must be translated by each school system into more specific criteria that take into account the considerations discussed in the remainder of this chapter.

THE SCHOOL AND YOUTH-SERVING AGENCIES

The broadened concept of educational purposes so widely accepted by both educators and laymen in recent decades was interpreted by many to mean that the school had exclusive responsibility, or nearly so, for facilitating all aspects of children's development. This was a logical interpretation in a day when the school was society's only organized agency for dealing with children and youth, as was largely the case when the "Seven Cardinal Principles" were first enunciated.

The Expansion of Services for Youth

In the period since then, however, other social institutions or agencies have been modified or created in response to the same changing conditions that were reflected in the schools. Many of these agencies have provided services for children and youth, either specifically or through programs offered to the community at large. Public health organizations, social work agencies, and community recreation programs, for example, were established in many cities and states. In rural areas, federal agencies sponsored 4-H Clubs and the Future Homemakers of America, organizations that serve social as well as certain educational needs of their members. Nondenominational youth organizations, such as Boy Scouts, Girl Scouts, and Junior Red Cross increased their activities to reach larger numbers of both urban and rural children and youth. In many religious groups the role of the church in society was re-examined and broader programs of education, recreation, and youth services were developed. Many public libraries added lectures, recorded concerts, art exhibitions, and other special events, some of them specifically designed for children and youth.

Adult Education

New agencies now provide types of popular and adult education which have implications for school programs.[8] The mass communications media are powerful agents of informal education with both positive and negative aspects. Programs of adult education, under the sponsorship of states and communities, offer older youth as well as adults opportunities that range from recreational activities and cultural studies to technical training. Some labor unions now sponsor educational programs for their members and their families. A number of large corporations conduct extensive educational programs for their employees, including basic technical training. The old idea that "you can't teach an old dog new tricks" has given way in the face of evidence that power to learn persists through the adult years.

Thus the secondary school no longer provides students who are not college bound with their final opportunity for organized study. In recent years, too, dramatically larger proportions of high school graduates have continued their formal education beyond the secondary school, whether in a four-year college, a technical institute, or a multipurpose community or junior college. Some of the things the school teaches may now be postponed until the years after high school.

Reconsidering the School's Functions

The school's function in the total education of young people today needs reconsideration in the light of the multiplication of youth-serving agencies and the expansion of adult education programs. Duplication of effort may be avoided, and better coordination of programs may be arranged by clarifying the school's relationship to these other organizations and programs. Such a re-examination need not and should not, in the opinion of many educators and laymen, lead to a narrowing of educational purposes and opportunities for pupils. Rather it should result in closer cooperation among all youth-serving agencies in the local community, including the school. More adequate attention to the full range of educational purposes can result as each agency concentrates on the services it can render most effectively. To the extent that other agencies are indeed caring for social, psychological, physical, and vocational needs of pupils, the school can reduce its efforts in those areas and focus its resources on its more traditional functions.

However, communities vary widely in the health facilities, social work organizations, recreational opportunities, and other services that are provided outside the school. In some communities, for example, many supervised social activities for teen-agers are provided through churches, civic clubs, and tax-supported recreation programs in parks and youth centers as well as by families of the children. In others the school may be the only agency that is concerned with such activities, and most parents may ignore the need for them. In middle or upper income communities, parents are likely to take the initiative in arranging physical examinations and medical care for their children. In slum areas such health care will not be provided for a majority of children and youth unless the school takes the lead. Even where an impressive range of privately sponsored organizations and tax-supported programs are operating such services, their coordination and the question of what proportion of the children are reached by them—or can be reached—needs study.

Whether a school system should maintain, expand, or reduce its provisions for the social, emotional, and physical development of its students is a local decision. This decision is not a matter of national policy, nor can it be made at the state level. Rather, the role of the school depends on the extent to which other agencies in the immediate community, including the families of pupils, are providing the experiences and services needed by children.

The school should be expected to take the lead in assessing students' needs and in arranging for coordination of activities of existing youth-serving agencies in the community. It should also take the initiative in stimulating the provision of additional services needed by students which the school cannot provide from its own resources.

The foregoing discussion, as well as that in Chapter Three, suggests that the question of what shall be included in and excluded from the school program must be answered differently in different communities. The educational needs and purposes of pupils and the work of nonschool youth-serving agencies condition the answer. Yet there are certain educational functions that only the school is called on to fulfill in American society. It is these functions, which will not and perhaps cannot be carried on effectively outside the school, which constitute its distinctive responsibilities. Every school is expected to include in its program the subjects and activities that are necessary to carry out these responsibilities which include introducing the child to his cultural heritage in a systematic manner, developing his skills of communication and rational thought, reinforcing moral and spiritual values, giving him information about the world of work, and developing aesthetic appreciations.

In addition to providing for these distinctive responsibilities, each school needs to examine its unique student body and community setting to determine what other functions it should undertake in order to serve the educational needs and purposes of its student body. The functions that are identified as a result of this examination may be classified as the shared responsibilities of the school, since the school may be one of several social agencies that participate in meeting these needs of students.

No hierarchy of subjects or activities is to be associated with the classifications of distinctive and shared educational responsibilities. Every school should give attention to both categories. Subjects that carry out the shared responsibilities are not fads and frills; indeed, they may be just as essential for pupils of a particular school as are those that implement the school's distinctive functions.

Areas of learning which are recognized by the National Committee of the Project on Instruction as distinctive responsibilities of the school are reading and related language arts; social studies; science and mathematics; literature and the arts; health instruction and foreign languages, which may not be studied by all pupils but which should be available. There is less agreement about how these studies should be organized, on the relative emphasis among them, and as to the school levels at which they should be taught.* There is evidence, as indicated in the preceding chapter, that these studies must be handled differently for children of different levels of ability and from varying cultural backgrounds, if pupils are to profit fully from the instruction. There is consensus, however, that the program of every school should include these areas of learning. Simpler elements will be drawn from them and organized to constitute most of the general education portion of the curriculum common to pupils in the elementary and secondary school. More advanced and specialized courses in most of these fields will be offered in the secondary school for college-bound students, as a basis for advanced study.

Areas of learning representative of the shared responsibilities of the school are specialized vocational and business education, work experience, social development, basic cultural experiences for pupils of impoverished backgrounds, driver education, consumer education, and home and family living.

The proportion of the total program devoted to the distinctive and the shared areas of learning will differ considerably from school to school. The ratio depends on such factors as the socioeconomic backgrounds of the student body, the long-range educational goals of the students, and the services available to them from social institutions and agencies other than the school.

Thus the suburban school, 75 percent or more of whose graduates enter a four-year college, properly places greatest emphasis on academic subjects drawn from the distinctive areas of learning. It selects from the shared areas of learning those subjects and activities that are appropriate for its students and that are not provided by other agencies in the community. Driver education, for example, may fill an important need for a teen-age student body

* Problems of priority and balance in the curriculum are discussed in Chapter Five. For discussion of curriculum organization, see *Planning and Organizing for Teaching.*

in which many pupils have their own cars or regularly drive the family vehicle. This need may not be met unless the school does so. This does not mean that driver education should replace another basic subject in the student's program.

A school serving a slum neighborhood, on the other hand, may wisely emphasize enriching cultural experiences, personal orientation, and social development, including recreational activities, if these needs are not adequately met by other agencies. Its program may stress specific vocational preparation and work experience. Through such emphases, the school in a low socioeconomic neighborhood may enable its pupils to gain much more from their studies in the areas that are the school's distinctive responsibility at the same time that they are gaining saleable vocational skills. All students, however, should study a basic core of knowledge and develop the fundamental skills constituting the distinctive responsibilities of the school.

The school may fulfill aspects of both its distinctive and its shared responsibilities through cocurricular activities as well as through organized courses. In the secondary school, for example, student publications can provide stimulating writing experiences. Subject matter clubs and seminars, such as science or art clubs, can deepen pupils' interest and knowledge in these fields. Activities contributing to social development and aesthetic appreciations may hold a prominent place in the cocurricular schedule. For many adolescents, participation in cocurricular activities seems to satisfy a need for affiliation with age-mates in their own projects and also to enhance students' performance in their formal studies. These considerations suggest that cocurricular activities of a nature appropriate to the needs and interests of the student body should be included in the school program.

SOCIAL TRENDS AS CURRICULUM CONTENT

In considering the problem of inclusion and exclusion in program planning, one question that is sometimes raised is whether information about social forces and trends is appropriate curriculum content. The impossibility of drawing an exact blueprint of American society as it will exist in the 1980's or in the twenty-first century—the world of tomorrow in which today's pupils will live—is generally admitted. Our culture is changing too rapidly for that to be possible. The generation now in school will almost certainly live their adult years in a society as radically different from today's as the society of the sixties is different from that of the early twentieth century.

Social scientists and scholars in related fields, however, have identified some of the basic forces that are shaping today's culture into new patterns. They have pointed out emerging social trends and some of the associated problems that are already apparent. These trends include the continuing development of science and the accelerating technological revolution, the changing patterns of economic growth, the continuing urbanization of our culture, the growth of international tensions and the increasing international interdependence, and the rapidly multiplying world population.*

Inducting youth into the culture of their society includes acquainting students with such prominent social forces and emerging trends as those named. It includes helping youth learn to apply the processes of rational analysis and critical thinking to consideration of contemporary social problems. No one expects that students will "solve" any of the problems they study, in the sense that solving requires definitive action. But through such study young people can gain better understanding of the issues of this decade and thus be better prepared to react intelligently to critical problems of the future. Although today's youth cannot be given a blueprint of their adult world, with specific descriptions of its achievements and tensions, they can learn how to approach both the achievements and the problems rationally and constructively. They can gain a background of information that

* See *Education in a Changing Society* for a more detailed discussion of these social forces.

will help them understand new problems as they emerge in specific forms, for the critical problems of tomorrow will be directly related to basic forces and trends that are in operation today.

To provide for effective study of social forces, trends, and problems in the school program, three considerations should be kept in mind.

Identifying social trends is a matter of predicting from available evidence. As evidence is accumulated, the prediction may be reinforced or it may be modified. The study of social trends in the schools should be based on factual information about emerging developments. The study should also include sufficient attention to the methods of analysis used by scholars in their investigations so that pupils will understand how the conclusions were derived and that they probably will be modified in the light of future developments. Such study will prepare youth to better understand new social trends that may emerge during their lifetimes.

The study of social forces and trends affects many and perhaps all areas of the school curriculum, although the heaviest load of content relating to emerging developments falls to social studies courses. For example, some aspects of the impact of science and technology on the culture will be studied in science courses, others in courses in literature and the arts, and others in health and physical education classes. Vocational and commercial courses also include consideration of this emerging trend. Analytical study of the social problems resulting from this and other social trends, however, falls into the realm of the social studies. The Program for Improving the Teaching of World Affairs, which has been conducted in Glens Falls, New York, in recent years, is an example of how the study of a major problem area may pervade the entire school program.*

Finally, the inclusion of social trends and problems as curriculum content demands classroom study about selected controversial

* See *Current Curriculum Studies in Academic Subjects* for a summary description of this program.

issues. The serious tensions and problems that are interwoven with basic social change are subjects of controversy among different groups in society. Almost every contemporary social problem sufficiently important to justify its study in the schools will have controversial aspects. To ignore this fact is to mislead youth about the realities of social change and to rob them of stimulating opportunities to develop skill in rational analysis. The question of teaching about controversial issues is discussed more fully in Chapter Six, where criteria for the selection of problems to be studied and for ways of conducting the study objectively are presented.

Including study of social forces, trends, and problems in the curriculum does not replace nor minimize the necessity for teaching about our cultural heritage. On the contrary, the study of contemporary trends and problems should be firmly based in a comprehensive knowledge of the past. In this way, a study of this nature can serve to vitalize the pupil's understanding of his cultural heritage.

RECOMMENDATIONS OF THE NATIONAL COMMITTEE

The views of the National Committee concerning what should be included in the school program and what should be excluded are summarized in two major recommendations. Each of these recommendations is addressed to a specific issue that bears upon the general question of the function of the school in American society today. The first deals with the division of responsibility between the school and other youth-serving agencies; the second, with the school's responsibility for introducing youth to political, economic, and social forces that are shaping the present-day world. A third related recommendation, which is elaborated more fully in Chapter Six, deals with teaching about controversial issues.

DISTINCTIVE AND SHARED RESPONSIBILITIES

RECOMMENDATION: *Priorities for the school are the teaching of skills in reading, composition, listening, speaking (both native and foreign languages), and computation . . . ways of creative and disciplined thinking, including methods of inquiry and application of knowledge . . . competence in self-instruction and independent learning . . . fundamental understanding of the humanities and the arts, the social sciences and natural sciences, and mathematics . . . appreciation of and discriminating taste in literature, music, and the visual arts . . . instruction in health education and physical education.*

Responsibilities best met by joint efforts of the school and other social agencies include development of values and ideals . . . social and civic competence . . . vocational preparation.

The decision to include or exclude particular school subjects or outside-of-class activities should be based on (a) the priorities assigned to the school and to other agencies; (b) data about learners and society and developments in the academic disciplines; (c) the human and material resources available in the school and community.

CURRENT SOCIAL FORCES AND TRENDS

RECOMMENDATION: *To help the student think critically about current issues, the curriculum should provide opportunities for adequate instruction concerning social forces and trends. Attention commensurate with their significance in modern society should be given to issues such as international relations, economic growth, urbanization, population growth, science and technology, and mass media.*

CONTRO-
VERSIAL
ISSUES

RECOMMENDATION: *Rational discussion of controversial issues should be an important part of the school program. The teacher should help students identify relevant information, learn techniques of critical analysis, make independent judgments, and be prepared to present and support them. The teacher should also help students become sensitive to the continuing need for objective re-examination of issues in the light of new information and changing conditions in society.*

CHAPTER FIVE

ESTABLISHING BALANCE AND PRIORITIES

Dimensions of Curriculum Balance
Current Problems in Achieving Balance
The Reading Program
Foreign Languages in Elementary School
Developing a World Perspective
Recommendations of the National Committee

What is a balanced school program? What hierarchy of priorities should be recognized in scheduling student time for various subjects and school experiences? There is no set of specifications for a balanced curriculum which can be applied to every school in the United States, just as there is no uniform prescription to determine what should be included and excluded from the school program. The same factors that the local school faculty must consider in deciding what to teach must also be studied as a basis for establishing balance and priorities in its curriculum. These are society's demands on the school, the abilities and life goals of the students, and the community services available to children and youth. Even more fundamental is the hierarchy of educational purposes of the individual school.

Indeed, a balanced curriculum is one that will lead pupils to achieve the educational goals that have been set. Priorities in the curriculum must parallel priorities among the goals. Establishing balance and priorities in the curriculum is thus an extension of the process of determining what should be included or excluded in planning the school program.

Although it is not feasible to describe *the* balanced school program nor to set a hierarchy of priorities that every school should adopt, there are common, continuing problems in planning for a balanced program. Some specific problems have assumed special urgency today. Some leading priorities should be considered by every school staff, with appropriate adaptations to the immediate situation. This chapter is devoted to discussion of such problems and priorities.

DIMENSIONS OF CURRICULUM BALANCE

Alexander and Moorer have identified two dimensions of balance in the school program.[1] The first describes what the school provides, the "curriculum planned"; the second has to do with what individual pupils actually experience, the "curriculum had." Both dimensions deserve the thoughtful attention of curriculum planners.

The school's provided curriculum sets the limits within which pupils may select. If the program offered is narrow, with obvious gaps in the subjects or experiences that are available, the curriculum that pupils actually study will have the same shortcomings.

Thus the elementary school program that includes little or no science restricts children's opportunities to learn about this important field. If instruction in health and physical education consists of more or less supervised recess periods, children receive little help in developing desirable attitudes and habits for healthful living. If experiences with music and art are limited to those that can be tied into the study of other subjects, children are handicapped in developing related aesthetic appreciations. If social studies is taught as a textbook subject, with uniform assignments for all, children are robbed of opportunities to develop habits and skills of rational analysis and critical thinking.

In the secondary school balance in the provided program is usually judged by the nature and amount of required course work, the range of electives, and the breadth of the cocurricular program. The high school that provides only, or chiefly, a college preparatory curriculum fixes on all students a pattern of studies which may be well balanced for college-bound youngsters but may penalize others in their preparation for adult life. The secondary school in which extraclass activities are dominated by interscholastic sports restricts students' opportunities to explore personal interest activities.

Two of the recommendations of the 1960 White House Conference for Children and Youth, taken in conjunction, suggest a measure for judging balance in the provided program of the school:

"That the curriculum provide opportunities for the student to develop—appreciation and understanding, at a behavioral level, of the dignity and worth of all individuals; knowledge, understanding, and appreciation of the fine and practical arts; the humanities; and the natural, physical, and social sciences; basic skills, such as reading, writing, and the use of numbers; special abilities and talents; a healthy and realistic concept of self; the best possible physical and mental health; ability to analyze critically and constructively; constructive civic attitudes, and appreciations basic to the worthy use of leisure time; insights into the ethnic and religious sources of American life; character, discipline, responsibility, and a commitment to spiritual, ethical, and moral values.

"That the curriculum include—education for political responsibility (by stressing democratic values, current issues, civics and economics, national defense needs and current military obligations, obligations as citizens of locality, State, Nation, and world); instruction in our own diversified culture and the culture of other peoples through such disciplines as literature, social sciences, art, and music; with additional emphasis on languages and social sciences of the non-western world; greater emphasis on the humanities; an expanded program in music and art to encourage creativity; exploration and preparation for further educational and vocational opportunities; a program of motion picture and drama appreciation; physical education of high quality for all students at elementary and secondary levels; health education and nutrition at the junior high level; mental hygiene education, based on its moral, social, and biological aspects; education for family life, including sex education and greater emphasis on the causes of human behavior, through discussion and participation in appropriate experiences at all age levels."[2]

If the program provided is comprehensive, each student still needs adequate guidance to select a curriculum that is balanced for him. To a large extent the problem is that of meeting both the type differences among groups of students and the unique differences among individuals (see Chapter Three).

In the elementary school, where pupils usually follow a common program, this guidance is largely the classroom teacher's responsibility. Thus children are helped to choose between alternative assignments, study materials, and activities related to the various school subjects. To give such guidance effectively, the teacher must know the interests, strengths, and weaknesses of each pupil. The teacher can best provide the needed guidance if the school day is planned flexibly and a variety of study materials is available.

In the secondary school, the student needs help in planning his total program of studies so that it will be balanced for him. Individual program planning, as described on page 75 (Chapter Three), can provide this help. The secondary student also needs guidance within each of his courses to see that he uses materials and completes assignments that are within his grasp and yet challenge him to exert his best efforts. In addition, the adolescent student needs stimulation to participate in extraclass activities that are suitable for him.

A rich and flexibly administered *provided* program, then, is an essential first step in achieving curriculum balance for students. This step must be followed by guidance to help each pupil develop a program of studies and activities which will be appropriate for him.

CURRENT PROBLEMS IN ACHIEVING BALANCE

Criteria for determining balance in the school curriculum change from time to time. The brief review of the changing school curriculum in the United States since colonial days (see page 88, Chapter Four) illustrates how changing demands from society result in changing conceptions of the desirable curriculum to be provided. The summary comment on conflicting philosophies of education (see pages 86-88) noted a second element that enters into determination of curriculum balance. Evidence such as that presented in Chapter Three concerning the nature and needs of today's school population is basic to the formulation of criteria for determining balance in the school program. Throughout all the publications of the Project on Instruction the point is made that the school program of the 1940's and 1950's is neither adequate nor appropriate for the 1960's and 1970's.

To achieve a balanced school program that is appropriate for the sixties and seventies, educators must resolve many issues and problems. Three seem especially critical, in view of society's needs and the temper of the times. They are (a) achieving a balance among the sciences, the social sciences, and the humanities; (b) achieving a balance between the academic and applied subjects; and (c) utilizing extraclass activities as a means of achieving a balanced school program for individuals.

Balance Among Sciences, Social Sciences, and Humanities

Introducing youth into their culture through study of the humanities, the social sciences, and the sciences has been described in Chapter Four as one of the distinctive responsibilities of the school. Most educators and laymen agree that these fields of knowledge are essential sources of content for the elementary and secondary school curriculum. Elements drawn from these fields constitute much of the general education or common core of knowledge for all pupils. It is also agreed that more advanced study in each of these fields should be available in the secondary school, so that students with particular interest and aptitude in one or another field can pursue it to greater depth than is appropriate in the general education segment of their schooling. The special contributions of each of these broad fields have often been described and need only be summarized here.

Science and Mathematics. The scientific base and the complex technology of modern society make it imperative that all citizens in a democracy attain minimum literacy in the natural and physical sciences and in mathematics. They need to do so if they are to understand the natural and social world in which they live and grasp the implications of public policy decisions about matters involving such technological problems as automation of industry or the control and use of nuclear energy. Information from these fields is essential for many vocations as well as for safe and healthful life in an urbanized culture. The nation's need for scientists, engineers, and competent technicians, if it is to maintain its leadership in world affairs and its high standard of living at home, has been widely and sensationally publicized. While the elementary and secondary schools cannot and should not attempt to produce scientists and engineers, they can help young people explore their interests and aptitudes in scientific fields.

Social Studies. The knowledge and patterns of thought needed by citizens to understand society's institutions, contemporary social trends, and the problems faced by our democratic system today are derived in large part from study of social science materials. The effective operation of American democracy—indeed, its very survival as a system of government and a way of life—depends on a citizenry that has achieved an adequate understanding of such knowledge, together with the ability and will for rational consideration of society's increasingly complex problems. The crucial dilemmas of the modern world arise from man's failure, thus far, to create social mechanisms that are capable of handling his rapid advances in science and technology. The urgent need for social scientists who can push back the frontiers of knowledge and reduce the tensions resulting from this uneven development is keenly realized by thoughtful Americans, although this need has not received the popular notice that has been given to the need for scientists. In this connection, the schools' obligation is not to produce scholars in the social sciences but to help young people discover their potential capabilities for advanced study in these fields.

The Humanities. In a society that is becoming increasingly standardized and mechanized, the individual needs a sense of personal self-realization more than ever before. This he can achieve to a considerable extent through the humanities—literature, language, and the arts. To live richly and sensitively, he needs a sense of direction and integrity of purpose that can be derived only from values he himself has formulated or discovered and accepted. He needs to develop his ability to react with aesthetic and moral discrimination to the array of stimuli that bombard him constantly in the fast-paced culture of modern America. Without such discrimination, his vocation is likely to have little meaning beyond the bare provision of material things, and his leisure is apt to bring mere escape from the routine of daily living. Spirituality, morality, and aesthetic appreciation are as basic to the humanness of man as are intelligence and physical well-being.

While literature, the languages, and the arts also have their practical uses, probably their unique contribution for most people is the enrichment they can bring to everyday living. Thoughtful analysts of modern society have pointed out the long-range result when a nation becomes so preoccupied with physical survival as to ignore the question of "survival for what?" Then its people are divested of essential elements of humanity and condemned to a life that is only half lived. Humanists, as well as scientists and social scientists, are urgently needed by American society. The schools should help young people with interest and talent in the humanities to discover their potential. At the same time, the school program should enable all students to enrich their lives through study of literature, languages, and the arts.

Is a New Imbalance Being Created? In recent years there has been an unprecedented effort to strengthen instruction in the sciences and mathematics, fields that had been relatively static in the school curriculum for many years. This effort has been supported by public opinion that was aroused to a great extent by Soviet achievements in space technology and a resultant fear that U.S. leadership in science and technology was threatened. To many, including members of the U.S. Congress, national survival seemed to be at stake. Federal funds for instruction have been allocated primarily to sciences and mathematics since 1958 through the National Defense Education Act and the National Science Foundation. The funds have been used for experimentation, development of new courses of study, and retraining of teachers in these fields. In addition, private foundations have supported major curriculum projects dealing with various aspects of science and mathematics instruction in schools.

Meanwhile, efforts to improve school programs in the social sciences and humanities have made relatively little headway. In spite of activities carried on by educational specialists in these fields, the necessary financial support for experimentation could not be obtained either from public or private foundation sources. A notable exception has been the case of modern foreign languages, a field that has been given a similar priority to science and mathematics on the basis of its potential contribution to national survival. Modern language instruction in the schools has been revitalized by programs comparable in scope to those in science and mathematics and drawing financial support from the same sources.

One measure of the relative emphasis in the school program which the sciences, the social sciences, and the humanities have received in recent years may be found in the number of nationally oriented curriculum projects that have been carried on in each field. A review of such curriculum studies made early in 1962 revealed that 25 were in progress or had recently been completed in the fields of science and mathematics; 4 were reported in the English language arts, 7 in the social studies, and none in the arts.* Since that time, limited federal funds have been granted for projects in English and social studies, and one major foundation grant has been made for a project in music. However, only a beginning has been made in providing for studies in these recently neglected fields.

Current planners are thus faced with a situation that threatens their efforts to achieve a balance among the sciences, the social sciences, and the humanities in the school program. Many educators recognized that instruction in the sciences, mathematics, and modern foreign languages was urgently in need of revision to incorporate up-to-date content and teaching methods. The enormous resources that have gone into revisions in these fields may have corrected an imbalance that existed in the decade of the fifties and the years before. The question that must be faced in the sixties is whether a new imbalance is being created, with the humanities and the social studies becoming neglected areas at a time when their special contributions are needed in American society more urgently than ever before.

* See *Current Curriculum Studies in Academic Subjects.*

It would seem that a crucial problem in the sixties and the years beyond will be that of providing a school program that gives balanced treatment to the sciences, the social studies, and the humanities. In its recommendations, the National Committee of the Project on Instruction has stressed the urgency of helping all pupils understand critical economic, social, and political problems of the nation today and of helping each student develop interests and resources for personal self-realization. These goals cannot be attained unless the curriculum includes adequate treatment of materials drawn from the social sciences and humanities as well as from the sciences. If adequate financial support for intensive curriculum experimentation and for in-service study by teachers in any of these fields is not forthcoming from federal or private foundation sources, state and local educational authorities will have a special obligation to give priority in budget and program to the fields that are neglected.*

Balance Among Academic and Applied Subjects

As the school curriculum has been expanded in efforts to meet changing needs of society and of a school population drawn from all socioeconomic classes, a number of applied subjects have become an essential part of the school program. Some contribute to the general education segment of the curriculum, the body of subjects which all pupils should study. Elements of these are included in both the elementary and secondary schools. Other applied subjects have been introduced in the secondary school to help students, especially those who are not college bound, prepare for a vocation.

Health Education and Physical Education. Health education and physical education have become increasingly important in the general education portion of the elementary and secondary school curriculum in the last half century. Urbanization, changed social

* See Chapter Seven (Who Should Make Curriculum Decisions?) for discussion of the effect on the school program of federal special aid measures, such as the National Defense Education Act.

conditions, and technological advances have created new health problems as well as benefits, both for individuals and for the community. Their satisfactory solution depends on popular knowledge of scientific information and fundamental principles in the area of health as well as on the work of health specialists. The school, as the only social institution that reaches all children and youth, has responsibility for teaching the basic information and for helping young people develop the habits and attitudes essential for healthful living. Effective health education begins in early childhood and continues as a cumulative program through the elementary and secondary school years. It stresses the application of rational thought processes to health problems as well as the teaching of essential knowledge.

The need for a systematic school program of physical development has also been intensified because of conditions created by urban living and technological change. Today most children and adolescents do not engage in the vigorous muscle-building activities that were a part of daily living for earlier generations. Modern transportation facilities encourage them to ride instead of walk, for example, and most of the muscle-building home chores in an agricultural society are no longer part of the daily routines of family life. The introduction to active sports that provide healthful recreation for adults living in urban centers may or may not be provided unless the school undertakes this responsibility.

To meet the requirements of these new conditions, specialists in health education and physical education have planned activity programs based on research concerning growth patterns of children and youth.[3] Such programs, it is held, should begin in the early elementary school years and continue through the high school, with every normal child participating. They should include activities that help pupils to build physical fitness and also to develop a continuing interest in sports as recreation which will carry over into a healthy adult life. Physically handicapped children need physical education programs adapted to their particular conditions and needs.

Industrial Arts. A second applied subject that is considered a basic part of the general education of children and youth is industrial arts. This field has been defined as "the study of industrial tools, materials, processes, products, and occupations pursued for general education purposes in shops, laboratories, and drafting rooms."[4] Its purposes do not include direct preparation of pupils for an occupation, although study of industrial arts provides opportunity for the pupil to explore various industrial activities. Such exploration leads some pupils to an informed decision to enter a specialized vocational education program in the high school, and it helps others find satisfying leisure-time activities in later life.

Modern industrial arts programs stress experiences that help students gain understanding of the technological society in which they live. In the elementary school pupils engage in construction activities involving the use of simple, easily manipulated tools and materials. These activities are frequently tied into other parts of the elementary curriculum. Older pupils, in the junior and senior high school years, explore the areas of drafting, electricity and electronics, graphic arts, industrial crafts, metalworking, power mechanics, and woodworking. They learn how industrial products are made, used, and maintained. They develop skills needed to work with technical and mechanical things, skills that are useful in the home and that give students a basis for later avocational activities in working with wood, metals, ceramics, and other materials. Students learn to handle tools safely and to anticipate common hazards. An integral part of industrial arts instruction is the application of problem-solving processes to the solution of technical problems that everyone meets at one level or another in the modern world. Once thought of as a subject to be studied only by boys, industrial arts in the modern school contributes to the general education of all pupils.[5]

Home Economics. The changes in American society which made health, physical, and industrial arts education a part of general education have also made home economics or family life education an accepted part of the common core of school studies as well as a secondary school subject taught in a more specialized form for vocational preparation. The problems of family life in an increasingly urbanized culture have become more complex, involving new economic, social, and psychological factors. Home economics, once thought of as consisting mainly of the skills of food preparation and clothing construction, assumed new dimensions in response to the changing conditions of the American family and the increasing body of scientific knowledge related to those conditions.

The modern home economics program, while still including instruction in the skills of cooking and sewing, places major emphasis on such areas as nutrition, consumer education, child rearing, housing problems, relationships among family members, and personal development. Once thought of as a subject for girls only, home economics materials are now contributing to the general education of both girls and boys at the elementary and junior high school levels and to some extent at the senior high school level. This change has resulted partly from the expanded content of the field and partly from the changing roles of men and women in family life, as more and more mothers have found employment outside the home.

In the elementary school, home economics materials, like those from industrial arts, are merged with other aspects of the curriculum rather than being taught as a separate subject. The emphasis is on the child and his life in the family. In the junior high school, where home economics may be presented as a separate subject or as "home living" in the block or core course, the focus is on the role and responsibilities of the adolescent in the family. The emphasis in the general education courses in senior high school, whether for girls or boys, is on developing the abilities and attitudes needed to achieve a satisfying family life.[6]

Vocational Subjects. Vocational education subjects are offered as specialized electives in the senior high school to help a large proportion of youth acquire saleable skills. Vocational education is intended for both the students who enter full-time employment and those who must support themselves partially or wholly while in college. With the steady decline in the number of unskilled and semiskilled jobs, vocational education programs have become more and more important as the gateway to independence and a satisfactory life for youth who lack the interest, aptitude, or financial resources to complete the long period of advanced studies required for the professions. Thus, vocational education helps meet society's need for increasing numbers of skilled workers in various technical and other occupational fields. Programs preparing young people for employment in office, technical, industrial, and distributive occupations as well as for work in agriculture and homemaking are provided.

In modern vocational education programs, the specialized vocational training constitutes only a portion, although a substantial part, of the student's high school curriculum. Complementing and supplementing the essential general education studies, vocational courses prepare the student both broadly and specifically for proficiency in his particular specialty. They include attention to technical knowledge, understandings, attitudes, and related information needed for success in this field as well as to specific skills. Specialists in vocational education point out that the nature of the content and the methods of instruction in these courses provide many opportunities for identifying and solving problems through the application of rational thought processes.[7]

Excellence Through Applied Subjects. This brief review indicates that in their modern format the applied subjects go far beyond the teaching of specific skills. Each of them has a body of intellectual content drawn from related academic fields and applied directly to problems of modern living. For most if not all pupils these subjects provide a needed bridge between the general and the specific, the principle and its application. They help students relate school experience and life in the out-of-school world. Each of these subjects, when developed according to modern standards, helps students move toward the educational goals of learning how to learn, developing interest in learning and in using rational processes, exploring values in new experiences, and understanding concepts and generalizations. They help students apply their school learning directly in the areas of home and family living, physical and mental health, use of leisure, personal self-realization, and occupation. Less directly but in important ways, they contribute to children's growth toward effective citizenship.

These values of the applied subjects should be considered by curriculum planners as they seek to provide a balanced school program to satisfy the educational requirements of children and youth in the decade ahead. Some recent critics of the school have spoken with a bias for the academic without apparent knowledge of the nature, purposes, and values of the applied disciplines. In some circles a climate of opinion has been created in which excellence is equated with achievement in academic subjects to the practical exclusion of the applied fields. When the realities of contemporary American society are considered, it becomes clear that both academic and applied fields of study contribute to the achievement of excellence in the intellectual life and in the daily behavior of citizens. The applied subjects should be represented in the general education segment of the program. The proportion of time given to them should be determined by analysis of the needs of students of the local school and of the community setting in which the school operates. In the high school, a similar analysis of the aptitudes and vocational goals of students will indicate the extent and range of vocational education courses which should be included in an adequate program of studies.

Extraclass Activities in a Balanced School Program

The potential values of extraclass activities in achieving balance, both in the school's provided program and in the student's individual program, have been widely recognized for at least a generation. Indeed, such activities were first introduced in an effort to meet youth needs that were not clearly related to conventional school subjects. Exploration of interests, civic participation, and personal self-development were among the adolescent needs that extracurricular activities were intended to satisfy. As the usefulness of extraclass activities for older students was demonstrated in secondary schools, service and special interest activities that were not directly related to a school subject were introduced in some elementary schools.[8]

A number of studies have indicated that extraclass activities are considered by students, parents, and teachers to be an important part of the total school program.[9] Participation in them has been found to increase student interest in the more formal aspects of their schooling. These activities have also helped students make better use of leisure, extend their circles of friends, learn to work more effectively with others in group enterprises, gain confidence in their ability to handle interpersonal relations, and acquire useful information beyond that studied in school subjects.

Such results as those cited support the view that extraclass or student activities are an important component of a balanced school program at both the elementary and secondary levels, although the emphasis on them is greater in the secondary school. In some cases certain of the shared responsibilities of the school, as identified in Chapter Four, may be partially or even largely met by extraclass activities. The school's success in carrying out its distinctive responsibilities also may be enhanced through an appropriate extracurricular program. Some critics of the schools have denounced extraclass activities as wasteful of student time and of public money. They fail to understand that this aspect of the student's school experience can provide him with many opportunities to apply rational thought processes to projects of immediate importance to him and to explore values in new and realistic situations. These activities also enable students to investigate areas of knowledge which they frequently cannot include in their formal studies, either because of limits on their own time or because the school does not provide such courses.

If extraclass activities are to make their potential contribution to a balanced school program, however, certain problems that have been all too common in the past must be avoided. The pupils who most need such activities in order to gain a well-rounded education frequently do not participate in them effectively.[10] For example, students from culturally deprived homes take much less part in extraclass activities than do those from a more favored environment. Too frequently the extraclass program has emphasized activities for students whose interests and abilities in a particular area, such as athletics or dramatics, were already well developed and neglected other pupils who had greater need for such opportunities. For example, in some schools financial support and teacher energy have gone to the varsity athletic team to the neglect of an intramural sports program for all or to public performances in music or dramatics by talented students instead of to a program that invites exploration of these fields by many pupils. Sometimes the range of extraclass activities made available in a school has been determined more by the interests of teachers or by pressures from the community than by the interests and needs of the students themselves.

As the total program is reviewed and revised in the light of the goals of an individual school, existing extraclass activities should be examined for their usefulness in achieving a balanced offering for the student body. Such a study can reveal what additional activities, shifts in emphasis, or guidance provisions are needed to make the extraclass program a more effective part of the total school curriculum.

THE READING PROGRAM

There is no controversy over the importance of reading instruction in the school program. The ability to read is essential for learning in every field of knowledge, and the child who reads poorly is handicapped in almost all school subjects. Without adequate skills in reading he falls further behind each year, and frustration and maladjustment go hand in hand with his repeated failures. The importance of a good foundation in reading and the continued development of reading skills for success in school can hardly be overemphasized. In the modern world, the ability to read is as important for vocational success and personal enjoyment in adult life as for progress in school, a view that has been stressed in earlier parts of this volume. There is no question among educators and laymen that reading instruction must be given the highest order of priority.

The Reading Controversy

Agreement as to its importance notwithstanding, reading instruction is the subject of heated and continuing controversy. The debate has developed around two closely related foci.

How Well Do Children Read? The claim is made that today's children learn to read less well than did those of earlier generations.[11] Comparative studies of children's achievement in reading today and 20 or 30 years ago, however, indicate that this assertion is not justified.

Apparently those who take a pessimistic view of the success of reading instruction today do not take into consideration the changes that have come in the American school population. Many pupils who are in today's upper elementary and secondary grades would not have been there a generation ago. The later school-leaving age that has been set in many states, better enforcement of compulsory attendance laws, and freer promotion policies have operated to carry many slower students further up the grade level ladder. Also, children tend to proceed through the elementary and secondary grades at a somewhat earlier age than formerly. Taking these factors into account, Gates, after careful investigation of fifth graders' reading performance in 1937 and 1957, concluded that today's children are at least a half year ahead of "pupils of equivalent intelligence, age, and other related factors twenty years ago."[12] Other studies confirm the fact that there has been progressive improvement in the reading attainment of young people in general.[13]

Although the charges of extremists have been refuted by evidence, few educators are satisfied with the present reading achievements of children and youth. The significant question is not whether today's reading instruction is as effective as that of a generation ago, but whether it is as effective as it can be. Many educators believe it is not. They suggest that better beginning reading instruction followed by a program of developmental reading through the secondary school could improve the reading growth of students materially. They point to the fact that relatively few adults read widely and suggest that this reflects the need for more stimulating reading experiences in school.[14] The findings from a half century of research concerning reading processes and how to develop them are not, say some reading specialists, effectively applied in many school classrooms.[15]

How Can Reading Instruction Be Improved? A second center of the reading controversy is found in the varied proposals for improving reading instruction. Many of them deal with beginning reading. They range from one-dimensional solutions, such as basing elementary reading instruction on a specific system for teaching phonics, to multidimensional proposals calling for flexible methods and varied materials to be adapted to the backgrounds and learning styles of individual pupils.

When the range of proposals is examined together with their sources, an interesting comparison emerges. Most of the one-dimensional proposals for solving problems of reading instruction are advanced by persons whose background and experience lie outside the field of reading instruction. In contrast, most reading specialists hold the view that effective teaching of reading depends on an analysis of the many factors and processes that are involved in learning to read. They call for a many-sided program of reading instruction based on this analysis.

In several cases the single-dimensional proposals could be implemented only by the use of a particular book, series of books, or set of materials that has been prepared by the proponents. Participants in a recent conference of reading experts, which was chaired by James B. Conant and included persons with diverse views on aspects of reading instruction, commented on this situation in the conference report: "On one matter we think we should offer a note of caution. We have recently witnessed some highly publicized attempts to force the favorable attention of the public on one or another reading book and its brand of teaching reading as though it were the single and indispensable answer to all of our reading concerns. Often these attempts have been made by persons who know little or nothing about the teaching of reading.

"We are convinced that there is *no one* book, and its brand of teaching reading, that is so superior to all others as to render it imperative for school systems to adopt exclusively that one book and brand of teaching as constituting their entire reading program."[16]

What Is Reading?

At the heart of the reading controversy is the question, "What is reading?" Is it the ability to recognize, pronounce, and understand the meaning of written words? Is it the ability to get and repeat the main ideas from printed paragraphs, chapters, or books? Is it the ability to go beyond comprehension of ideas and facts presented by an author, to evaluate them and fuse them with previously gained knowledge and experience?

To most reading experts, reading is all of this and more. Reading is "the meaningful interpretation of verbal symbols";[17] it is "securing the meaning intended by the author and reacting to it."[18] Recognizing the words on the printed page is an essential first step, to be sure, but it is only the beginning of reading. Reading is not a single skill; it is a group of many interrelated skills that the reader must apply simultaneously and selectively according to his immediate purpose in reading. Reading skills are part of a larger complex of communication skills. They are closely related to the skills required for effective listening and for oral and written expression.

A pupil does not learn to read in one year or in all his elementary school years. Learning to read is a cumulative process that continues through the secondary school and college program and indeed throughout the reader's lifetime, because an effective reader achieves an increasingly mature command of reading skills.

He continually expands his reading vocabulary, almost automatically applying appropriate skills of word attack. He becomes increasingly proficient in organizing what he gains from reading, relating it to his previous knowledge, and reacting to it critically. He identifies his purpose for reading particular material and adapts his rate and method of reading to that purpose.

Stages of Reading Instruction

There are successive stages or periods in learning to read. Planning for reading instruction can be made more efficient when the stages have been identified. Five such stages were described in 1925 by the National Committee on Reading of the National Society for the Study of Education. This description remains useful more than a generation later. The five stages are not to be regarded as rigidly separated but as overlapping.[19]

Reading Readiness. First comes the period of preparation for reading or the development of reading readiness. This stage has been accomplished when the child has reached a level of general maturity which enables him to react to formal reading instruction successfully and without excessive difficulty. The nature and quality of experiences during preschool years affect the child's development of reading readiness. Parents can do much to help the child gain this readiness. They can read to him, showing their own interest in reading. They can teach him to listen attentively and to express himself in correct language. They can encourage the child's curiosity and, in general, provide a rich variety of experience.

It is the school's responsibility to pick up where the family has left off. Teachers must plan systematically to help children develop the visual and auditory perception skills, the command of oral expression, and the interest in reading that will enable them to move easily into the next stage and begin to read. For children whose home backgrounds have been impoverished and inadequate, the school can take special measures such as those described on page 57. Intentional development of reading readiness instead of "waiting for the child to grow" is thus an important part of reading instruction.

Because of individual differences among children and their backgrounds, there are inevitably great differences in the rate of progress through this first stage of learning to read. A few may enter kindergarten fully ready for formal reading instruction; a few may not have developed adequate readiness until they have entered the second grade or even later. Many, probably most, children can be helped to achieve a satisfactory level of reading readiness and move into the second stage during the early weeks or months of their first grade year.[20]

Initial Reading Instruction. During this stage, when systematic reading instruction begins, children relate printed symbols to meanings. They learn to follow left-to-right progression across written charts and printed pages. They develop a sight vocabulary and begin both oral and silent reading. They begin to develop word-attack skills including the use of configuration and context clues, phonic and structural analysis, and combinations of these approaches. At the same time comprehension skills are taught, for the emphasis is placed on getting meaning from the printed page rather than just naming individual words. Simple exercises are used to give children practice in following a sequence of events or ideas, selecting main thoughts, relating details to main ideas, and drawing inferences from what is read. The basic skills of reading are thus introduced during this second period. The stage of beginning to read is accomplished by most children in American schools during their first grade year.

Rapid Progress in Reading Skills. During the third stage of learning to read, which for most children is accomplished during the second and third grades, the basic skills that were introduced in the initial period of reading instruction are reinforced and expanded. There is systematic instruction in using word-attack skills at a more mature level, leading to greater independence for the reader and to a rapid expansion of his reading vocabulary.

Comprehension skills are stressed throughout, and children are given continued practice in both oral and silent reading. They are encouraged to consult a variety of sources so that they become aware of different types of books and begin to select the type that will best serve the purpose at hand.

Wide Reading. As children progress through their intermediate grade years, their reading program provides for wide reading to extend their interests and experiences into many fields. They give a higher proportion of school time to silent reading, with attention to increasing speed without sacrificing comprehension. They receive systematic instruction in using the index, table of contents, and other parts of a book efficiently and in locating information in encyclopedias and other special references. They are helped, through review and reteaching, to reinforce and expand their command of word-attack skills and the skills required for organizing what is read. In this stage, independent reading for both recreational and study purposes is emphasized.

Refinement of Reading Skills, Habits, and Tastes. If the student has accomplished successfully the previous stages of learning to read, he enters the secondary school with a firm foundation of the skills and habits needed for most reading tasks. With each succeeding year in the secondary school and in college, he will be required to read more intensively, more extensively, and more independently. He needs continued help in refining the total range of his reading skills and habits, with special emphasis on organizing, evaluating, and interpreting the material he reads. He needs systematic instruction in how to solve the special reading problems he encounters in the various content fields, in developing library skills, and in adapting reading rate and method to specific reading purposes.

This stage of refining reading skills, habits, and tastes is never finally accomplished by even the most superior reader; it continues through adult life. A reader may retrogress, losing ground once gained, and then may be able to forge ahead again. The ultimate limit for this stage of refining reading abilities is not known.

Each Stage Is Important. An adequate program of reading instruction provides attention to each of these stages of learning to read. There is danger that current controversies about reading, which spotlight the beginning stage mainly, may contribute to neglect of the equally important readiness period and later stages of the program. To the extent this occurs, young people will be handicapped in learning to read effectively.

Components of the Reading Program

Within each stage of the process of learning to read, beginning with the readiness period, the pupil needs guidance in three related but distinct components of the reading program. The first is the *developmental* aspect, devoted to improving the learner's control of the mechanics of reading and of comprehension skills. The second consists of *functional* or *work-type* reading and includes activities to develop ability to locate pertinent reading material as well as special applications of comprehension skills and study skills in the various content fields. *Recreational* reading, in which enjoyment, broadening of interests, and development of discriminating taste are the goals, comprises the third component of an effective reading program.

In the earlier stages of learning to read, the developmental component receives heaviest emphasis. Work-type and recreational reading are also given attention, however. Children use reading materials that are either work-type or recreational in nature, as they are taught the mechanics of reading and gain comprehension skills. By the later elementary grades, as children enter the stage of wide reading with a grasp of basic reading skills, the functional and recreational components are emphasized. Nevertheless, activities to teach or reinforce specific reading skills should be used throughout the upper elementary and secondary school whenever learners need them. Teachers of science, social studies, and the other content areas share responsibility with the language arts or English teacher for continuing the developmental component of the reading program. Their main attention, however, is given to helping students with special reading problems in their particular content field.

Thus in an effective reading program, according to most reading specialists, the learner is helped at each stage to expand his grasp of a range of reading skills. He is taught to apply these skills to work-type reading materials. He is also encouraged to read for entertainment and to develop standards of appreciation and taste in his selection of recreational reading materials.

This view is not held, however, by certain critics of the methods now widely used to teach beginning reading. They would limit the reading program in the early stages to teaching the mechanics of reading, following the particular system that they have endorsed.[21]

Specific Issues Concerning Reading Instruction

In the current debate about the teaching of reading, several specific issues are frequently and vigorously discussed. Outstanding among them are these: Should systematic reading instruction for all children, as distinguished from readiness programs, begin earlier than grade 1? What is the place of phonics in teaching beginning reading? Should individualized reading replace group instruction in elementary school reading programs? Is remedial reading instruction a necessary part of a school's reading program, or can improvement in the teaching of reading render it unnecessary? Any consideration of reading in the school program must take account of these specific issues.

When Should Systematic Reading Instruction Begin?[22] It has already been noted that general practice in American schools places the first systematic reading instruction in grade 1, when the child is about six years old. In Europe the practice differs from country to country. In Scotland children receive systematic reading instruction from the age of five, and English children usually begin at six. In the Scandinavian countries and the Soviet Union children enter the first grade at age seven and then begin to learn to read. A study of a group of six-year-olds in Scotland made about a decade ago showed that the children had achieved on the average a level of reading that typical American children do not reach until they are about seven and a half years old.[23]

Currently, there are in the United States various proposals and experimental programs based on the assumption that most if not all children can learn to read effectively long before the age of six. Fries, an outstanding linguist, argues that "*any* child can learn to read within a year after he has learned to 'talk' his native language successfully" [24] and outlines a proposed method of instruction which has not, as yet, had widespread trial. Using a completely different approach, Omar K. Moore has conducted a widely publicized experiment in which children from two to five years old are taught to read through procedures utilizing elaborate equipment.[25] First grade teachers in American schools know from experience that some children have learned to read before they enter school.

Thus there is evidence to suggest that some but not all children *can* begin to learn to read at an earlier age than is customary in American schools. It may be that television viewing, travel, and other enriching experiences to which many of today's young children are exposed help make these youngsters ready for systematic reading instruction at an earlier age than was true in previous generations. More experimentation is needed to determine whether or not this is true.

Meanwhile, specialists in early childhood education and in reading point out that there is no evidence that children gain in the long run from very early reading instruction, even when they can respond to it effectively. A successful beginning in school is basic to the child's development of a positive self-concept and level of aspiration. Initial failure and frustration may color his total approach to learning tasks. Instead of being exposed to formal instruction at an early age, it is urged that the young child's energies are better used in relatively informal experiences that contribute to his social development and help him learn to work independently, to concentrate, to experiment, to work out simple problems, and to follow successfully a daily program in school. It is especially important to note existing evidence that children for whom systematic reading instruction is delayed *learn to read rapidly and successfully when they do begin and soon catch up with those who started earlier.*

A number of studies have compared the progress in reading of children who received early systematic instruction with the progress of those who began it later. The results show, in general, that by the end of the primary grades late beginners for whom a reading readiness program is provided will overtake children who are given formal reading instruction earlier. In later school years, the late beginners frequently surpass the others in reading skill. Indeed, one study showed that upon reaching the eighth grade, a group for whom systematic instruction had been delayed until the middle of the second grade were a year and a half ahead of control groups who had started learning to read at the beginning of grade 1.[26] The investigator in another longitudinal study concluded that children who began to learn to read after the age of six not only made more rapid progress but also developed more liking for reading than children who began earlier.[27]

Today's reading specialists make it clear, however, that there should be no clear-cut line between the reading readiness program and the beginning of systematic instruction. The first should phase into the second easily, naturally, and as rapidly as children show they can handle beginning reading activities with success. The readiness program will continue parallel to the more formal instruction. In this way children can progress at their own rate, confident from the early stages that they are learning to read.

In summary, the following conclusions about an early beginning of systematic reading instruction seem defensible:

1. Careful, controlled experimentation with methods and materials for the early beginning of systematic reading instruction should be encouraged, with adequate safeguards for the welfare

of children who are involved. Special attention should be given to the immediate effects on children's total development and to whether an early beginning gives any long-range advantage in their reading achievement.

2. Until such experimentation gives conclusive evidence in favor of a generally earlier beginning in reading for children and reveals how it can be given effectively, schools should not introduce reading instruction on a formal, systematic basis below the first grade. The existing evidence that beginning too early may lead to failure and negative attitudes toward self and school and that early formal instruction gives little or no advantage for later reading achievements is too strong to be ignored.

3. Children should never be held back from beginning to read when they give evidence that they are ready. The reading program should be handled with flexibility, allowing beginning reading instruction to start gradually and informally along with reading readiness activities.

What Is the Place of Phonics in Teaching Beginning Reading?[28]
Much of the controversy about reading instruction concerns the place of phonics in teaching beginning reading. Too often the debate has been couched in terms of the phonics method, in which the child is taught the sounds of individual letters as a means of building words vs. the sight-word or look-and-say method in which the child first learns to recognize printed words that are already in his oral vocabulary. Although this statement of the issue has received widespread publicity, it is inaccurate and misleading. No recognized reading authority has advocated teaching beginning reading by the sight-word method alone; the need for phonics as one tool for word recognition is almost universally recognized. Specialists in reading and early elementary education have pointed out repeatedly that phonics *is* taught in American schools as one part of the reading program. On the other hand, many of the advocates of emphasis on phonics have recommended a phonics program as an essential part of the total reading program, but not as the sole component.[29] Most of this

group have complained that too little attention is given to phonics, that instruction in phonics does not begin early enough, and that the procedures used in many schools to teach phonics are ineffective. Only a few extremists have seriously claimed that the schools use a sight-word method exclusively.

The issue, then, is not phonics vs. sight-words but rather when phonics should be introduced, with what emphasis, through what procedures, and in what relation to other reading tools and skills.

An exception that must be noted is the position of certain linguists, well expressed by Bloomfield and Fries.[30] Defining phonics as matching individual letters in a word with the sounds those letters "say," these men hold that this approach has no place in beginning reading instruction. Learning to read, they contend, is a process completely different from learning to write and does not involve spelling or sounding out of individual letters. Instead, reading is a matter of transferring from reception of oral language "signals" to reception of written signals. Words are one form of such signals. The reader must learn to respond, not to individual letters that comprise words, but to the phonemes or "bundles of sound contrasts that constitute the functioning units to identify our word-patterns."[31] Thus children should never be taught to sound out "t" as a separate letter; instead they must learn to recognize and differentiate letter shapes, but they do not necessarily need to know the "names" of the letters of the alphabet and certainly should not be encouraged to associate individual letters with isolated sounds. It is the view of these linguists that as the child becomes able to relate the written representation of phonemes to their sounds as he hears them in words, he learns to read.

Since there are at least 26 different systems for teaching beginning reading through an emphasis on phonics, each with its vigorous proponents, any generalization about the systems has exceptions. Some elements are common to most of them, however. In general, those who would emphasize phonics say that intensive drill in phonics should start at the very beginning of the reading program and constitute the major part of initial instruction. This emphasis on phonics should be maintained through the primary grades. As children learn to match sounds to written letters, they build word-identification skills that make them independent in vocabulary development. With this approach, it is claimed, a readiness program as such is not needed.[32]

Admitting that English is not completely phonetic, advocates of the phonics approach point out that a high proportion of the language is in fact phonetic and that mastery of basic speech sounds will give children the ability to unlock a vast majority of the words they will encounter. Wingo states that, by learning 44 basic speech sounds in the first year of instruction and reviewing them for fixation in the second and third years, children will be able to control 87 percent of the words they encounter.[33]

Reading specialists who urge a more gradual introduction to phonics, with initial emphasis on developing a sight vocabulary and getting the meaning of thought units, base their recommendations on research studies that have been made during the past 40 years.[34] These studies do not verify the claims that have been made for various systems of beginning reading instruction which emphasize phonics as their major element. The research studies do show, in general, that pupils get off to an earlier start in recognizing and pronouncing words when phonics is emphasized in initial instruction but that this advantage is not maintained through the later primary and intermediate grades. For example, one study showed that a group of fourth grade children who had been taught through a balanced program, with phonics treated as one aspect, earned better scores on tests of word meaning, reading rate, and paragraph comprehension than those who had been taught with initial emphasis on phonics.[35] Other studies have shown no significant difference between the two methods so far as word recognition is concerned, when judged by children's reading performance in the early intermediate grades.[36]

Advocates of a balanced approach to initial reading instruction point out that mastery of phonics enables the child to pronounce words but not necessarily to understand their meaning. While phonics thus provides one means of attacking an unknown written word, other methods of word recognition such as getting the meaning from context, using configuration clues, and analyzing the structure of the word are also useful. For independence in reading, the child must be able to employ all of these approaches and do so in a flexible manner, always seeking the meaning of the thought unit in which the unfamiliar word is found. Furthermore, children vary in the approaches they find most useful and need to be acquainted with different tools from which they can select.

Proponents of a balanced program of beginning reading also urge that a one-sided approach, in which overemphasis on phonics or any other element causes neglect of other basic reading skills and abilities, contributes to serious problems in reading rate, comprehension, and interpretation in the learner's later school years. To make adequate progress in the later stages of reading, when skills should be refined at increasingly higher levels, the learner needs to commence the development of a broad range of skills and abilities during the period of beginning reading.

The following conclusions as to the place of phonics in the beginning reading program seem to emerge from the current debate:

1. Phonics is generally recognized as deserving an important place in initial reading instruction as one of several word recognition tools to be taught *along with* other reading skills and abilities. Those who insist on debating phonics vs. no phonics are merely boxing with shadows, and the layman may properly be suspicious of their knowledge of reading instruction, if not of their motives, in pursuing a meaningless question.

2. A balanced initial reading program in which phonics is introduced systematically during the first and second years as one of a range of reading skills contributes to long-range development of efficient reading. Children who receive intensive training in phonics at the very beginning stage of reading seem to make more rapid initial progress in word recognition than children who are introduced to phonics as one of several word recognition tools, but the early advantage is not retained beyond the first or second year of reading instruction.

3. If overemphasis on phonics leads to neglect of other reading tools and skills during the period of beginning reading, children will be handicapped in their development as effective readers.

4. The various special programs for beginning reading instruction, including those based on the linguists' structural analysis of the language, should be tested through careful experimentation. As yet, there is not sufficient evidence to justify the discard of a balanced program of beginning reading instruction for a one-dimensional system of teaching beginning reading.

Individualized Developmental Reading or Group Instruction? The question of individualized vs. group instruction in the elementary school reading program has not been given the same widespread public attention as the two issues just discussed. It is currently a leading issue, however, among reading and curriculum specialists. The question at issue concerns only the developmental component of the reading program, that devoted to teaching mechanics of reading and comprehension skills. An individualized approach to functional (work-type) reading and to recreational reading has long been widely accepted in principle, although practice has lagged behind the approved theory.

The teaching of basic reading skills through individualized instruction was first suggested in the 1930's and aroused controversy among reading specialists in the 1940's and 1950's. Few schools have introduced individualized developmental reading across the board, although a number have conducted experiments in its use.

In group instruction in developmental reading, a basal reading series is ordinarily used. Such a series begins with reading readiness books, preprimers, and primers. These texts are followed by graded readers. The vocabulary employed throughout the series is carefully controlled, and new words are introduced with spaced repetition. In basal readers; in the accompanying teacher's manuals; and in correlated charts, workbooks, and other materials, systematic provision is made for developing word-recognition tools and other specific reading skills. The procedures outlined in the teacher's manuals usually include preparation of the class for the reading assignment; guided reading and discussion of the material; oral reading; practice exercises on specific skills; and related activities involving dramatization, music, or art experiences.[37]

When the basal reader method is used, some of the pupils' reading period is given to whole-class instruction, but much of the time the children work in reading groups to which they are assigned on the basis of their reading achievement. The teacher meets with each group in turn, providing other activities for the rest of the class while he is busy with a group. Each group uses a reader the teacher judges to be appropriate for the children's level. The groups may be reconstituted from time to time, in an effort to accommodate the varying rates of progress of individual children.

When developmental reading is taught on an individualized basis, systematic group instruction with basal readers is eliminated. Instead each child, from the beginning, chooses from a classroom library the books he will read. The teacher guides this selection to the extent he considers desirable. A wide range of materials thus takes the place of the basal reader. During the scheduled reading period each child reads by himself in the book he has selected. When he encounters words he cannot identify by himself or another problem, he turns to the teacher or to a classmate for help. At intervals—one to three times a week—he has an individual conference with the teacher to discuss his reading. During the conference, which may last five to ten minutes, the teacher may have the pupil read aloud. He may use part of the time for skill instruction that he judges the child needs. He keeps careful records of each child's progress.[38] From time to time the teacher calls together several children who have common problems and helps them with a specific reading skill. At appropriate intervals, also, the entire class meets together to discuss books the children are reading or to have a session on a particular skill.

In individualized developmental reading, then, pupil interest and initiative are emphasized, and each child is encouraged to proceed at his own rate. Seeking, self-selection, and pacing are the key concepts. Proponents of individualized developmental reading emphasize the need to fit instruction to the growth of each child. They stress the importance of pupil interest and self-motivation in developing positive attitudes toward reading. In the individualized program the teacher uses a variety of procedures, tailoring them to each pupil's needs and helping each child work toward his own goals. The situation is not one of *laissez-faire,* but one in which each child is guided to make continual progress. The classroom library must include materials on many subjects and at various levels of difficulty. An adequate collection, it is suggested, will contain at least three times as many books as there are class members.[39]

The individualized method as yet has not been used widely enough or long enough, and too few efforts at controlled evaluation have been made to justify firm conclusions about its results. Nevertheless, several studies have compared standardized reading test scores of children taught in an individualized program with those receiving group instruction with basal readers.[40] The results indicate that the basal reader method usually does as well as the individualized approach or better. Some studies have shown that superior and average readers advanced about equally under the two approaches but that slow readers made better progress with the basal reader method.

It is important to remember, however, that some of the values claimed for the individualized approach cannot be measured by standardized tests. There are many reports that children in an individualized program read more, read more widely, and demonstrate more enthusiasm for reading than those taught by the basal reader method.

In summary, it seems that—

1. Much more comparative data, including evidence from longitudinal studies, are needed before definitive judgments about the two approaches can be made.

2. For the present, a combination of the basal reader method and individualized procedures seems desirable for the developmental aspect of the reading program. As Harris has pointed out, "A combination of whole-class activities, group reading, and individualized reading is more likely to be able to achieve all the varied objectives of reading instruction than can be attained by using just one of them."[41]

Questions Concerning Basal Readers. Related to the issue of group vs. individualized teaching of reading skills are the criticisms of basal reader series that have been made in recent years. The criticisms are focused chiefly on the limited vocabulary found in the readers and on the nature of the content.

Without question the vocabulary used in basal readers is narrowly limited, when compared with the oral vocabulary of the children for whom the books are prepared.[42] New reading words are introduced at a planned rate and with frequent repetition to build a reading vocabulary of which children gain thorough command. The total number of different words used in basal reader series has been decreased since the 1920's. The number of words judged to be of high functional value has increased, however, and the new words are introduced at a more uniform rate with more repetition. The total number of running words has also been increased considerably. Basal readers today, as compared with those of earlier generations, "provide an easier introduction to reading, much more reading material, and more frequent contact with specific words."[43]

Some reading specialists question the need to limit vocabulary in basal readers as drastically as is the current practice. At the same time, they defend the use of a controlled vocabulary in basal reading material. The essential range of reading skills can be developed more systematically and efficiently when close controls are maintained, they say, and this is the purpose for which basal readers should be used. In an adequate reading program children also use a wide variety of informational and recreational reading books that enable them to develop a much larger vocabulary than is presented in the basal readers.[44] Reading experts also point out that in vocabulary counts cited by critics of basal readers, each "new" word includes the common variants of the stem word. Some highly inaccurate comparisons of the total vocabulary of American basal readers and those used in foreign schools have been made because the word count of the foreign readers included each variant as a new word.[45]

The content of basal readers has been criticized on several counts. One criticism has been that the selections fail to stress social and moral values.[46] Comparative analyses of modern readers and those used by earlier generations of Americans indicate, however, that the same basic values continue to be emphasized in these basal reading materials.[47]

Another criticism stresses the lack of literary quality in school readers. Still a third, which is receiving increasing attention, is directed to the problem of stereotyped content that is oriented toward the white, upper middle class, suburban sector of American society. Such orientation, it is held, gives children a false picture of their social world and damages the self-concept of children whose way of life may be in sharp contrast to that presented in the "smiling, fair-skinned world" depicted in their readers.[48]

The following conclusion, which has been reported as the position of the New York State Education Department on these points, suggests directions in which the improvement of basal readers should move: "School readers . . . have been oriented too extensively to the culture of our prosperous middle class. Our school readers should undoubtedly be more realistic. They should recognize that America is a land of plural cultures, that all our families do not have Anglo-Saxon names, that Americans are representative of varying races, nationality backgrounds, and religious faiths. School readers will need to make greater use also of selections from the very best juvenile writings. We shall need to invest our school readers with some of the richness of vocabulary and content that is characteristic of the finest children's literature."[49]

Can the Need for Remedial Reading Instruction Be Eliminated? Some critics of current reading instruction have contended that the need for remedial reading work can be eliminated by drastic changes in methods of teaching beginning reading. They have supported their view by citing the absence of remedial reading instruction in the schools of the nineteenth and early twentieth centuries.[50]

Most reading specialists, on the other hand, believe that the need for remedial instruction can be reduced by improved instruction but never completely eliminated. In their eyes the provision for remedial reading instruction in modern schools merely indicates the progress that has been made during recent decades in dealing with a persistent, long-standing problem. They point to an enormous body of research that indicates the causes of poor reading are complex, vary from child to child, and include factors that are beyond the control of the school.[51]

As has been noted earlier, children who encounter difficulty with initial reading instruction because of their own immaturity or lack of experience are likely to have continued difficulty in reading. More adequate programs of reading readiness would undoubtedly reduce the need for remedial instruction in later school years. Improving initial reading instruction and providing a continuing, well-balanced reading program through the upper elementary and secondary school years can also reduce the number of pupils who need remedial help. In addition to these factors, which can be affected by changes in the school program, there are many other causes of reading difficulty which can be dealt with only through special corrective help.

Children whose mental growth is slow usually fall behind agemates in reading accomplishment. Many of the children who are reading "below grade" are in this group. While children of slow mental growth are not considered subjects for remedial instruction in the technical sense unless they are reading below their own intellectual level, they nevertheless require special help in reading if they are to make the best progress of which they are capable.

Children with defects in hearing or eyesight frequently encounter difficulty in reading, and special approaches are needed to help them learn. Children with generally low vitality are likely to make slow progress in all school learning, including reading. Other physical conditions that cause frequent or prolonged absences prevent normal progress in reading. A very small proportion of slow readers suffer from special brain defects that contribute to reading disability. Children with such physical handicaps as these must have special assistance in reading, as in other school work, if they are to progress.

There is a high correlation, although not necessarily a cause-effect relationship, between emotional disturbance and reading difficulty. Indeed, in some cases of severe disability, the child must be helped to resolve his emotional problems before he can make much progress with learning to read. Such extreme cases are the exception, however. Many pupils who are victims of instability in family relationships or are struggling with other emotional problems are also retarded in reading and can benefit from remedial help.

Reading problems are often encountered by children whose school attendance has been interrupted for one reason or another—for example, because their families moved frequently—so that their school experience has lacked continuity. These children, too, need special help if they are to develop their reading skills.

This brief survey of common causes of reading difficulty indicates that if the school is to help all children learn to read as effectively as possible, corrective and remedial help must be available to pupils who need it. Such assistance must be based on careful diagnosis of the pupil's specific difficulties. Much of the corrective teaching can and will be done by the classroom teacher within the regular class period. A teacher trained in remedial techniques is needed, however, to diagnose the nature of pupils' reading problems and to teach children who have more severe reading disabilities. This remedial reading specialist should also serve as a consultant to the classroom teachers who will carry major responsibility for improving the reading of all students.

The question of whether or not to add instruction in foreign languages to the elementary school program has received much attention in the past decade and many school systems have decided affirmatively. The number of elementary school pupils studying a foreign language rose from about 145,600 in 1953 to about 1,277,000 in 1959-60, an increase of about 742.5 percent.[52] The debate as to the desirability of foreign language study by younger children still rages, however.

Arguments in Support of FLES

Arguments in favor of foreign language study in the elementary school, commonly referred to as FLES, may be summarized as follows:[53]

• Many language specialists, with the support of certain neurologists, psychologists, and child development specialists, urge that the optimum time for beginning foreign language learning is between the ages of four and eight. During these years, it is held, "the brain seems to have the greatest plasticity and specialized capacity needed for acquiring speech."[54] This capacity includes ability to mimic speech and to manipulate language patterns easily.

• An early beginning of foreign language study will facilitate later and more systematic study of the language. Proficiency in use of a language requires study and use over an extended period of years.

• Foreign language study is interesting and enjoyable to children and can enhance their interest in the total school program. Although it should be pursued in a separate time period, it can be related to other curriculum areas of the elementary school, particularly social studies, art, and music. There is no research evidence that studying a foreign language hinders pupil progress in other subjects.

• Elementary school children can begin to gain acquaintance with another culture—one of the benefits of foreign language study. Favorable attitudes toward the people whose language is studied can be developed as a result of the study.

• Study of another language can improve understanding of one's own language.

Arguments Against FLES

Those who question the desirability of introducing foreign language study in the elementary school years have presented the following points in support of their view:[55]

• There is no conclusive evidence to support the claim that the optimum time to begin study of a foreign language is in childhood; in fact, there is disagreement among both neurologists and child development specialists as to the accuracy of this claim.

• Results of an early beginning in foreign language study to date have been disappointing. Even pupils who have had as much as six years of elementary school foreign language study seldom gain more than a year of advanced placement when they enter the high school foreign language program. Relatively little evidence on this point is yet available, however, since in most schools the FLES program has not been in operation long enough to affect sizeable numbers of pupils.

• Evidence is accumulating that from 10 to 20 percent of elementary school age children do not make satisfactory progress in the study of a foreign language. There does not appear to be a direct relation between academic intelligence and success in foreign language study. This suggests that if foreign language study is introduced in the elementary school, it should not be scheduled for all pupils or as enrichment for all pupils of superior ability.

• The elementary curriculum is already crowded. Some areas, such as science and the arts, now do not receive as much attention as is generally considered justified. If a foreign language is introduced, pupil time and energy must be taken from other subjects. Financial support must be taken from other aspects of the program to provide the materials and teachers for foreign language study. Even if it is proved conclusively that foreign language can be learned more easily when its study is begun in childhood, the question remains: Is foreign language study the most desirable use of the pupil's time and of the school's limited resources?

- Progress has been made in developing a unified program of studies in the elementary school and in reducing fragmentation of the school day into many separate subject periods. To introduce foreign language study, which language specialists say must be conducted as a separate subject with its own time period, is not in keeping with this desirable trend.
- There is no evidence that children will gain a better acquaintance with other cultures or develop more constructive attitudes toward other people through foreign language study than through spending the same amount of time, with adequate learning materials, in direct study of other peoples of the world.

Criteria for Decisions About FLES

Curriculum planners must weigh these arguments and the evidence on which they are based in deciding what priority to assign to foreign language study in the elementary school program. Language specialists have warned against faddish aspects of the FLES movement and have expressed dismay that in many communities FLES has been introduced without adequate preparation. A FLES program, whether for selected groups or for all pupils, should be introduced only when the following conditions are met: "1) It is an integral and serious part of the school day; 2) it is an integral and serious part of the total foreign language program in the school system; 3) there is close articulation with later foreign language learning; 4) there are available FL specialists or elementary-school teachers with an adequate command of the foreign language; 5) there is a planned syllabus and a sequence of appropriate teaching materials; 6) the program has the support of the administration; 7) the high-school teachers of the foreign language in the local school system recognize the same long-range objectives and practice some of the same teaching techniques as the FLES teachers."[56]

In determining what priority is to be given to foreign language study in the elementary school, evidence about the particular student body and the community the school serves should be studied. If the decision is to include foreign language in the elementary curriculum, the school that acts responsibly will meet the conditions stated above before instituting a FLES program.

DEVELOPING A WORLD PERSPECTIVE

Many of the public issues and national policy decisions to which citizens must react in present-day America can only be understood if viewed in the total world setting. The increasing interdependence among nations and the close relationships between domestic and international problems which have created this situation are discussed in other volumes of this report.* Members of the National Committee of the Project on Instruction are convinced that a leading responsibility of the schools in the decades ahead is to help students develop the world perspective needed by citizens of a democratic nation.

This responsibility has been recognized as a valid educational goal for at least a generation. During and after World War I it was suddenly realized that most citizens of the United States had extremely limited knowledge of other parts of the world and of international relations. Since the 1920's, schools have tried various approaches to help young people gain more understanding of world affairs. During the decades of the twenties and thirties some schools introduced more study of other regions of the world and of relations among nations. The "international friendship" approach received considerable emphasis during the 1930's. Many schools, however, remained relatively untouched by these efforts,

* See *Schools for the Sixties* and *Education in a Changing Society*.

and those that were affected gave almost exclusive attention to Western cultures.

Events of World War II again forced the realization that many U.S. citizens were abysmally ignorant about important regions of the world. The neglected geographic areas that received little or no treatment in most school programs included eastern Asia, the Soviet Union, the Middle East, Africa, and Latin America. Since World War II and especially since the late 1950's, considerable progress has been made in introducing into the school curriculum some study of these geographic areas.

A Program for Developing a World Perspective

From a generation of exploration and experimentation by a minority of schools, it is possible to identify four elements that contribute to the student's development of a world perspective. These elements are so interrelated that they cannot be separated from one another in the school program, but they are defined separately here for purposes of clarity.[57]

Information about other peoples, regions, and cultures of the world and about relations among nations is the first element. To achieve a realistic view of world affairs and of U.S. policies in the world setting, a person must have some perception of why other peoples and nations act as they do—even when that action seems undesirable in the eyes of the United States. To gain this perception, a person must realize that each national group has developed its own structure of traditions, attitudes, and value patterns from its experience as a nation. The student should acquire factual information about the experiences of other nations and the resulting viewpoints of their people. For example, the long struggle against colonialism of such nations as India or Ghana has given the people of those nations a particular set of mind about their relations with the rest of the world and especially with former colonial powers. Actions of other nations that appear from our own national frame of reference to be contradictory, mistaken, or short-sighted at best may be quite comprehensible when viewed against the background of their experience and culture. Armed with such knowledge and understanding, the citizen is able to consider more realistically his own nation's policies and their probable reception by other peoples.

Information about the channels of communication and negotiation among nations helps the citizen evaluate how national policies are carried out. The UN system is the most comprehensive agency for conducting international relations today. Young people should learn about its problems and progress along with their study of other channels for handling foreign affairs and the operation of such forces as trade and cultural exchange in the modern world.

The development of cultural empathy for other peoples is a second element in gaining a world perspective. Cultural empathy involves the ability to comprehend the people of another culture as live human beings with their own patterns of customs, hopes, and fears rather than as mere statistics or as quaint characters living in a far-off land. Personalized information about other peoples, about the differences as well as the similarities among cultural groups, can help students become capable of cultural empathy. Firsthand contacts with persons of another culture and school-to-school exchanges of letters, toys, books, and even of pupils and teachers can contribute to this element.

Efforts to develop cultural empathy should not be confused with the international friendship approach to study of other peoples. The goal is not to have everybody "like" everybody else but to help children realize that people of other cultures are flesh-and-blood human beings who have worked out their own life patterns. Nor is the goal to create an attitude that all patterns of living are equally worthy or desirable; rather it is to develop an understanding that differences among life patterns from culture to culture are normal and must be taken into account in seeking solutions to international problems.

A third element in developing a world perspective is the application of rational or critical thinking processes to the area of international affairs. Leading issues concerning international relations and U.S. foreign policies should be studied *as issues,* with objective examination of the arguments and proposals advanced by various parties to the disagreements, rather than as presentations of our national policies as the only way of dealing with the problems underlying the issues. Because stereotypes and prejudices concerning other peoples block rational consideration of their part in world affairs and of related U.S. policies, students should be helped to recognize and avoid common stereotypes and prejudices in their own thinking about world affairs.

Understanding one's own culture is the fourth element in developing a world perspective. By helping students achieve an objective appreciation of the traditions and strengths of their own nation as well as comprehension of its unsolved problems, the school can provide a firm basis for viewing the cultures and policies of other nations objectively. Young people who are secure in their own culture are unlikely to be either blindly disparaging or uncritically enthusiastic about the achievements and policies of other nations. Instead, they will be free to evaluate objectively the differences they observe among the institutions, traditions, and policies of the various nations of the world.

Provision in the Curriculum. Responsibility for helping students develop a world perspective is shared by many fields of the curriculum and by both the elementary and secondary schools. The four elements described above should be woven into existing subjects and activities, not presented as a new course or sequence of courses.

Much of the basic information about our own institutions and heritage, about the cultures of other peoples, and about world affairs will be presented in social studies classes, if an adequate and up-to-date program has been developed. Study of contemporary issues in world affairs will be an important part of such a social studies curriculum. The program in language arts and English will include study of the literature of other cultures as well as that of England and the United States. This may begin with the use of folk tales and children's stories from many lands in the elementary school and proceed to study of world literature in the secondary school. Selected examples of the music and art of other cultures should be included at appropriate points in the school program. Foreign language study may be developed in order to stress the culture of the group whose language is being learned.

In a recent experimental program in the teaching of world affairs,[58] it was found that still other curriculum areas such as science, physical education, home economics, industrial arts, and business education had important contributions to make to pupils' development of a world view. Indeed, in that experiment the study of other cultures and of world affairs permeated almost every aspect of the elementary and secondary school program, including some extraclass activities. A program of in-service study for the entire faculty of the school system and the involvement of various lay groups in the community were basic to the success of the project.

In many schools helping young people develop a world perspective will require a reorientation of much familiar curriculum content rather than drastic changes in the program of studies. Most schools, however, may find they also need to add some new content and experiences, especially for more adequate study about non-Western cultures.

RECOMMENDATIONS OF THE NATIONAL COMMITTEE

The National Committee believes there is no uniform prescription for establishing curriculum balance and priorities which will apply in every school and for every pupil. The Committee has, however, identified basic principles that local school systems may apply in achieving a balanced school program for their particular students and in determining curriculum priorities. These are stated in the following broad recommendation.

WAYS OF ACHIEVING BALANCE

RECOMMENDATION: *The school can provide and maintain a curriculum appropriately balanced for each student by offering a comprehensive program of studies, making early and continuous assessment of individual potentialities and achievements, and providing individualized programs based on careful counseling.*

To avoid the imbalance that can result from limiting financial support to certain selected subjects and services, general financial support should be provided for the total program. This applies to local, state, and federal support.

The need for balance, both in the provided program of the school and in the curriculum each pupil actually studies, is recognized in this recommendation. In planning the courses to be offered, a proper balance should be maintained among the humanities, the social sciences, the natural and physical sciences, and mathematics. The recent heavy emphasis on science, mathematics, and modern foreign languages has probably corrected a former neglect of these fields in the schools. One problem in many school systems, now and for the immediate future, will be to prevent neglect of the other academic areas. Before decisions are made to increase the amount of school time devoted to a particular subject or to introduce new subjects, such as foreign language in the elementary school, the effect of such changes on pupils' total school experience should be carefully considered.

Another problem that curriculum planners must face is that of achieving a sound balance between the academic and the applied subjects in the education of children and youth. All pupils need both types of studies if they are to be equipped for life in the modern world, although the relative emphasis on the academic and applied subjects will vary from student to student.

In this recommendation the Committee re-emphasizes the importance of identifying the potential talents and learning problems of each pupil as early as possible, a need that is treated more fully in Chapter Three. Effective instruction in reading, which deserves high priority in the school program, requires that the individual differences revealed through such early identification of talents and problems be taken into account. This principle applies with equal force to the other areas of the curriculum. The older student, in order to select studies that will be appropriate for him, needs guidance that is based on a thorough knowledge of his abilities, his progress in school, and his long-range goals. Cocurricular activities as well as organized courses should be drawn upon to plan a program of studies and activities which will be balanced for the individual pupil.

Two other comprehensive recommendations that have been discussed in earlier chapters apply to the problem of establishing balance and priorities in the school program and therefore are repeated here. One deals with the need to base all curriculum planning on a clear statement of educational objectives (see Chapter Two). The other proposes guidelines for distinguishing between the distinctive and shared responsibilities of the school (see Chapter Four).

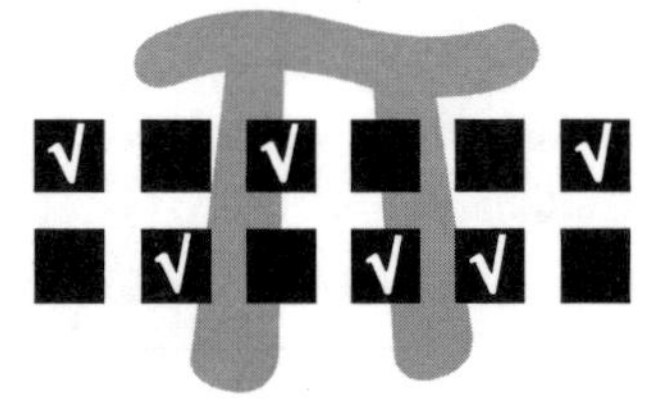

CHAPTER SIX
CONTROVERSIAL ISSUES IN THE SCHOOL PROGRAM

Studying Controversial Issues
Teaching About Communism
Recommendations of the National Committee

One recommendation of the National Committee of the Project on Instruction that has been already emphasized is that "the curriculum should provide adequate instruction concerning major social forces and trends of the present time." Schools that seek to implement this recommendation will include, in many curriculum areas and at all grade levels, content dealing with controversial issues.

A variety of problems is likely to arise when controversial issues are dealt with in the school. The first part of this chapter is devoted to a discussion of guiding principles that the school may apply in handling those problems. The second part of the chapter discusses an urgent contemporary problem, teaching about communism, which schools are currently dealing with in a variety of ways—some good, some bad. The guiding principles for teaching about controversial issues are applied to this problem.

STUDYING CONTROVERSIAL ISSUES

A controversial issue involves a problem about which different individuals and groups urge conflicting courses of action. It is an issue for which society has not found a solution that can be universally or almost universally accepted. It is an issue of sufficient significance that each of the proposed ways of dealing with it is objectionable to some sector of the citizenry and arouses protest. The protest may result from a feeling that a cherished belief, an economic interest, or a basic principle is threatened. It may come because the welfare of organizations or groups seems at stake. When a course of action is formulated that virtually all sectors of society accept, the issue is no longer controversial.

Controversial issues arise most often in social studies, because this field is devoted to the study of man and his society. Many other school subjects, however, deal with topics or problems that are at least potentially controversial. For example, certain topics in science or health education lead naturally to the question of birth control or of fluoridation of the community water supply.

In the English class the study of standard literary works, both classic and contemporary, often leads to discussion of controversial problems. Thus, the decision to treat controversial issues in the classroom may affect many parts of the school program.

The Debate About Study of the Controversial

There is not universal agreement that controversial issues should be studied in the school. Those who believe the curriculum should be focused sharply on our heritage from the past hold that today's unsettled issues do not lie within the compass of the school. Others argue that school time is so limited that at best much valuable noncontroversial material has to be omitted. To give time to controversial issues would force still more of the standard content out of the curriculum. The argument is also heard that school age children and youth are not sufficiently mature to weigh evidence and arrive at reasoned conclusions about issues on which their elders are in conflict. Fear that young people may become indoctrinated with questionable viewpoints on political, economic, or social problems is also voiced.

Those who favor the study of controversial issues in the schools point to the dynamic nature of American society. The rapid change in social conditions and institutions makes controversy among various groups and organizations inevitable, when satisfactory adjustments of evolving problems are sought. If democratic values and institutions are to survive, citizens must learn to resolve issues through rational, independent thought. They must learn how to get and evaluate evidence and to listen to and weigh opposing views. They must learn to draw conclusions based on the available facts or suspend judgment until adequate facts are available. The attitudes and skills essential to this process of rational inquiry should be taught systematically in the context within which citizens are called on to apply them, it is urged. "If training in the consideration of controversial issues is left to the unplanned experience of the average individual, there is little to guard him against blind acceptance of his own prejudice and the acceptance of an inadequate technique for reaching enlightened judgments."[1] Thus preparation for citizenship, along with development of rational thinking, is a primary reason for including study of controversial issues in the school program.

Truly controversial issues are rarely settled in a brief time. Those that are sufficiently significant to deserve study in the classroom are likely to persist into adult life, although the specific form they take may shift. As controversial issues are treated in the classroom, students begin to build a background of factual information for understanding them in their evolving forms. The study of leading issues rooted in investigation of underlying social forces and trends thus becomes one part of the student's introduction to his society. Only a small proportion of school time devoted to controversial topics can make study of related noncontroversial materials more vital.

As for the question of pupils' maturity, those who favor treatment of controversial issues in the classroom agree that the materials selected for study at any grade level must be those which pupils can comprehend and handle rationally. Indoctrination should be prevented by objective treatment of the issues.

In recent years many groups of professional educators, academic scholars, local school boards, and lay citizens[2] have adopted the view that the study of controversial materials and issues is an inherent right of pupils and a way for them to learn about significant aspects of their culture. This view has been incorporated in policy statements of many boards of education in terms such as this: "The pupils of Armijo Joint Union High School District have four rights to be recognized [in connection with study of controversial issues]:

"[1.] The right to study any controversial issue which has political, economic, or social significance and concerning which (at his level) he should begin to have an opinion. Among others these issues might include such topics as local government problems, labor unions, party political ideologies, United Nations and Unesco.

"[2.] The right to have access to all relevant information, including the materials that circulate freely in the community.

"[3.] The right to study under competent instruction in an atmosphere free from bias and prejudice.

"[4.] The right to form and express his own opinions on controversial issues without thereby jeopardizing his relations with his teacher or the school." [3]

Selecting Issues for Classroom Study

Since the study of controversial issues constitutes only a small portion of the total curriculum in any school subject, the issues should be carefully selected with both pedagogical and social factors taken into account. The following five criteria provide a guide for the selection of controversial topics to be studied in the classroom. They apply to both the elementary and the secondary school and to all subject areas.

Is the Issue Suitable for Pupils of the Maturity and Backgrounds Represented in the Class? Can the pupils comprehend the problem, understand the concepts and values that are involved, grasp the varying points of view, and interpret factual information on which these viewpoints are based? Issues that involve relatively technical information, such as a proposed reorganization of the federal tax structure, would not be appropriate for younger children to study in depth. They can, however, grasp simpler aspects of such topics as conservation of resources or medical care programs. They can become aware of disagreements in the adult society and begin to develop the attitudes and skills required to deal with them rationally. Secondary school youth may appropriately study such unsolved problems of society as civil rights, inflation, and the role of the United States in international organizations.

Most senior high school pupils are mature enough to study significant issues of the day, including those that are hotly debated in the community. There may be times when a particular issue must be handled with special care because of community attitudes. In such cases, the teacher can consult with members of the school administration to plan how to approach the study and when to schedule it. Issues that are extremely controversial locally can usually be studied by mature pupils with reasonable objectivity if such precautions are taken.

One test of the appropriateness of an issue for study by a particular class is how significant it seems to the pupils. Some topics such as proposals for solving problems of juvenile delinquency or the question of lowering the voting age spark immediate interest with certain age groups. The teacher should stimulate interest in others. To limit the treatment of controversial issues to those in which students happen to express interest spontaneously is as educationally unsound as waiting to introduce an arithmetic process until pupils have asked for it. Unless substantial interest in an issue can be aroused, however, it is doubtful that pupils will gain from its study. Since there are more appropriate controversial topics than there is time to study them in depth, only those of greatest potential interest to class members should be selected.

Will Study of the Issue Help Students Achieve Course Objectives? The principle of vertical and horizontal coordination of students' school experience should be respected in choosing controversial issues for a particular course. The pupil who studies problems of juvenile delinquency in two or three succeeding years, for example, is probably wasting time. Selecting issues that grow out of the course content usually avoids duplication from one year to another or from one school subject to another.

Only occasionally should issues be studied merely because they are prominently in the news. Leading issues of the day can be treated as current events topics in all social studies classes, but most of the controversial topics selected for fuller study are best chosen in relation to the course work. The Presidential election is one clear exception to this general rule. During this event, which occurs just once during a student's high school career, opinion about basic national problems is often crystallized. The experience of analyzing campaign issues in the objective atmosphere of the classroom is an important one for every young American.

Is the Issue One for Which Adequate Study Materials That Present Various Points of View Can Be Obtained? Materials appropriate to the pupils' reading level and general maturity are essential. They should include reasonably full presentations of the various widely held viewpoints. This criterion may require that study of an issue arising in class be postponed until materials can be gathered. Or it may require that the issue be treated only as a current event, with students aware they are not studying it in depth.

Is the Issue One Which Is Important and Likely To Be of Continuing Significance? Since reasonably full study of a few issues will be more valuable than brief study of many, a selection has to be made among those that meet the foregoing criteria. Just as some historical or scientific facts are more important than others and therefore are more worth studying, so some controversial issues are more significant than others and deserve priority. Also, a problem that promises to be of continuing importance is more significant than one which is ephemeral in nature. U.S. policy concerning foreign aid, for example, meets the tests of both current significance and probable continued importance.

Is the Issue One That the Teacher Is—or Can Become—Adequately Prepared To Handle Fully and Objectively? A teacher without adequate background in economics may properly avoid full-scale study of economic issues until he can become better prepared. If his own knowledge of international relations and foreign affairs is limited, he needs to make careful preparation when a controversial issue in this area is selected for study. The teacher is not required, however, to have a specialist's knowledge of a specific issue before it can be taken up in his classroom. If he has essential background relating to the issue and demonstrates how to study the specific problem, students may profit enormously from the example thus provided. An adequately prepared teacher, of course, has the necessary background for most current issues.

Study of Controversial Issues

As the foregoing discussion indicates, the teacher has definite responsibilities for guiding the study of controversial issues. He helps pupils understand and seek the values of such study. He leads pupils in creating and maintaining the calm atmosphere in which rational analysis proceeds. He helps pupils learn to disagree courteously, avoiding acrimonious comments or ridicule of unpopular opinions, and to respect the right of others to disagree with them. The teacher can do much to create the desired behavior by setting the example of respect for others.

The wise teacher, of course, does not attempt to indoctrinate pupils with his own point of view. This does not mean that he may not express his own opinion. He may properly do so, provided pupils understand that it is his view and provided students are made to feel truly free to arrive at their conclusions independently. Many teachers prefer to withhold any statement of their own views until pupils' study has been concluded. As students become well acquainted with a teacher, however, they are likely to sense his opinions. Hence, as pupils become certain of their freedom to disagree, an objective atmosphere may be maintained more effectively through a straightforward statement of the teacher's views.

The teacher sees that all widely held views about the issue are presented and considered honestly by the class. If one or more sides of the question are being neglected, the teacher himself may present these. Another useful procedure may be to have students present the case for views with which they disagree. The emphasis should be on objective evaluation of evidence and formulation of conclusions from the evidence within the context of recognized values. Students are thus helped to distinguish among facts, assumptions, and value judgments. They learn that opposing conclusions may be drawn from a body of factual data because the evidence is approached from different value positions.

While students should understand the citizen's responsibility to arrive at reasoned conclusions on current issues, they should also learn that a prior conclusion needs reconsideration as new evidence becomes available. The teacher need not and frequently should not urge pupils to draw a firm conclusion about the issue under study. Sometimes a pupil may gain more by summarizing the evidence for and against leading proposals for dealing with the problem than by coming to a conclusion about it. This procedure may be especially useful in considering an issue in which the community has much emotional involvement.

The need for materials presenting a range of positions deserves further comment, because many attacks on public education in recent years have been focused on controversial materials in school libraries or classroom collections. Effective study of controversial issues requires that partisan materials as well as balanced, objective treatments be read and analyzed by students. Some, perhaps much, of the material needed for study of controversial issues may not have been prepared specifically for school use. The pertinent questions to be asked in reviewing a collection of materials, therefore, are these:

1. Are the materials adaptable to the range of reading ability among students who will use them? Some material should be easier and some more advanced than the average reading level of the class to provide for the inevitable range of individual differences.

2. Is there in the collection a balance among various points of view on the issue?

3. Are some objective accounts that are balanced within themselves included? If not, is it because none is available?

4. As partisan materials are used, are students made aware of the nature and purposes of the organization or individual responsible for the material?

5. As partisan materials are used, are students helped to analyze persuasion techniques, faulty reasoning from evidence to conclusion, and other characteristics of this sort? [4]

Questions such as these need to be kept in mind by school authorities as they authorize the procurement of materials and by citizens who may be concerned with teaching about controversial issues.

The Need for Stated Policies

Although the right of students to learn to deal with the controversial has been widely accepted, that right cannot be fulfilled unless teachers are free to include controversial materials in the curriculum. Some school officials and teachers have avoided the controversial, consciously or unconsciously, because of possible repercussions in the community. In a few cases, individual teachers who led their pupils in study of controversial issues have come under criticism with resulting injury to their professional careers. If pupils are to enjoy their right to study controversial issues, teachers and school administrators must be protected against unjust pressures from partisan groups.

One means of providing this protection is for the board of education to develop a specific written policy to govern the teaching of controversial issues. The teacher who works responsibly within such a framework has assurance of support from the school administration, including the board of education, should unfair attacks be made. An increasing number of boards of education have adopted such policy statements. Examples are given in the recent publication of the National Education Association, *Controversial Issues in the Classroom.*

Examination of a number of these statements and of reports of professional educational organizations [5] suggest that such a policy statement should—

- Be written in clear, unequivocal language.
- Include a positive endorsement of classroom study of controversial issues.
- Be stated in terms of general policy rather than list specific issues to be studied.
- Indicate the principles that should govern activities of administrators and teachers in relation to classroom study of controversial issues.
- Guarantee support to school personnel who, while acting responsibly, encounter unexpected difficulties in connection with classroom study of controversial issues.
- Be thoroughly publicized so that both school personnel and members of the community are fully aware of the school's policy.

The adoption of such a policy statement by the board of education in no way prevents citizens from expressing legitimate interest or concern about this or any other aspect of the school program. They are free to raise questions or ask for information through proper channels, which should be established clearly by the board. The policy statement can serve as a protection for the public, the school board, and school personnel against irresponsible accusations. It can do so, however, only if it is implemented in spirit as well as in letter by all concerned with the operation of the school.

TEACHING ABOUT COMMUNISM

In recent months, a number of national citizen groups have gone on record as favoring teaching about communism in the schools. Two leading organizations have issued widely circulated policy statements. In its bulletin, *Instruction on Communism and Its Contrast with Liberty Under Law,*[6] the American Bar Association urged its members to work in their own communities to achieve treatment of the subject in the schools. The joint committee of the American Legion and the National Education Association in July 1962 published *Teaching About Communism—Guidelines for Junior and Senior High School Teachers.*[7] Also, legislation requiring that units or courses on communism be introduced in the high schools has been passed recently in some states.

The reasons for teaching about communism in the schools may be summarized quickly. The communist movement is a critical force in world affairs today. Ignoring it will not cause it to go away. Citizens of the United States need to understand communism's basic tenets and techniques of operation in order to evaluate developments in the cold war and give rational support to appropriate national policies concerning our foreign relations problems. Hand in hand with an understanding of communism comes deeper insight into the system of constitutional government and freedom under law that the United States has developed. Even if no critical situation existed in world affairs as a result of the conflict between communism and democracy, the study of communism would still be, as the report of the American Bar Association states, a sound educational requirement. "The history of much of this century is incomprehensible without a considerable knowledge of the Communist movement and its history, doctrines, objectives, and tactics."[8]

A Trend Reversed

This development of popular approval for teaching about communism is in sharp contrast to the situation that prevailed widely through much of the 1950's. During that decade in many parts of the United States, the schools were effectively if informally prohibited from presenting information about communism and its chief proponent, the Soviet Union. In some schools that introduced even minimal treatment of these topics, teachers and administrators were subjected to attack from highly vocal special interest groups, although such groups seemed to represent only a small segment of the citizenry.

Throughout this same period, however, some voices called for the study of communism, particularly as developed in the U.S.S.R., as important in the development of a well-informed citizenry. In many communities where public opinion permitted, units on democracy and the isms, including communism, were taught in twelfth grade social studies courses or in world history, and the Soviet Union was studied in courses in world geography and world history. A few materials on communism suitable for use by high school students were published in the early fifties.[9] Teaching about communism and all forms of totalitarianism was urged by the National Education Association in a resolution adopted at its annual convention in 1951.[10] President Eisenhower in 1956 recommended that students be taught to understand differences between the American and Soviet forms of government.[11] In an address to the National Education Association's annual convention the next year, the Assistant Secretary of State urged that schools teach the facts of communist theory and practice.[12] Sessions on teaching about the U.S.S.R., with attention to its economic system, its form of government, and its foreign policies, were included in annual conventions of the National Council for the Social Studies throughout the 1950's; and in 1958 an entire issue of the organization's official journal, *Social Education,* was devoted to the Soviet Union and teaching about communism.[13]

Facts or Propaganda?

The current trend of public approval for treatment of communism in the schools has contradictory possibilities. It can develop in a positive fashion if those who endorse teaching about communism support factual, analytical study of the subject, with emphasis on free, rational inquiry. If it is interpreted to mean indoctrination based on propaganda, however, or if it is used by special interest groups to cover irresponsible attacks on all who disagree with them about public issues, the effects could be destructive indeed.

Responsible citizens, both in and out of the schools, are aware of the weakness of the indoctrination approach and of the danger of misuse by extremist groups. The report of the American Bar

Association stressed the importance of a factual study of communism, one involving the method of rational inquiry: "The importance of viewing this particular program as education—rather than some form of counter-propaganda—should be emphasized. In America, the educational process is closely and properly related to a principal objective of our society—freedom of the individual. This obviously includes freedom of the mind, and this in turn includes freedom and capacity to think and make rational choices. In the light of these great traditions, the subject of Communism (like any other subject) should be taught factually, thoroughly and objectively. This is, indeed, in our national interest as American students jealously reserve to themselves the right to make rational choices, and they would be the first to resent—or later to be disillusioned by—teaching which departs from these traditional standards." [14]

The joint committee of the American Legion and the National Education Association has taken a similar position: "Our loyalties must be rooted in knowledge and understanding, not in ignorance and prejudice. Thoughtful American citizens realize that our institutions will not suffer by comparison with those of any communist country or of any country under the domination of communism . . . in the realm of free thinking, nothing is so potent as simple truth." [15]

In spite of such endorsements for a factual study of communism in the schools, Hechinger found that "right-wing indoctrination" characterizes at least some of the programs.[16] In one state, for example, he found that a resolution of the state legislature called for all high school students, as a requirement for graduation, to view a filmstrip that "implies that the United States, Spain, and Switzerland are the only non-Communist nations of the western world."

Another survey that was limited to one state revealed that extremist pressures had been brought on the schools.[17] In one community an effort was made to censor study material prepared by a reputable scholar dealing with the non-Western world. The social studies teachers in one large high school were required to distribute to their classes "highly partisan materials designed to fight communism with captions such as, 'Will you be free to worship by Easter?' "

Many public leaders as well as educators believe that the important purposes of teaching about communism in the schools will be defeated if such tactics prevail. The reasoning behind this view is indicated above and presented more fully in the discussion of characteristics of an adequate program of instruction about communism.

State Action Concerning Teaching About Communism

A survey completed in the fall of 1962, with responses from the chief state school officers of 50 states, revealed that in 27 states the state education department had developed programs for teaching about communism or were doing so.[18] Laws concerning the matter had been passed in 3 states, and resolutions had been adopted by 2 state legislatures. In 2 states, New York and California, the laws permitted but did not require such instruction. The Florida law and Louisiana resolution included a definite requirement for a special unit or course on Americanism vs. communism. The resolution adopted by the Georgia legislature also called for a separate, required unit on this topic.

Legislative acts requiring specific courses or units in any subject violate the widely accepted principle that there is a proper division of responsibility in educational matters between the lay government and the educational authorities. It is the responsibility of the state legislature to set general goals for the schools, not to legislate specific courses or curriculum content, and to delegate to the appropriate educational authority the power to implement the stated goals. Responsibility for deciding what and how to teach about communism should lie in the hands of the teachers and school administrators of the local community—supported by the school board and by public opinion—who should use the resources of scholarship and professional consultation on the subject. Well intended as laws requiring teaching about communism may be, such specific prescriptions do not lead to competent teaching. The teaching profession furnishes the best guarantee there is that young people can be taught wisely about communism without being misled as to its values and ideals.

Evidence that teaching about communism is included in the school program without legislative requirement is found in states where no specific legislation has been passed. In Connecticut, for example, the high school curriculum recommended by the state education department since 1959 and generally followed in the schools includes study of communism in connection with these topics: Soviet Russia and Communist China in grade 10 and democracy and authoritarianism in grade 12. In Maryland a special state-wide committee appointed by the state superintendent of schools recommended that study of totalitarian ideologies be included in the junior and senior high schools, with emphasis in senior high school history and problems of democracy courses. This recommendation was approved by a resolution of the state board of education. Many counties in Maryland have developed or are developing materials for teaching about communism in the context of the social studies program. Similar examples could be cited from other states.

An Adequate Program of Instruction About Communism

From discussions of educators, historians, political scientists, economists, and specialists on the U.S.S.R. and from materials that have been used effectively in the schools, seven characteristics of an adequate program of instruction about communism may be identified.[19]

The Study Should Be Conducted Factually and Unemotionally, Stressing Rational Inquiry and Objective Comparisons of the Communist and Democratic Systems. The basic differences between the closed society of communism, with its imposed conformity to a single system of belief and control, and the open society of democracy, with its toleration of individuality and diversity, are dramatic and will stand for themselves. To exaggerate the conditions of communist society while painting American society as perfect in all aspects only leads to disbelief, questioning of the honesty of the instruction, and cynicism on the part of the student.

The achievements as well as the negative aspects of communist societies should be presented. To do otherwise would be contrary to the method of rational inquiry. Furthermore, unless the content studied in the classroom includes facts about Soviet industrial and technological progress, for example, one of two negative results follows. Some students may fail to grasp the critical nature of the world-wide competition between communism and democracy and the reasons communism appeals to the people of some underdeveloped regions. They may think that the communist influence can simply be talked away. More likely, as pupils learn about the Soviet achievements in certain areas such as space technology from the public press, they will dismiss as unrealistic and slanted any classroom treatment that ignores such significant accomplishments.

Although the major treatment of communism should come in the secondary school years, some aspects of communist societies may be studied in the later grades of the elementary school. Certainly younger children are likely to raise questions about the Soviet Union and other communist countries as they hear current news stories. Their questions should be answered with the same factual, objective approach that is recommended for older students.

The problems as well as the achievements of the American democratic system and the progress being made to solve the problems also require realistic treatment in classroom study. All that is done in the elementary grades as well as in the secondary school to develop understanding of the freedoms, rights, and responsibilities of citizens in our democracy and to teach the process of rational thinking can help to educate citizens who will make objective comparisons of the communist and democratic systems.

The Study of Communism Should Be Set in the Perspective of Study of the Modern World. As pupils are wisely guided to learn about both Western and non-Western cultures, about highly industrialized and the underdeveloped nations, they come to understand that there are other forms of democratic government besides that of the United States and other forms of authoritarianism besides Soviet communism. In their study of a range of economic systems,[20] they can learn about the historical development of communist theory and understand its basic elements of historical materialism, dialectical materialism, surplus value, and the class struggle. In this study, students can be guided to realize semantic differences in interpretation of such terms as democracy, capitalism, and imperialism in various cultures, including the communist.

The study of communism in the U.S.S.R. should include attention to factors in Russian history before 1917 which have influenced the development of the totalitarian system of the Soviet Union. Petrovich suggests 10 major themes from Russian history which can throw light on conditions in the world's leading communist state today:

"1. The vast masses of the Russian people have been traditionally disinterested in participating in government and have been politically passive.

"2. The Russian peasant way of life is traditionally based on social democracy and communal living.

"3. Russian society has for centuries consisted of a small ruling class on top, the vast peasant masses below, and only a thin layer of middle class and workers between, and then only in relatively recent times.

"4. For centuries the State has been the prime mover in Russian history, and most of the great changes in Russian life have been effected from above.

"5. The Russian State has been ruled like an armed camp for centuries.

"6. Russia has long pursued certain basic aims in its foreign policy that have become a part of Soviet foreign policy.

"7. Russia has long felt the ambivalence of its relation to the west.

"8. There has long been an idea in Russian history that the Russian nation has a mission to fulfill that is destined to go beyond the borders of Russia.

"9. The Russians are and have been an extraordinarily gifted and creative people [in art, music, science, mathematics].

"10. . . . it is necessary . . . to realize the strength of Russian patriotism, quite apart from Communism."[21]

In learning about the U.S.S.R. today, students need to become familiar with its governmental and economic systems, making comparisons with those of the United States and other selected nations. They should investigate the strategy and tactics of recent Soviet foreign policy. In addition, they can investigate such aspects of Soviet life as the status of civil liberties, the position of ethnic minorities, the condition of the arts, educational opportunities, family life, religion, and social class structure, again comparing conditions in the Soviet Union with those in the United States and other selected nations.

Approaches such as these will help to avoid black-and-white comparisons of democracy and communism, comparisons that will only defeat the purpose of the study. They can guide students to realize that the relative appeal of democracy and communism to the uncommitted peoples of the world is affected by conditions under which those peoples live. These approaches can also help pupils see that while communism takes advantage of deprivation, ignorance, and repression wherever those conditions are found such conditions in most parts of the world are rooted in causes lying far outside communism. Understanding this fact gives students a basis for appraising communist techniques and for considering U.S. policies intended to combat the spread of communism.

Although attention may well be given to the history of the Communist Party in the United States, study that is narrowly focused on this topic will not achieve the major purposes of instruction about communism. Indeed, study so narrowly directed may actually obscure the real issues and problems that communism presents to the modern world.

Instruction About Communism Should Be Provided for All Students Including the Slow Learners and the Culturally Deprived As Well As Their More Favored Peers. It may well be, as Fischer has suggested, that the greatest need for study of communism is among the intellectually and culturally disadvantaged, since it has been "the ignorant, the ill informed, and the maladjusted who often are most likely to be impressed by its forcefulness and to yield to its deceptive promises."[22] To make this point does not suggest that more able students should be neglected in plans for teaching about communism. What is implied is that varied approaches and varied materials for the study of the topic must be developed. Many curriculum guides appearing today stress relatively abstract concepts and recommend relatively difficult materials that may not be useful for slower learners. The solution is not propaganda for the dull and rational inquiry for the bright, however. Pupils should be helped to apply whatever abilities they possess to reasoned study about communism.

Instruction About Communism, As About Other Topics, Should Be Planned To Develop Basic Concepts Based on Specific Examples or Facts. Concepts that students build from the facts learned about communism (as any other topic) can serve as tools for analyzing and ordering any new facts encountered. A grasp of underlying concepts can help to identify the half-truths, the partial information, and the illogical reasoning that characterize communist or other propaganda.

In the Study of Communism a Range of Materials Should Be Used, Including Slanted As Well As Objective Treatments, and Pupils Should Have Experience in Evaluating These Study

Materials. A variety of material about communism—books, pamphlets, periodicals, and films—is available from different sources. It is important, of course, to use a range of study materials in order to adapt the instruction to pupils' abilities. In addition, students can gain experience of lasting value through analyzing materials to identify propaganda techniques and through evaluating the materials with regard to such factors as reliability of source, logical presentation, and evidence of authenticity. Authentic factual accounts will constitute the core of the material, but partisan materials from communist and other extremist groups are also needed. The teacher has the responsibility of leading pupils in objective analysis of all materials.

A Program for Study of Communism Should Include Provision for Developing Community Support, But Avoid Sensational Approaches That May Play into the Hands of Extremist Elements. Study of communism in the school should have the publicly stated approval of the board of education and the sympathetic understanding of the lay public if it is to be carried on successfully. Sensational headlines in the local press or involvement in the classroom of spokesmen for extremist groups, whether of the left or the right, should be avoided. Such procedures may create a highly emotional atmosphere that would make it difficult or even impossible to study about communism in a rational manner.

A Program of Instruction About Communism Should Include Provision for Preparing Teachers To Handle the Topic. Effective study about communism depends to a large extent on the skill and knowledge the teacher brings to the instruction. Few teachers now in the schools had opportunity, in their preservice education, to study communist theories and institutions or the societies in which communist systems have developed. Only in recent years have a sizable number of colleges and universities introduced courses dealing with the history and institutions of the U.S.S.R. and Asiatic cultures, for example. This trend is growing at the college level. Future teachers will undoubtedly be better prepared than those now in the schools to handle instruction about communism. There is urgent need, however, for in-service study opportunities for the teachers concerned, even for many of the most recent college graduates.

The teachers' study about communism should be conducted in the same atmosphere of objectivity and rational inquiry that is appropriate for the school classroom. It should enable them to become thoroughly grounded in the history and institutions of communist societies as well as in communist theories. They need to become acquainted with available instructional materials on these topics and to make critical evaluations of these materials.

A mere lecture series by volunteer spokesmen, who themselves are too often not thoroughly informed about the topics cited, will not be sufficient for in-service preparation of teachers. Local school systems can cooperate with their state education department and with nearby colleges and universities to set up in-service study opportunities that meet the suggested criteria.

Placing Study About Communism in the Curriculum

Information about the topic of communism should be introduced at appropriate points throughout the social studies curriculum or a special unit might be introduced in some cases.

Aspects of the topic to be studied in world history include the historical development of communist theory, the history of Czarist Russia, the Revolution of 1917, and the development of the Soviet system since 1917. In some schools a unit on democracy vs. dictatorships in the modern world may be included in this course, although such a unit is more commonly placed either in U.S. history or the twelfth grade government or problems course. This unit gives opportunity for specific comparisons between the governmental systems of the United States and other democracies and the communist and fascist systems. In geography courses information about land, climate, resources, and population of the Soviet Union may be presented along with some attention to the economic system. A more detailed analysis of the Soviet economic system can be made in economics or modern problems courses in the eleventh or twelfth grades.

Communist foreign policies, both within and outside the United Nations, may be treated in connection with current affairs study throughout the high school. A systematic analysis of communist strategy and tactics in foreign affairs can be made in the eleventh grade U.S. history course, in a unit on U.S. foreign policy, or in the twelfth grade course in government or modern problems. The history of the Communist Party in the United States may be studied in these same courses.

An arrangement such as this facilitates the objective study of communist theory and practices, because it puts the study of communism in a realistic setting of modern world affairs. It contributes to the pupil's development of basic concepts through his secondary school years and gives him opportunity for repeated use of these concepts as analytical tools in dealing with increasingly complex materials. It avoids the useless duplication with courses in U.S. history, world history, geography, government, and economics that may result in a separate course on communism unless such a course is planned carefully.

The social studies staff of the local school can ensure that teaching about communism is carried on systematically and objectively by reviewing the total social studies program and allocating appropriate parts of the study to the various courses that are offered. Local schools can develop an effective study about communism by all pupils if two conditions prevail. First, the community needs to support such study. Second, the community should recognize that it is the responsibility of the professional staff of the school to determine how and where, in the total curriculum, this study should be carried on.

RECOMMENDATIONS OF THE NATIONAL COMMITTEE

Three recommendations of the National Committee are related to teaching about controversial issues and communism.

RECOMMENDATION: *Rational discussion of controversial issues should be an important part of the school program. The teacher should help students identify relevant information, learn techniques of critical analysis, make independent judgments, and be prepared to present and support them. The teacher should also help students become sensitive to the continuing need for objective re-examination of issues in the light of new information and changing conditions in society.*

The view that controversial issues should be studied in school by American youth as part of their preparation for citizenship has gained widespread though not unanimous approval. The National Committee believes that controversial issues should be studied by American youth for two reasons. First, American society has many unresolved problems that are controversial issues because they are as yet undecided. As one part of their induction into their culture, youth should study about these issues—although no one expects that pupils will resolve them. Second, study of controversial issues provides excellent opportunities to develop students' powers of rational thought, a primary responsibility of the educational system. The emphasis in study about controversial issues should therefore be on learning how to understand significant unsolved problems of society and arrive at rational conclusions about them.

Generally accepted criteria for the selection of issues to be studied have been formulated. They are listed and discussed on page 166. It is agreed that the teacher has responsibility for conducting classroom study of controversial issues in an objective manner and for refraining from indoctrination of pupils. Study materials should include partisan as well as objective accounts in order that pupils may learn to analyze materials for bias and draw conclusions from evidence. To safeguard the right of students to study important issues and to protect teachers against unfair attack, school authorities should formulate and enforce clear policies about classroom study of controversial issues.

Many school systems have done so, and the National Committee urges that their example should be followed by all.

CURRENT SOCIAL FORCES AND TRENDS

RECOMMENDATION: *To help the student think critically about current issues, the curriculum should provide opportunities for adequate instruction concerning social forces and trends. Attention commensurate with their significance in modern society should be given to issues such as international relations, economic growth, urbanization, population growth, science and technology, and mass media.**

This recommendation was presented in Chapter Four and is repeated here to emphasize the Committee's view that problem areas such as those mentioned should be given priority in the school program. The conditions of modern society require that these and other contemporary issues be studied in world perspective as well as be treated as domestic problems. Hence the school's responsibility for helping American youth develop a world view is emphasized both in this chapter and in Chapter Five.

The task of curriculum modification to provide adequate attention to problem areas of our society is not a simple one to carry out, but such change is so urgently needed in most schools that its achievement deserves a high priority. Two problems connected with this task deserve special comment.

The change can be accomplished only by teachers who themselves are well informed about leading issues of modern society. Many present-day teachers had little opportunity during their preservice preparation for study of some of these topics. Programs of in-service study to repair this deficiency are needed.

The other problem, which may be more apparent than real, is that of finding time in the school program to develop the needed attention to current societal problems. In part, the required emphasis may be achieved by new approaches in handling topics

* These topics are discussed in *Education in a Changing Society*.

already in the curriculum. Current experimentation with new instructional media and other efforts to find more efficient ways of teaching and learning, which are discussed in depth in another volume of the Project Report,* may also give clues for solving this problem.

TEACHING ABOUT COMMUNISM

RECOMMENDATION: *The school curriculum should include a study of political and social ideologies focusing upon communism. The methods of rational inquiry should be stressed. The study should be set in the perspective of the modern world and be incorporated into the instructional program at appropriate points. If a special unit on communism is deemed desirable in the secondary school, it should supplement and complement earlier study of these topics.*

As with other areas of the curriculum, decisions about what to teach *and* how to teach *about these topics should be based upon policies developed by school administrators and teachers of the local school system. In the formulation and implementation of such policies, school personnel should utilize the resources of scholarship and be supported in their decisions by the school board and by an informed community opinion.*

A critical problem of the day is the world-wide conflict between democracy and communism. There is no controversy in American society about the relative merits of democratic values and institutions as opposed to those of totalitarian communism and other authoritarian systems. There is disagreement, however, as to how American youth shall be guided in their study about communism.

The National Committee believes that all youth in the schools of the United States should have opportunity to study about communism and other totalitarian systems and compare the institutions of these systems with those of democratic nations. Through

* *Planning and Organizing for Teaching.*

such study American youth can gain a deeper understanding of their own society where freedom under law is the prevailing idea. Such study is needed, also, to give youth a realistic picture of the world in which they are growing up, in which they will live during their adult years, and in which they must strive to defend the basic values they hold.

The National Committee welcomes the growing popular approval for study about communism in the schools but warns against legislation that prescribes specific courses or units and against an emotional, propagandistic approach to the topic. The characteristics of a balanced program of instruction about communism that are discussed on pages 167-73 should guide the schools in planning for teaching about this topic. The Committee joins the many leaders in American life who have urged that the public must support objective instruction about communism. A slanted approach that is limited to persuasion techniques defeats itself by denying the very essence of the democratic way. Knowledge rests on established facts, and attitudes should result from an open yet critical mind. These are America's greatest strengths. Wise teaching will strengthen American democratic traditions and thought in the minds of our students.

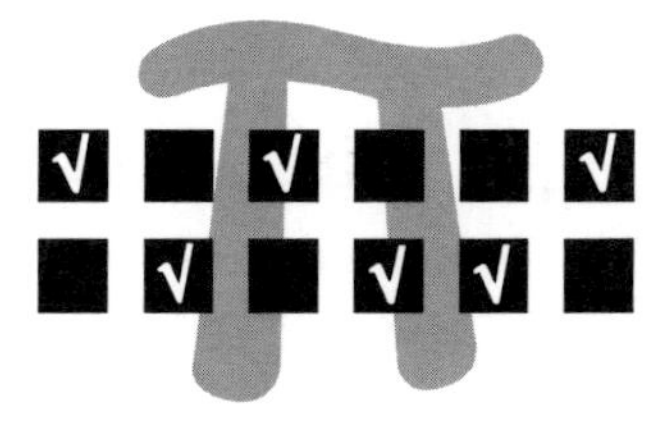

CHAPTER SEVEN

WHO SHOULD MAKE WHAT CURRICULUM DECISIONS?

Legal Framework for Curriculum Decisions
Factors Affecting Curriculum Decisions
What Influences Are Crucial?
Recommendations of the National Committee

Who should decide what the schools should teach? The answer to this question is as complex as the question is seen to be when analyzed. Both the question and its answer must be studied in the light of the variety of factors that affect decisions about the curriculum which are made in our schools today.

Analysis of the curriculum-making process reveals that there are various levels and types of decisions to be reached in determining what the schools shall teach. Every day schools are in session teachers make *instructional* decisions that set the specific curriculum pupils will study. At a level more remote from the learner, teachers and administrators make *institutional* decisions that structure the general pattern of the curriculum. At a third level, still more remote from the student in the classroom, *societal* decisions about the curriculum are made by school board members, state legislators, and federal officials.

These three levels and types of decisions about the curriculum are interrelated yet distinctly different in nature. Each of them requires kinds of data and involves specific considerations that do not apply directly to the others. Wise decisions about what the schools shall teach depend on recognition of this situation. The question becomes *who* should make *what* curriculum decisions? The answer in each case depends on the *nature* of the decision to be made and the *kinds of data* required to make it intelligently.

A variety of forces operates at each level of decision about the curriculum. Some can be readily identified by describing the legal framework within which our schools are conducted. Other forces operate more or less informally but may have a powerful influence on the individuals in whom the legal responsibility is vested. All of these must be considered to get a realistic understanding of how curriculum decisions are made today and to plot a course for the future.

LEGAL FRAMEWORK FOR CURRICULUM DECISIONS

Public education in the United States is a function of the several states by virtue of the Tenth Amendment to the Constitution which reserves to the states all powers not delegated to the federal government nor prohibited to the states. State policies concerning education including the general scope of programs of study are defined in some state constitutions. In other states they are formulated by the legislatures directly through legislation or indirectly through state educational authorities to whom decision-making powers are delegated.

Varied Patterns Among the States

Extensive powers to operate the schools, including authority to make many curriculum decisions, are vested in the local boards of education which must work within the framework of the state education laws. These laws vary from state to state. In some cases curriculum decisions are left almost entirely to the local school system, while in others the state prescribes considerable parts of the program. Even where a substantial portion of the program is set by the state, the requirements tend to be so general that major responsibility for specific curriculum development still rests with the local school system.

The diversity among the states with respect to the allocation of legal responsibility for curriculum planning between state and local authorities was documented in a recent survey made by the U.S. Office of Education.[1] In general, the states prescribe, by law or by ruling of the state education department, the basic program of studies for the elementary school, including reading and other language arts, arithmetic, geography and American history, science, health, physical education, art, and music. State prescriptions concerning the secondary school tend to focus on a limited number of areas instead of describing the entire basic program. In most states specific subjects or fields of study are mandated by the state as requirements for high school graduation. The subjects most frequently required are American history and English, but about two thirds of the states also require for graduation some work in mathematics, science, health, and physical education. Many states also require secondary school instruction in such subjects as government (national, state, and local), state history, driver education, first aid, fire prevention and safety, conservation, and the effects of alcohol and narcotics. The proportion of the total secondary school curriculum thus specified varies considerably from one state to another.

The manner in which the state educational authorities are required by law to implement the curriculum requirements set by the state also varies. In some cases the state education department is legally responsible for preparing courses of study for the required subjects and topics. In others it must approve curriculum materials that are developed locally and adopted by the local board of education. In still others the state department's legal responsibility is limited to inspection of the local school to ascertain whether state requirements are met.

Responsibilities of State Education Departments

In most states, in addition to duties specifically described by law, the state education department has a general responsibility to provide leadership for improvement of the instructional program in local schools. In better school legislation a qualifying phrase, such as "on and with the advice of the state school superintendent," is usually found. The trend in recent decades has been toward greater emphasis on the leadership role of the state education department in curriculum development.

The responsibility of the state education authority for professional leadership is carried out by a variety of means. These include publication of curriculum materials developed by state-wide committees of teachers, sponsorship of conferences and workshops for discussion of curriculum problems by instructional leaders from local school systems, and consultant service to local curriculum committees. In more than one fifth of the states a director of curriculum is in charge of state-wide curriculum projects; in others the directors of elementary, secondary, and vocational education carry this responsibility. Many state education departments follow a schedule for periodic review and revision of the instructional program in each subject field.

Legal Responsibility Is Shared

In summary, the legal responsibility for curriculum decisions is shared by state and local educational authorities. This arrangement has its roots in the national tradition that places control and operation of the schools in the hands of the people at the state and local level. The ultimate responsibility lies with the state, but many specific decisions about curriculum are made by officials of the local school. The present tendency is for the state to exert more fully its leadership in matters of curriculum as well as in other aspects of school operation.

FACTORS AFFECTING CURRICULUM DECISIONS

The decisions of those officials legally responsible for deciding what the schools shall teach are affected by factors that are not specified in state education codes. Some of them, such as tradition or public opinion, are intangible but powerful. Others, such as the efforts of organized groups to implement particular ideas, are identifiable. They have varying degrees of influence which cannot be measured exactly. Many of these factors are nationwide in their scope and influence, others operate locally. The directions in which these influences would move the curriculum are as varied as the influences themselves.

Tradition

The experience of the past, crystallized into tradition, exercises a powerful and conservative influence upon what the schools shall teach, as it does on all human affairs. Tradition carries much that is essential and desirable, representing as it does the culture patterns that earlier generations have found workable and rewarding. As basic changes take place, however, and as new knowledge becomes available, the patterns of the past may be inadequate for the new conditions. Nevertheless, traditional elements may persist in schools and other social institutions long after they have outlived their usefulness. To hold on to the good in traditional practices while adjusting to new needs is a never-ending task in curriculum making.

To perform this difficult task successfully, the curriculum planner must possess not only information-based insights into social trends and needs but also the ability to cut away the obsolete even when it is familiar and comfortable. Teachers, administrators, and parents alike share a tendency to prefer the type of curriculum with which they have had experience. But just as much as medicine, industry, and agriculture have changed significantly in recent decades in response to new knowledge and new conditions so—and to some extent—has education. What was adequate for the 1920's or 1940's is not adequate for the 1960's and 1970's—whether the area of concern be medicine, industry, agriculture, or education.

The National Community

The development of a national community, with a concomitant lessening of local and even regional differences in American life, is a force affecting curriculum decisions. Modern methods of communication, especially the mass media, carry information and ideas to all sections of the country almost instantaneously. Modern means of transportation contribute to a degree of population mobility, including the movement of school children, hitherto unknown in man's history. The patterns of economic life have become national in scope, and fluctuations in any basic industry or in one region affect the whole. In the realm of political life, the growth of a national community has extended the functions and powers of the federal government. Differences between rural and urban living, between life in the North and the South or the East and the West, have become less distinct, although they still exist.

Because of the nature of modern life in the United States, the problems of education have become national in scope. What the schools in California or Mississippi or elsewhere teach becomes important to the entire nation, for the general welfare of the nation is involved. Interdependence within the national community, an outgrowth of increasing specialization within an expanding economy, influences curriculum decisions. Like tradition, its effects are intangible and not subject to precise measurement but are nonetheless all-pervasive.

Regional and Local Differences

Regional and local differences continue to a degree, however, and constitute another factor affecting curriculum decisions which must not be overlooked. While there is no local mathematics or physics, the way such subjects can be taught most effectively to different groups of pupils may vary with their backgrounds. While the major body of such subjects as history, geography, music, and literature is not local, there is a local and regional aspect to each of these fields that may be worthy of study by children and youth of the locality or region.

Public Opinion and Politics

Public opinion constitutes still another kind of influence on curriculum decisions—one that is closely related both to tradition and to the growth of a national community. The effects of public opinion are diverse. On most questions, educational or otherwise, the American public is divided in its opinion so that several conflicting views may have substantial support. As opposing views become crystallized, each with substantial citizen support, their proponents in the local and state community exert both indirect and direct effects on curriculum planning.

Public concern about our schools has developed rapidly during the past decade, and several prominent citizens and educators have articulated their points of view. Some of these spokesmen have little knowledge of the schools, and some are well informed on the subject. Their statements have provided focus for opposing views. For example, some laymen have called for a more selective system of secondary education modeled on European patterns, placing heavy emphasis on subject matter mastery. James B. Conant's recommendations, based on a review of many school programs and a broader conception of the school's role, favored a comprehensive high school with a diversified program of studies. Other spokesmen from various walks of life—college professors of science or history or other academic disciplines, businessmen, government officials, novelists, and educators—probably have attracted less widespread attention as individuals than Conant, but they have played a part in creating the public's views of what the schools should teach.

Public opinion about school problems has been crystallized by the attention given to educational issues in recent political campaigns. In 1956 and again in 1960 the Presidential candidates stressed educational policy as a major issue. School problems have also been an issue in state and local elections. While the question of financing the schools has had priority in the campaign discussions of education, the instructional program has received considerable attention.

Fuller coverage of educational issues by the mass media also contributes to the formation of definite points of view by citizens, frequently through an appeal that is dramatic rather than thoughtful. Popular journals, television, and radio serve a mass audience and seek colorful methods of presentation to hold it. Controversy and criticism attract and retain popular attention more effectively than reasoned analysis. Thus it is not surprising that the treatment of education by mass media has sometimes verged on the "good guy" vs. "bad guy" kind of presentation in which the real meaning of the issues cannot be explored fully or thoughtfully. A public aroused to a recognition that changes in educational programs are needed, but having only superficial understanding of the problems involved is likely to demand changes that will be ineffective or actually harmful in their results.

The situation with regard to educational reporting in newspapers is apparently mixed. A recent survey of 19 "well-known community newspapers" showed that the local press tends to limit its coverage of educational news to school sports events, which are fully and effectively reported, and to "housekeeping" news such as teacher appointments, the school budget, and scholarship awards and other honors that students have received. Relatively few newspapers carry stories of national scope about important issues and developments in education.[2]

A more constructive side of the mass media's increased attention to educational issues is the development of a new kind of reporter, the education reporter, found today on the staffs of many major newspapers and of some popular journals. The education reporters are often persons who spend their full time studying schools and writing about them. In 1962 there were almost one hundred full-time education reporters in the United States. With their enriched background of information about educational problems, they are providing the public with more thoughtful discussions of the issues.

Education-related lay groups, such as the Parent-Teacher Association and citizen advisory committees, contribute to an informed public opinion at the local, state, and national levels. Their potential influence is indicated by the numbers of persons involved. There are 47,000 local Parent-Teacher Associations in membership with the National Congress of Parents and Teachers. There were 12,000 known citizens advisory committees at work in 1957. Many persons active in these groups have made a careful study of educational problems and policies including issues related to curriculum. Their recommendations have carried some weight with at least a segment of the general public, and their explanations of these have informed other members of their communities.

Commercially Produced Learning Materials

Commercially produced learning materials affect curriculum decisions directly and indirectly. These materials include textbooks;

workbooks; classroom newspapers and magazines; pamphlet materials; recordings; and a variety of maps, charts, and other audio-visual materials. Programed instructional materials, whether for use in teaching machines or as programed textbooks, are appearing. Of the commercially produced materials, conventional textbooks wield the greatest influence on curriculum, but other materials have become increasingly important.

The authors and publishers of learning materials, by the selection and organization of content, affect the plans developed by curriculum committees and the implementation of those plans by teachers in the classroom. Conversely, the authors and publishers of instructional materials are influenced in their selection and presentation of content by their judgment as to what will be accepted by their customers, the schools.[3] In planning school textbooks, educational films or filmstrips, or other basic learning materials, most producers study existing curriculum bulletins and courses of study, review recommendations of professional education organizations, and examine surveys of school practice. The topics selected for treatment in a textbook or film are determined largely by what the schools are teaching in the subject at a given grade level. The depth of development of each topic depends in part on the customary time allocation given it in current school practice. The manner in which the topic is presented reflects accepted ideas about arousing pupil interest and making the content learnable.

Learning materials produced for a nationwide or even a regional market thus tend to perpetuate existing curriculums rather than to encourage change, although there have been a few notable exceptions. This is especially true of textbooks, chiefly because production costs are so great that the publisher is eager to satisfy a considerable sector of the market to make his venture as profitable as possible.

On the other hand, authors and producers of learning materials are alert to curriculum changes in the schools and to recommendations of national professional groups[4] and react comparatively rapidly to these changes as they prepare new materials or revise old ones. Where the authorship includes competent scholars in the subject field, recent discoveries and new interpretations are introduced. The range in school curriculums, from those with a high proportion of traditional content and practice to those in which considerable change has been introduced, is reflected in the range of available learning materials.

Special Curriculum Studies

One result of the renewed interest in the disciplines as a basis for planning the school program (see Chapter Two) has been a number of special curriculum studies in various subject areas. The reader will find descriptions of the major studies in another publication of the Project on Instruction* and in a recent bulletin of the Association for Supervision and Curriculum Development.[5]

Each of these studies has developed or is developing recommendations for the part of the school curriculum with which it is concerned. Most of them have been financed entirely or largely by grants from federal government sources and/or private foundations. A few were largely supported by professional education associations or by such associations in cooperation with scholarly societies in the related disciplines and by the contributed services of members of the organizations. Some of the projects were started by academic specialists; others, by specialists in education.

The greatest number of these special studies has been devoted to science, mathematics, and the modern foreign languages. More recently, the number in the fields of social studies and English language arts has increased, now that Project English and Project Social Studies have been launched with federal funds. One in the field of music, begun early in 1963, is the only major curriculum project currently underway in the field of the arts.[6] The School Health Education Study is an important

* *Current Curriculum Studies in Academic Subjects.*

project that deals with a school subject not usually classified as academic.[7]

These projects have common characteristics. One goal of most of them is to close the gap between recent research findings in the academic fields and the related subjects as they are taught in the schools. To this end, academic specialists are heavily involved in most of the projects.

The special curriculum studies differ from each other in many ways, however. Some of them, such as the projects in science and certain ones in the social studies, are focused on a single school subject. Others of broader scope are planned to develop recommendations for a total curriculum area such as foreign languages, mathematics, or social studies. In some cases, the project has produced specific course plans and learning materials through which the plans can be implemented. In other cases, the product consists of more general recommendations that can serve as guidelines for curriculum planners and for authors and publishers of learning materials. The projects in science, mathematics, and foreign languages deal with subject areas in which the school curriculum had changed relatively little for many years. Others are concerned with subject areas in which school programs have been revised considerably during the past two generations.

In most of the special curriculum studies the concern, at least initially, has been with the subjects at the secondary school level. Some of the projects, however, have focused on treatment of the subject in the elementary school; in a few the sequence in the subject area throughout the elementary school has been or is being studied. Many of the projects are concerned primarily or entirely with the college-capable student, but some are designed to influence programs for all students from the slow to the gifted. The underlying philosophy of education, theory of learning, and concept of curriculum development seems to vary considerably from study to study.

Some of the projects are in the beginning stages; in others there has been substantial progress toward completing the study.

A few, chiefly those in operation for a number of years, already have had considerable impact on school programs throughout the United States, as will be shown later in this chapter. The influence of the others remains to be seen.

Programed Instructional Materials—A Potential Factor

The potential influence of programed instructional materials is not clearly defined as yet, because the development of such materials is still in an early stage. There are indications that their influence may be quite significant. Programed materials, as presently planned, are primarily subject-centered in that they place major emphasis upon associative connections among items of content and upon sequential ordering of content in a given subject field with relatively little attention to the nature and needs of learners. Individual differences in ability and experience background are taken care of, it is held, by presenting the content in such minute steps that any child within the range of normalcy can comprehend each step and move ahead successfully. The pupil will be motivated, according to the view of some leaders in programming, by the sense of achievement he will gain from his continuous progress.

There is a question as to whether all curriculum areas or all aspects of any curriculum area can be programed. If it proves feasible to program a subject completely, it seems that the effect would be to reduce the need for local curriculum planning in that subject; scope, sequence, and specific content would be determined by the programmer as he constructed the program. Other planning would consist of choosing the particular programed material to be placed in the hands of the pupils, and instruction would be reduced almost to checking as the pupil works through the program at his own rate.

As experimentation with these materials proceeds, however, they may be found useful only for parts of the school program in any subject area. Ways may be discovered to relate study of the programed material to other types of learning activities. Then the problem of integrating the programed materials with other learning experiences would become crucial and give new urgency to effective over-all planning by the school staff.

Colleges and Universities

Colleges and universities influence school curriculums in several ways. In the early days of publicly supported high schools, the entrance requirements of the colleges were the determining factor in the courses offered in secondary schools. That influence has continued, although larger high schools have broadened their course offerings considerably. College and university faculty members, especially those of teacher education institutions, frequently serve as consultants to state or local curriculum committees. State-supported institutions often have an active field service program for the schools of their state, usually operating through the professional education faculty. In some cases these institutions cooperate with the state education department in state-wide curriculum programs. Some universities maintain instructional centers or curriculum laboratories where individual teachers or curriculum committees have access to the collection of curriculum bulletins, textbooks, and other curriculum materials. By the kinds of academic and professional courses they provide for future teachers, those colleges and universities that prepare teachers exert a long-range effect on what shall be taught in the schools.

Professional Education Organizations

Most professional education organizations, state and national, are concerned with curriculum development either directly or indirectly and have potential influence on the decisions of local and state curriculum planners. Association members affect opinion on curriculum issues through their numerous publications and conferences. Recommendations concerning curriculum which have been formulated by an organization through its committees or other special groups are usually publicized. Since the leaders in educational organizations tend to include the leaders of state and local school systems, there is often a close relation between the organization's recommendations and practices in the schools that have conducted active curriculum development programs. Recommendations of professional organizations may also disseminate research results from the fields of educational psychology and human development, as they apply to curriculum planning.

Some professional organizations, such as the elementary and secondary school principals associations and the Association for Supervision and Curriculum Development, are oriented to consider the school program broadly. Others are concerned with specific subject areas such as science, social studies, or business education.

The subject-oriented groups frequently attempt to bridge the gap between what is taught in schools and recent developments in the related academic field by bringing to their members information about recent research and new interpretations. Their recommendations regarding the school curriculum, usually limited to their own particular subject field, may propose new content and ways of presenting it or new sequences of content. Such recommendations do not always take into account the pupil's total school experience.

Because of the differing orientation of the various professional groups, conflicting recommendations may be made. A subject-oriented group is likely to demand more time for its field of study in both the elementary and secondary school program and to approach the problems of curriculum and instruction with emphasis on what has been called the "subject matter point of view." Recommendations from groups that are concerned with the total school program, on the other hand, have tended to stress the needs of the learner as one of the important criteria in curriculum planning.

Regional Accrediting Associations

The regional accrediting associations of secondary schools and colleges, which review member school programs at periodic intervals, have in the past exerted influence on curriculum decisions of secondary schools and continue to do so. By implication, the actions of the accrediting associations may affect elementary school curriculums as well. State education departments usually cooperate with the regional accrediting group in matters of curriculum development.

Foundation Grants and Special Financial Arrangements

Special provisions for financing aspects of school programs affect curriculum planning, if only to insure that those fields of study for which extra funds are available will receive attention. Subject area projects supported by foundation grants, such as the curriculum studies carried on in the fields of science and mathematics, have a direct impact on curriculum decisions at the state and local level. These projects not only influence what the schools will teach but may also affect the proportion of student time devoted to the particular subjects. The same result occurs when state or federal legislation makes funds available for some aspects of the curriculum and not for others. Examples of such special financing by the federal government are found in the laws supporting vocational education and the activities of the National Science Foundation and in the National Defense Education Act.

Government Agencies

Certain state and federal agencies, although not directly related to education, nevertheless exert some influence on what the schools shall teach in particular subject areas. Agency personnel may serve as consultants to state or local curriculum committees. In some cases government agencies publish materials for use by teachers, such as teaching units or collections of resource information, or materials for student use. At the state level the departments of health, safety (highway patrol), conservation, agriculture, welfare, labor, and commerce are among those most frequently involved. The U.S. Department of Agriculture and the Bureau of the Census are examples of the many federal agencies that prepare and distribute materials for school use.

The U.S. Office of Education, operating as an information-gathering and advisory agency, includes among its publications reports of promising curriculum developments. It also sponsors conferences in which educational personnel from all parts of the nation meet to discuss curriculum problems and formulate recommendations for dealing with them. The work of the U.S. Office of Education in administering federal funds for vocational education and NDEA projects is significant for the curriculum areas that receive this financial support.

Testing Programs

Testing programs that are state-wide or nationwide in scope frequently affect the curriculum by influencing the content that is emphasized in particular subjects. While most of these external testing programs are administered at the senior high school level and have the most direct effect on the high school curriculum, elementary school programs are also influenced. Of the 50 states, 23 carry on some type of state testing program, although participation is compulsory for all schools in only 4 of them. There are more than 20 nationwide testing programs in which secondary school students may participate, most of which are administered for college admissions and scholarships. Among the most influential are those administered by the Advanced Placement Program and the College Entrance Examination Board.

Special Interest Organizations

A great variety of groups that are not directly related to education seeks to influence what is taught in the schools. These include organizations representing businessmen, such as the United States Chamber of Commerce and the National Association of Manufacturers; trade institutes, such as the American Meat Packers Institute; individual corporations, such as Westinghouse;

labor unions; the American Legion; and intercultural groups, such as the National Conference of Christians and Jews. Most of these groups prepare and distribute to the schools, often without charge, learning materials dealing with their field of special interest.

The Interaction of Legal and Nonlegal Factors

Clearly, while curriculum planning is legally the responsibility of state and local school authorities, decisions about what the schools shall teach result from a complex combination of many forces and groups that directly or indirectly influence the decision makers.

The nonlegal factors that affect the school curriculum in the United States are not separate and discrete in nature, although they have been treated separately in this discussion for clarity of presentation. Public opinion, for example, reflects and expresses the influence of other factors such as tradition and the needs of the national community. It is less important to categorize and describe the various factors precisely, however, than to recognize the wide range of influences that enter into curriculum decision making.

WHAT INFLUENCES ARE CRUCIAL?

Recognizing the wide range of factors that affect curriculum decisions, it is pertinent to inquire into their relative influence. It is not possible to discover the exact weight each one carries in particular situations. Nevertheless, some indication of the factors that are perceived by school officials as highly influential has been obtained through a survey of opinion about school programs conducted by the Project on Instruction, in cooperation with the Research Division of the National Education Association. A random sample of principals of elementary and secondary schools, selected so that schools of various sizes in all regions of the country were represented, participated in the questionnaire study. The responses to selected questions dealing with curriculum decisions are available in another publication of the Project on Instruction for readers who wish to study them in detail.*

Causes of Pressure for a Heavier Student Load

In the Project survey a large majority of the principals of both elementary and secondary schools reported increased pressure for a heavier student load, but the two groups perceived different causes for this pressure. Among elementary school principals the leading causes were considered to be, in the order named, higher standards for admission to college, the influence of critics outside the teaching profession, the scientific achievements of the Soviet Union, and general public opinion. Only a small minority of this group said demand from influential citizens of the community was a major cause of the pressure for a heavier student load.

Among the principals of secondary schools, higher standards of admission to college was the cause most frequently reported for an increased student load, although a substantial proportion of the group also named the other causes that were considered important by the elementary school principals. The wider use of standardized tests was considered by a majority of the secondary school principals and by a minority of those in elementary schools to have caused pressure for a heavier student load, although many believed it a minor rather than a major force.

Influences on Local Curriculum Decisions

The principals of both elementary and secondary schools of all sizes reported that local decisions about the instructional program have been, are, and are expected in the next five years to be most influenced by the local superintendent and his administrative staff. The school faculty was seen as the next most important

* See the following: *The Principals Look at the Schools: A Status Study of Selected Instructional Practices.*

influence in schools of all sizes. The trend over the past five years and the anticipated trend for the five years ahead was reported as an increasing influence on curriculum decisions by these two groups, with the superintendent and his administrative staff holding slightly more influence than the school faculty.

Research studies on learning and child growth and development were seen by the elementary school principals as third in influence, but the secondary school principals gave them a considerably lower place. Secondary school principals thought that next to the local superintendent's administrative staff and the school faculty, important sources of influence on the school program were national studies in the various subject areas, state school officials, federal programs such as those financed under NDEA, and prominent studies associated with individuals.

In their evaluation of the impact of these various national programs and studies on the curriculum, secondary school principals of large high schools indicated that the Advanced Placement Program had produced more marked changes in curriculum than any of the others. This estimate suggests the great effect a nationwide testing program can have, since curriculum changes that have occurred as a result of this Program have been reflections of the advanced placement test.

The influence of professional organizations was considered by both elementary and secondary school principals to fall below the other sources of pressure that have been mentioned. Other sources of pressure that the principals believed had relatively small influence on the instructional program included academic scholars, local community groups of laymen, and the school's PTA. While all three were seen as probably having a bit more influence in the next five years, the influence of academic scholars was expected to grow the most. Even so, the rating of anticipated influence for the scholarly group remained relatively low.

Resources Used To Develop the Curriculum

Curriculum decisions are influenced by the resources that are used in selecting and organizing content for the instructional program. The principals who participated in the Project survey listed textbooks as the top-ranking resource, although secondary school principals expected them to be in second place by 1966. Close behind textbooks in their degree of usefulness, according to the principals' estimates, were curriculum materials prepared locally by workshops, individual teachers, or the superintendent's staff. Courses of study and curriculum bulletins prepared by state education departments came close to the local resources in their estimated usefulness.

Curriculum materials prepared by state workshops, professional associations, educational foundations, national studies in subject areas, and reports such as the Conant and Trump studies were considered by elementary principals to be of only slightly more than minor usefulness, and their influence was expected to increase only slightly in the five years ahead. Much the same estimates were made of these resources by secondary school principals, except that they expect the national studies in various subject areas to exert more influence by 1966 but still to rank somewhat below local school resources and textbooks.

Nonlocal Forces Influence General Trends

The testimony of the school principals who participated in the Project survey indicated that the local school personnel and state education officials do indeed carry out their legal responsibility to make curriculum decisions. Many of the forces that lead local and state educational personnel to their decisions, however, are outside the purview of the local scene. Local groups of laymen, including the school's PTA, seem to exert relatively little specific influence. Many forces that have greatest effect on the decisions made by local and state school authorities come from the national level and are not controlled by those who have legal responsibility for deciding what the schools shall teach.

Public opinion appears to be a powerful force in determining general directions in which the educational program shall move. When there is sufficient unanimity on a particular question, such as the desirability of an increased work load for students, the schools respond. But it is only on broad issues such as this one that a widely accepted view develops among the general public, and when it does it seems to be based on the experiences of many citizens within their local school situations. Stiles[8] concluded, on the basis of a poll of selected experts on public reactions, that a national trend in public opinion about education seems to reflect rather than create local attitudes toward the schools.

College admissions standards, requirements, and practices such as advanced placement have a direct effect on the general direction of secondary school programs and, in some aspects, on the content of the program. The testimony of secondary school principals to this effect, cited above, is substantiated by comments of state education department officials in a recent survey conducted by the U.S. Office of Education.[9] Replies to the question, "To what extent do college entrance requirements and college entrance examinations affect the secondary school curriculum in your State?" indicated that the influence of such requirements was considerable. This was true especially with regard to the academic subjects and particularly in small high schools where the restricted number of courses which could be offered conformed to college entrance requirements. It is clear also that more rigorous college admission standards tend to influence the elementary school, although to a lesser degree.

Nonlocal Forces Influence Curriculum Content

Decisions as to the specific content of the curriculum in local schools are affected by forces that are nationwide in scope and character and not under the direct control of local or state school authorities. Predominant among these are textbooks, foundation-supported programs such as the special subject studies in mathematics and science, and special programs supported by the National Defense Education Act.

Textbooks. It is no surprise that textbooks are rated by the principals of both elementary and secondary schools as the most significant single resource in determining the content of the curriculum. Many educators believe that the indirect influence of textbooks is probably even greater, since many committees or individual teachers who are developing curriculum guides lean heavily on the texts used in the local schools. The pre-eminence of textbooks as a factor in curriculum decisions has several implications. These materials are one of the major forces for a national curriculum, or at least for a high degree of nationwide uniformity in curriculum. Their generally conservative nature serves more as a brake on curriculum change than an encouragement for it. If desired, curriculum changes for a particular subject can be agreed upon and introduced into leading textbooks; however, these changes will get into the local schools' curriculums rather rapidly. This possibility of effecting curriculum change through textbooks is underlined by the fact that national studies in selected subject fields have used considerable sums of their money grants to produce textbooks in order to implement their proposed programs.

Foundation Grants. Education foundations have considerable effect on the content of the school curriculum through the special programs that they finance. The special studies in mathematics, science, and foreign languages and the Advanced Placement Program are examples of the various projects that have received either initial or continuing foundation support. The nationwide impact of these projects is clearly indicated by the questionnaire study cited above, and this impact seems to be increasing as the programs are more fully developed and publicized. That these projects make detailed recommendations and, in some cases, supply materials to implement their recommendations undoubtedly helps to account for their widespread influence. As schools accept the direction indicated by a special project, commercially produced textbooks and other materials will follow the trend. Thus crucial decisions as to which areas of the curriculum shall receive attention, in what direction curriculum change shall proceed, and what philosophy of education shall be supported are made when the foundations allocate or decide not to allocate funds to programs.

Federal Financial Measures. The grant of federal support for selected aspects of the school program such as is extended by grants under the National Defense Education Act, while other parts of the curriculum are excluded from such support, is a form of curriculum decision making by Congress, an agency with no legal responsibility for such decisions. The impact of NDEA grants on the secondary schools is clear from the evidence of the questionnaire study cited above and from even a cursory survey of recent educational literature.[10]

Local and state educational authorities recognize the great benefits that come from strengthening the school program in the fields of science, mathematics, modern foreign languages, and guidance but are also aware of the dangers inherent in a patchwork of special aid measures. The Council of Chief State School Officers, for example, reflected this awareness in action taken at its annual business meeting in November 1960, where the question of the extension and revision of the NDEA was considered.[11] In spite of the financial benefits that schools have received under the law, one third of the chief state school officers opposed extension of the Act, although all favored legislation for general support such as that introduced in the first session of the 87th Congress. In testimony before the House Subcommittee on Education in June 1961, a spokesman for the Council pointed out that general federal aid to public education, in cooperation with the states and local school districts, can strengthen state and local autonomy. But to the extent that federal support for the school consists of "proliferation of special aids," state and local control of educational decisions will be weakened.

Again, in 1962, at its annual business meeting, the Council of Chief State School Officers urged that federal authorities provide general support for the schools rather than making special-purpose grants: "The Council believes that the interests of American public elementary and secondary education will be served best by permanent, broad-purpose federal financial support rather than by limited, emergency federal aid for special purposes. The Council opposes as a permanent policy the acceptance of the special aids approach.

"Special aids to education shall be opposed unless all three of the following conditions are present: a. The educational need is a major one. b. This need will not, as a practical matter, be met by more general federal support legislation. c. Passage of the special aid authorization will not interfere substantially with the passage of more general federal support legislation."[12]

Professional Associations. The evidence from the Project survey that principals believe professional organizations and critics within the profession exert relatively small influence on curriculum decisions deserves thoughtful consideration by the profession itself. A similar conclusion was drawn by Cummings and Mackintosh in their survey.[13] In his survey of "Who Speaks for American Education?" Stiles[14] found his jury believing that in the related area of public attitudes toward the schools professional organizations have little influence. Perhaps one reason for this situation is that, in general, national professional education organizations have hesitated to make definite recommendations about specific curriculum matters. Because of the tradition of local decision making and the range of views held by their members, these organizations have preferred to cite "promising practices," present evidence concerning curriculum issues, and suggest guidelines for decisions, much in the manner of the present Project report. If the principle of state and local autonomy in curriculum decisions is to be respected, this approach by the national professional organization is valid. But it is not an approach that exerts direct influence or pressure of the kind that a single-purpose group, such as a foundation-supported project, can achieve. At the same time, in estimating the influence of professional organizations, it must be remembered that their publications and conferences probably have considerable influence upon the thinking of individual leaders among local and state educational personnel and on that of authors of commercially produced learning materials. As a consequence, professional organizations probably affect curriculum decisions indirectly more than is realized.

RECOMMENDATIONS OF THE NATIONAL COMMITTEE

The foregoing analysis points up certain basic contradictions in American education which must be understood and resolved if the public schools are to carry out their responsibilities. Although legal authority to make curriculum decisions is in the hands of state and local educational officials, many of the forces influencing those decisions are independent of those persons and agencies. Does this mean that the tradition of local-state control of the school curriculum has outlived its usefulness in today's national community? Is local control in reality a myth, as some observers of the American educational scene have declared? Has local control been destroyed in substance though not in form by influences that are nationwide in their operation? Should this "reality" be acknowledged and dealt with by vesting legal authority for curriculum decisions in a national agency, either governmental or professional?

These questions pose in an extreme form the issue, who should make curriculum decisions for the public schools today? To raise them is to answer them negatively. But such questions point up the need to resolve the discrepancies between what has been the traditional picture, what is the actual practice of curriculum decision, and what should be the practice in the 1960's. A suitable resolution cannot be found by treating the issue in either-or terms. The question is not one of local *or* state *or* national control. Rather it concerns the part that educational authorities at each governmental level can most effectively take in the decision-making process and the role that professional education groups and other nationally oriented nongovernmental groups should take in deciding what the schools should teach. The goal is to improve the program of instruction for young people by drawing on all our resources, and it is best approached through a partnership of all who are involved.

In response to this question of who should make what curriculum decisions, the National Committee makes the recommendations which follow:

RECOMMENDATION: *Local school faculties should have the freedom and the authority to make decisions about what to teach—within state and local requirements—and how to teach. Final instructional decisions should be made by the teacher, taking into consideration recommendations from appropriate local, state, and national groups representing the teaching profession, academic scholars, and the public.*

LOCAL SCHOOL FACULTIES

Ultimately, the curriculum pupils study is determined by the teacher's decisions about daily classroom instruction. These decisions should be recognized as individual creative acts that are the responsibility of the teacher who makes them. Specific curriculum planning within the local school system can provide each teacher with the help and support he needs to carry this responsibility effectively.

Regional and local differences exist, although they are decreasing because of the development of a national community. Curriculum planning at the local level is needed to develop school programs that take these differences into account in constructive fashion. Experimentation in developing more effective school programs, urgently needed, is encouraged by the opportunity for planning at the local level. Although this opportunity has too often been overlooked, it should be maintained and efforts made to increase such experimentation.

A number of conditions must be observed, if curriculum planning within the local school system is to have positive results.

The nature and scope of curriculum decisions that are appropriately made at the local level needs to be agreed upon by both local and state educational authorities. Clearly the local decisions must implement the basic curriculum established by the state.

Rarely should a local school attack a curriculum problem as if it were making the first effort to solve it. Instead the local personnel should study work that has been done on the problem in other schools, judiciously screening recommendations by national study groups and professional organizations and considering other information that is available. The local curriculum task may sometimes consist of choosing between alternative programs that have been developed by state or national groups to whom rich consultative resources have been available, making a thorough study of the selected program, and planning how to adapt it to local conditions.*

A continuing liaison with nearby institutions of higher learning should be maintained, and their resources should be drawn upon for curriculum development. In too many communities there has been little communication and consultation between the public schools and a nearby college that is a potentially rich source of assistance.

Local curriculum development should be supported with adequate funds. If curriculum planning is carried on as an after-hours activity with no provision for materials and working facilities, only haphazard and superficial results can be expected. Some local curriculum planning programs have been ineffective or even harmful because too much was attempted with too few resources.

There should be wide participation in curriculum planning by the teachers who are to implement the plan in the classroom, with time provided for the curriculum work. It is impossible for teacher members of curriculum committees to work effectively either in program planning or in performing daily classroom duties if the committee work is simply added to an already arduous teaching schedule.

The schedules of supervisors and other members of the administrative staff who are to participate in curriculum planning needs

* See *Current Curriculum Studies in Academic Subjects*, pp. 86-93, for principles and procedures that may be applied in making such adaptation.

also to be arranged so that time is allocated for this work. Administrative personnel cannot carry out their leadership responsibilities for curriculum work unless they have time to make thoughtful preparation and to implement the decisions of the planning group.

Adequate funds for materials, consultant service, and clerical help should be provided for curriculum committees. The lack of funds has, in too many cases, restricted local curriculum planning to those aspects of the instructional program for which well-financed special-interest groups offered support. Lack of funds has too often prevented local curriculum committees from obtaining the specialized consultants, including academic scholars, who are needed if a committee is to do more than a cut-and-paste job of curriculum planning.

The development of cooperative projects among the schools within a region should be explored as a way of making more efficient use of available funds. The need for more adequate funds for curriculum development will not be solved, however, by such expedients. The budget of the local school system should carry the main burden of support.

LOCAL SCHOOL BOARDS

RECOMMENDATION: *Local school boards are the legal instruments through which the state fulfills its responsibility for education. The distinction between lay control of school policies determined by the board of education and implementation of these policies by the professional staff, with the leadership of the local superintendent, should be delineated, understood, and respected.*

The vigor of the school and the climate within which it operates depend upon the active support of the community it serves. Only as the public, through its local leaders, shares in the determination of policies for the school program within the structure set by the state will active interest and support be created and maintained in the community.

The lay board of education and the professional staff of the school each has its distinct role in conducting the school program.

These complementary roles should be understood and respected. The board of education should make decisions about policies. The implementation of those policies is the responsibility of the professional staff under the leadership of the local superintendent. For example, the decision to expand the school library materially is made by the board of education, but the selection of instructional materials should be made by the professional staff.

STATE EDUCATIONAL AUTHORITIES

RECOMMENDATION: *State educational authorities should establish standards for public school instruction, provide adequate resources for their achievement, and give dynamic leadership to curriculum development, experimentation, and innovation in local schools.*

The state educational authority, by setting minimum standards and providing leadership for the improvement of instructional programs in the local schools, can protect the children of every community from the potential dangers of provincialism and mediocrity that could develop in a given locality. The state authority can make certain that the educational interests of the national community are served.

State leadership should be exercised through procedures that have proved effective for stimulating improved instructional programs in local schools. Examples of such procedures include—

- Publishing curriculum materials that have been developed by state-wide groups with membership including (a) classroom teachers, (b) academic scholars in the subject field involved, (c) scholars in appropriate fields of professional education, (d) school administrators or supervisory personnel, and (e) if appropriate, lay citizens.
- Sponsoring state-wide or regional workshops and study conferences focused on particular curriculum problems, with membership from the groups listed immediately above.
- Providing local school personnel with information about available learning materials, proposals from projects, outstanding curriculum materials from other states, and evaluations thereof.

State education officials should use their resources and powers to encourage active programs of curriculum study and experimentation by local schools. Detailed curriculum prescriptions that are set forth and enforced by the state education department will leave little room for creative development of local initiative.

The state educational authority should stimulate curriculum experimentation through grants of funds for special projects; collection and dissemination of information about results of experimentation; and sponsorship of cooperative projects involving colleges and universities, local school systems, and state education personnel. The state educational authority may also take the lead in evaluating curriculum proposals from special curriculum projects, national study groups, and other such sources. For example, individual states might establish their own curriculum evaluation commissions or join with other states in the region to do so. Such commissions would review and evaluate various aspects of curricular research and study, seeking to adapt desirable features to the needs and interests of the states.

The staff of the state educational authority should consist of personnel who are well prepared in the various fields of the school curriculum and who are capable of providing state-wide leadership in their particular fields. Political considerations should play no part in the selection of members of the state's professional education staff. There is great variation from state to state in the number and quality of such specialists on the professional staff, and this variation is reflected in the amount and effectiveness of the state's leadership for curriculum improvement. Local school systems, especially the smaller ones, need the help that can be provided only by a strong professional staff at the state level.

STATE LEGISLATURES

RECOMMENDATION: *State legislatures should set forth general goals for the schools, provide adequate financial support, and delegate broad powers of implementation to the state and local educational authorities. The state legislature should* not *prescribe curriculum content or legislate specific courses.*

The distinction between lay control of educational policies, to be determined by the legislative and executive branches of the state government, and the implementation of those policies by the professional staff of educators under the leadership of the chief state school officer should be understood and respected. The state legislature is fulfilling its educational responsibilities when it enacts legislation describing general goals for the public schools, provides adequately for their support, and delegates broad powers of implementation to a staff of well-prepared professional educators.

The state legislature that legislates a specific pattern of curriculum organization, assigns the time of the school day among various subjects, and places upon the schools a multitude of special requirements such as holiday celebrations will hamper the development of effective programs of instruction. This principle was aptly explained in a minority dissent to the recommendations recently made to a state legislature by its citizens advisory committee: "A school curriculum shaped by state legislative action is likely to be too rigid to utilize effectively advances in knowledge and to lack comprehensiveness and balance. Decisions related to what is taught in the schools are of vital importance. They should be made only after the most careful consideration and the utilization of the best talents available, particularly those of classroom teachers. The school curriculum should be flexible enough to meet local and individual needs and encourage continual efforts for improvement."[15]

FEDERAL GOVERNMENT

RECOMMENDATION: *The federal government should provide the types of assistance needed to improve local and state systems of education. Two types of federal assistance should be stressed: (a) the federal government should provide general financial assistance for the improvement of public education; (b) the U.S. Office of Education should have an expanded role in stimulating experimentation and innovation in the schools, in providing statistical analyses of importance, and in disseminating information about educational problems and promising practices.*

The tradition of federal participation in education, which is almost as old as the nation itself, has been rapidly and greatly strengthened by the development of the national community. Beginning with the Northwest Ordinance of 1785 and continuing through the Smith-Hughes Act of 1917 and later support for vocational education, to the recent National Defense Education Act, the extent of federal participation in public education has grown in breadth and strength. The impact of cooperatively set standards on vocational education curriculums and of the NDEA as cited in a previous section demonstrates the nature of the very real though nonlegal controls that have developed as a result of federal support for particular programs.

The federal government is and should be a partner in the field of public education, taking its appropriate part along with localities and states. Its participation is inevitable because of the importance of education to the nation.

Federal activities affecting public education, now scattered through numerous branches and agencies of the government, should be coordinated under a strengthened federal educational agency and administered by it. This arrangement would minimize the expensive duplication of activities that now exists and, by subjecting all activities to the scrutiny of a staff of professional educators, would eventually result in the elimination of those activities that are educationally indefensible.

The range of activities of the strengthened federal educational agency should include—

- A broad range of consultative services to state and local school systems for the improvement of programs of instruction.

- Increased distribution of information concerning promising curriculum practices.

- Stimulation and coordination of research and experimentation concerning curriculum planning in schools across the nation.

- An expanded program of national conferences at which instructional leaders of state and local school systems, academic scholars, scholars in the various disciplines of professional education, and leaders of education-related and civic groups would meet together in order to consider particular curriculum problems.

The strengthened federal educational agency should have the status and administrative independence that would ensure long-term leadership by its chief educational officer, who should be a respected figure in American education, and continuity of service by a staff of well-qualified personnel. Whether or not the federal educational agency should be a department of education with cabinet status, as has been recommended,[16] or some other arrangement, the need for a strengthened federal educational agency is apparent.

Federal participation in the financial support of education has strengthened and will strengthen the public schools enormously, provided that it follows appropriate principles. Federal financial support for the schools should take the form of general funds allocated to and administered by the states rather than special aid measures. The latter are likely to result in unbalanced, even haphazard, instructional programs. Determination of what to teach and when to teach it according to federal appropriation of money is neither a rational nor a desirable method of procedure.

NON-GOVERNMENTAL GROUPS

RECOMMENDATION: *Efforts of nationally oriented, nongovernmental groups to stimulate curricular and instructional experimentation and innovation should be encouraged. Scholars in the academic fields and the teaching profession should be involved in such efforts.*

This recommendation can best be considered along with the National Committee's recommendation about how to use the results of curriculum studies carried out by nongovernmental groups.

NATIONAL CURRICULUM PROJECTS

RECOMMENDATION: *In making selections of content, school staffs should study the results and recommendations of curriculum projects sponsored by nationally oriented groups with a view to applying promising findings.*

There should be a systematic procedure for studying the results of these curriculum projects. The procedure should recognize the importance of balance and continuity in the total school experience of students and include the steps prerequisite to curriculum changes.

There is no doubt that benefits have come from many of the individual projects, study groups, and other special programs that in recent years have made recommendations about various aspects of the school curriculum. There is also no doubt that such individual projects have contributed to curricular imbalance in some cases. Some of them have resulted in the adoption, at least temporarily, of practices that have yet to be proved educationally sound and are considered unsound by substantial groups of qualified educators. In a few cases, independently financed projects have been designed to serve only the interests of self-seeking groups. The educational profession, as the element in national life best equipped by special preparation and continuing responsibility to provide coordination, guidance, and evaluation of such special programs, has a responsibility to attempt to bring some order out of the competitive chaos that is developing.

National commissions and committees sponsored by professional educational organizations or other educational groups can profitably make studies and recommendations on curriculum matters, especially in relation to providing balance in the total school program. With the numbers of special studies and programs of special support for one element or another in the curriculum, there is need for more national leadership on problems of the school program as an integrated whole. Nongovernmental commissions working on a national scale can be expected to balance the national as against the local interest and also to work for balance among the elements of the curriculum.

Two other recommendations of the National Committee which are discussed more fully in another volume of the project report, *Planning and Organizing for Teaching,* are significant for the question of who should make what curriculum decisions. They deal with financial provision for curriculum work by the faculty of the local school and with the need for regional centers to encourage and conduct curriculum research.

MONEY, TIME, AND PERSONNEL

RECOMMENDATION: *School systems should allocate an appropriate proportion of their annual operating budgets—not less than 1 percent—for the support of research, experimentation, and innovation.*

Adequate time should be provided for each staff member to participate in curriculum planning, research, evaluation, and other activities designed to improve the instructional program.

REGIONAL CURRICULUM AND INSTRUCTION CENTERS

RECOMMENDATION: *Adequately staffed and supported regional curriculum and instruction centers should be encouraged. These centers, located mainly in universities, should work in partnership with local schools to initiate innovation and conduct experimentation and research to improve the instructional program of the public schools.*

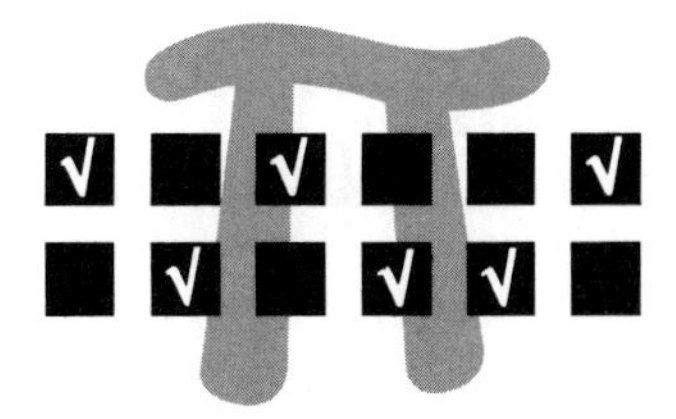

CHAPTER EIGHT

WHAT TO TEACH —A CONTINUING INQUIRY

"What shall the schools teach?" Knowledge and skills and values—these the schools shall teach. On this we are agreed, as earlier generations in many cultures have been agreed.

But what knowledge, what skills, what values? For what purposes? To whom? When? In what sequence and with what priorities?

These are questions that bring disagreement and excite controversy. They are questions for which earlier generations in America have found answers quite different from most that are advanced today. They are questions some contemporary societies respond to with solutions unacceptable to democratic America.

Questions that deal with such specifics as what, to whom, and for what purpose are basic and relatively unchanging; the answers are not. The answers change as society changes, as new knowledge is discovered, as the problems and goals of the people change. They change to reflect the beliefs, the values, and sometimes the prejudices of those who answer the questions. But the questions must be asked, again and again, and *the best answers for our times and our society must be sought* if children and youth are to be equipped for life in the modern world.

The National Committee believes that the most effective answers in the continuing inquiry about what to teach will be found by applying the processes of rational thought, within a framework of explicit values and goals.

The Committee has identified six fundamental values that it believes should serve as criteria for assessing present practices and for planning for improvement in our elementary and secondary schools.* They are—

- Respect for the worth and dignity of every individual.
- Encouragement of variability.
- Equality of opportunity for all children.
- Faith in man's ability to make rational decisions.
- Shared responsibility for the common good.
- Respect for moral and spiritual values and ethical standards of conduct.

* *Schools for the Sixties,* pages 7-8.

The Committee has also urged that the essential objectives of the school must be concerned with developing in pupils the ability and the will for self-teaching and self-renewal.* Unless curriculum planning is directed toward clearly identified values and goals, the changes that are made may only result in the school's doing effectively things it should not be doing at all.

If curriculum decisions are to be arrived at rationally, they must be based on the best evidence available—evidence about society and its needs, evidence about the learners and how they learn, and evidence from the fields of knowledge that learners are to study. The best evidence of one decade is likely to be outmoded, even obsolete, in the next, as social change proceeds at an unprecedented rate and as scholars in many fields push back the frontiers of knowledge. It is appropriate, therefore, to close this volume, *Deciding What To Teach,* by re-emphasizing two of the National Committee's recommendations for continuing research which have been presented in this volume and are also discussed in other volumes of the Project report:

MONEY, TIME, AND PERSONNEL

RECOMMENDATION: *School systems should allocate an appropriate proportion of their annual operating budgets—not less than 1 percent—for the support of research, experimentation, and innovation. Adequate time should be provided for each staff member to participate in curriculum planning, research, evaluation, and other activities designed to improve the instructional program.*

REGIONAL CURRICULUM AND INSTRUCTION CENTERS

RECOMMENDATION: *Adequately staffed and supported regional curriculum and instruction centers should be encouraged. These centers, located mainly in universities, should work in partnership with local schools to initiate innovation and conduct experimentation and research to improve the instructional program of the public schools.*

* See p. 216 (Chapter Four) and *Schools for the Sixties,* pages 8-9.

In both these recommendations, the Committee reaffirms its conviction that "sound decisions about the kind of education that is good for a given people at a given time in history rest upon information that is pertinent and accurate, upon thinking that is rational and objective, and upon values that are clear and compelling."*

The Committee calls on the American people and especially on the organized teaching profession to ensure that the continuing inquiry about what to teach be guided by the goals of education and be conducted through the processes of rational decision making. Only to the extent this is achieved will the youth of our nation receive the preparation for life that they need and that is their right in a democratic society.

* *Schools for the Sixties,* page 2.

APPENDIX A / *A Summary List of Issues and Recommendations*

Decision Area I

DECISION MAKING

Who should make what decisions about education?

Recommendation 1: Local school boards are the legal instruments through which the state fulfills its responsibility for education. The distinction between lay control of school policies determined by the board of education and implementation of these policies by the professional staff, with the leadership of the local superintendent, should be delineated, understood, and respected.

LOCAL SCHOOL BOARDS

Recommendation 2: The federal government should provide the types of assistance needed to improve local and state systems of education. Two types of federal assistance should be stressed: (a) The federal government should provide general financial assistance for the improvement of public education; (b) the U.S. Office of Education should have an expanded role in stimulating experimentation and innovation in the schools, in providing statistical analyses of importance, and in disseminating information about educational problems and promising practices.

FEDERAL GOVERNMENT

Recommendation 3: Local school faculties should have the freedom and the authority to make decisions about what to teach—within state and local requirements—and how to teach. Final instructional decisions should be made by the teacher, taking into consideration recommendations from appropriate local, state, and national groups representing the teaching profession, academic scholars, and the public.

LOCAL SCHOOL FACULTIES

Recommendation 4: State educational authorities should establish standards for public school instruction, provide adequate resources for their achievement, and give dynamic leadership to

STATE EDUCATIONAL AUTHORITIES

curriculum development, experimentation, and innovation in local schools.

STATE LEGISLATURES

RECOMMENDATION 5: State legislatures should set forth general goals for the schools, provide adequate financial support, and delegate broad powers of implementation to the state and local educational authorities. The state legislature should *not* prescribe curriculum content or legislate specific courses.

DECISION AREA II

RESEARCH, EXPERIMENTATION, AND INNOVATION

How can an extensive program of educational research, experimentation, and innovation be developed?

MONEY, TIME, AND PERSONNEL

RECOMMENDATION 6: School systems should allocate an appropriate proportion of their annual operating budgets—not less than 1 percent—for the support of research, experimentation, and innovation.

Adequate time should be provided for each staff member to participate in curriculum planning, research, evaluation, and other activities designed to improve the instructional program.

REGIONAL CURRICULUM AND INSTRUCTION CENTERS

RECOMMENDATION 7: Adequately staffed and supported regional curriculum and instruction centers should be encouraged. These centers, located mainly in universities, should work in partnership with local schools to initiate innovation and conduct experimentation and research to improve the instructional program of the public schools.

NON-GOVERNMENTAL GROUPS

RECOMMENDATION 8: Efforts of nationally oriented, nongovernmental groups to stimulate curricular and instructional experimentation and innovation should be encouraged. Scholars in the academic fields and the teaching profession should be involved in such efforts.

Decision Area III

EDUCATING ALL CHILDREN AND YOUTH*

How can the instructional program of the school be designed to develop the individual potentialities of all members of the school population within the framework of a society that values both unity and diversity?

THE INDIVIDUAL AND THE NATION

Recommendation 9: The instructional program should provide (a) opportunities for developing the individual potentialities represented in the wide range of differences among people; (b) a common fund of knowledge, values, and skills vital to the welfare of the individual and the nation.

To achieve these objectives, the instructional program cannot be the same for all. Provision for individual differences should be made by qualified teaching personnel through diagnosis of learning needs and through appropriate variety of content, resources for learning, and instructional methods.

Decision Area IV

ESTABLISHING PRIORITIES FOR THE SCHOOL

What are the distinctive responsibilities of the school in contrast to those that are distinctive to the family, the church, industry, and various youth-serving agencies?

What responsibilities should the school share with other institutions and with other youth-serving agencies?

What, then, should be included in the school program?

What should be excluded from it?

DISTINCTIVE AND SHARED RESPONSIBILITIES

Recommendation 10: Priorities for the school are the teaching of skills in reading, composition, listening, speaking (both native

* Decision Areas III through IX, including Recommendations 9 through 19, are related to "Deciding What To Teach."

and foreign languages), and computation . . . ways of creative and disciplined thinking, including methods of inquiry and application of knowledge . . . competence in self-instruction and independent learning . . . fundamental understanding of the humanities and the arts, the social sciences and natural sciences, and mathematics . . . appreciation of and discriminating taste in literature, music, and the visual arts . . . instruction in health education and physical education.

Responsibilities best met by joint efforts of the school and other social agencies include development of values and ideals . . . social and civic competence . . . vocational preparation.

The decision to include or exclude particular school subjects or outside-of-class activities should be based on (a) the priorities assigned to the school and to other agencies; (b) data about learners and society and developments in the academic disciplines; (c) the human and material resources available in the school and community.

Decision Area V

THE SCHOOL'S ROLE IN DEALING WITH NATIONAL PROBLEMS RELATED TO YOUTH

What is the school's role in dealing with serious national problems such as youth unemployment and juvenile delinquency?

YOUTH UNEMPLOYMENT AND JUVENILE DELINQUENCY

Recommendation 11: The schools can help to combat such serious national problems as youth unemployment and juvenile delinquency by (a) evaluating the intellectual and creative potential of *all* children and youth in the schools; (b) identifying early the potential dropout and delinquent; (c) developing positive programs to challenge these young people to educational endeavor; (d) participating in cooperative programs with parents and with community groups and organizations—business and industry, labor, service groups, government agencies, and the many youth-serving agencies.

DECISION AREA VI

TEACHING ABOUT CONTROVERSIAL ISSUES AND ABOUT COMMUNISM

What is the school's role in teaching about controversial issues and about communism and other ideologies?

CONTROVERSIAL ISSUES

RECOMMENDATION 12: Rational discussion of controversial issues should be an important part of the school program. The teacher should help students identify relevant information, learn the techniques of critical analysis, make independent judgments, and be prepared to present and support them. The teacher should also help students become sensitive to the continuing need for objective re-examination of issues in the light of new information and changing conditions in society.

CURRENT SOCIAL FORCES AND TRENDS

RECOMMENDATION 13: To help the student think critically about current issues, the curriculum should provide opportunities for adequate instruction concerning social forces and trends. Attention commensurate with their significance in modern society should be given to issues such as international relations, economic growth, urbanization, population growth, science and technology, and mass media.

TEACHING ABOUT COMMUNISM

RECOMMENDATION 14: The school curriculum should include a study of political and social ideologies focusing upon communism. The methods of rational inquiry should be stressed. The study should be set in the perspective of the modern world and be incorporated into the instructional program at appropriate points. If a special unit on communism is deemed desirable in the secondary school, it should supplement and complement earlier study of these topics.

As with other areas of the curriculum, decisions about *what to teach* and *how to teach* about these topics should be based upon policies developed by school administrators and teachers of the local school system. In the formulation and implementation of such policies, school personnel should utilize the resources of scholarship and be supported in their decisions by the school board and by an informed community opinion.

Decision Area VII

A BALANCED PROGRAM

How can the school provide a balanced program for the individual and maintain it amidst various pressures for specialization?

WAYS OF ACHIEVING BALANCE

Recommendation 15: The school can provide and maintain a curriculum appropriately balanced for each student by offering a comprehensive program of studies, making early and continuous assessment of individual potentialities and achievements, and providing individualized programs based on careful counseling.

To avoid the imbalance that can result from limiting financial support to certain selected subjects and services, general financial support should be provided for the total program. This applies to local, state, and federal support.

Decision Area VIII

SELECTING CONTENT

How can schools make wise selections of content from the ever-growing body of available knowledge?

BASES FOR SELECTING CONTENT

Recommendation 16: The objectives of the school, with a clear statement of priorities, should give direction to all curriculum planning. This applies to adding content, eliminating content, or changing the emphases on various topics and fields of study.

Recommendation 17: Each curriculum area should be under continuous study and evaluation and should be reviewed periodically. One purpose of such reviews is to determine whether recent findings in the academic disciplines are, or should be, reflected in the instructional program. These reviews should utilize the knowledge and skills of the teacher, the school administrator, the scholar in the academic disciplines, the scholar in the profession of teaching, and the lay citizen, each contributing his special competence to the total task.

KEEPING CONTENT UP TO DATE

Recommendation 18: In making selections of content, school staffs should study the results and recommendations of curriculum projects sponsored by nationally oriented groups with a view to applying promising findings.

NATIONAL CURRICULUM PROJECTS

There should be a systematic procedure for studying the results of these curriculum projects. The procedure should recognize the importance of balance and continuity in the total school experience of students and include the steps prerequisite to curriculum changes.

Decision Area IX

ORGANIZING CONTENT

How should the content of the curriculum be organized?

Recommendation 19: The content of the curriculum should be organized in such ways that students may progress, from early to later school years, toward an increasingly mature utilization and organization of their knowledge. Helping learners see interrelationships and achieve unity from the diversity of knowledge is basic to any organization of content.

BASES FOR ORGANIZING CONTENT

School staffs should experiment with a variety of ways of organizing content. The nature, meaning, and structure of the discipline and differences in the ways students learn should be taken into account in selecting a particular plan of organization and evaluating its effectiveness.

Decision Area X

ORGANIZING THE CURRICULUM*

How should the curriculum of the school be organized to give appropriate direction to the instructional process?

EDUCATIONAL OBJECTIVES

Recommendation 20: The aims of education should serve as a guide for making decisions about curriculum organization as well as about all other aspects of the instructional program.

The public, through the local school board, is responsible for determining the broad aims of education. The professional staff is responsible for translating the broad aims into specific objectives that indicate priorities and define clearly the behaviors intended for the learners. The local board of educaton has responsibility for seeing that an acceptable statement of objectives and priorities is prepared and for endorsing such a statement.

CURRICULAR SEQUENCE

Recommendation 21: In each curricular area, the vertical organization of subject matter should take account of (a) the logical structure of the subject; (b) the difficulty of material as related to the student's intellectual maturity; (c) the relation of the field to other fields.

Procedures and instruments for evaluating pupil progress must be specifically geared to the school's educational goals and to the curricular sequence in use in the school.

WHEN TO TEACH WHAT

Recommendation 22: The fact that very young children *can* learn relatively difficult aspects of science, mathematics, and other subjects is at best an incomplete answer to the question of whether they *should* learn them at this particular stage of their development. Decisions about *when to teach what* should be based on both the learner's ability to understand and the relative importance of alternative ways of using the learner's time at any given point in his school experience.

* Decision Areas X through XII, including Recommendations 20 through 33, are related to "Planning and Organizing for Teaching."

Decision Area XI

ORGANIZING THE SCHOOL AND THE CLASSROOM

How should the school and the classroom be organized to make the most effective use of the time and talents of students and teachers?

Recommendation 23: The vertical organization of the school should provide for the continuous, unbroken, upward progression of all learners, with due recognition of the wide variability among learners in every aspect of their development. The school organization should, therefore, provide for differentiated rates and means of progression toward achievement of educational goals.

NONGRADING, MULTI-GRADING, GRADING

Nongrading and multigrading are promising alternatives to the traditional graded school and should be given careful consideration in seeking to provide flexible progress plans geared to human variability.

Recommendation 24: The assignment of pupils to classroom groups should be based on knowledge about students and teachers and on understanding of goals to be achieved.

BASES FOR ABILITY GROUPING

Efforts to set up groups in terms of ability and/or achievement do little to reduce the over-all range of pupil variability with which teachers must deal. However, selective grouping and regrouping by achievement sometimes is useful, particularly at the secondary school level.

Recommendation 25: In order to provide individually planned programs for learners, taking into account the specific objectives to be achieved, the horizontal organization of the school should permit flexibility in assigning pupils to instructional groups that may range in size from one pupil to as many as a hundred or more. Well-planned cooperative efforts among teachers—efforts such as team teaching, for example—should be encouraged and tested.

TEAM TEACHING

Recommendation 26: The school should be organized in such a way that it provides opportunity for each student to (a) experience continuity and relatedness in his learning, and (b) have

SELF-CONTAINED CLASSROOM

a close counseling relationship with competent teachers who know him well. Various forms of organization should be explored to determine their effectiveness for these purposes.

The contributions of specialized personnel should be used as students progress through the elementary and secondary school. At whatever point specialized personnel are brought into the instructional program, their work should be coordinated with and related to the total program.

CLASSROOM GROUPING

RECOMMENDATION 27: In schools where the classroom is the unit of organization, teachers should organize learners frequently into smaller groups of varying types and sizes. Decisions as to size and membership of such groups should be based on knowledge about learners and on the specific educational purposes to be served at a given time for each learner.

DECISION AREA XII

INSTRUCTIONAL MATERIALS, TECHNOLOGY, SPACE

How can the quality of instructional materials be improved?

How can the products of modern technology be used effectively?

How can space be designed and used to support the instructional program?

INSTRUCTIONAL MATERIALS CENTERS

RECOMMENDATION 28: In each school system, there should be one or more well-planned instructional materials and resources centers, consisting of at least a library and an audiovisual center. In each school building, there should also be an instructional resources facility.

These centers should be staffed by persons who are adequately prepared in curriculum and instruction, in library service, and in audiovisual education.

ETV AND RADIO

RECOMMENDATION 29: The use of educational television (ETV) and radio to broaden and deepen learning should be encouraged. Such use should be accompanied by a vigorous program of research and experimentation.

RECOMMENDATION 30: Schools should make use, with proper supervision, of self-instructional materials and devices (programed instruction) that facilitate varied learning opportunities and continuous progress for learners of widely divergent abilities. The use of programed instruction should be accompanied by a vigorous program of research and experimentation.

PROGRAMED INSTRUCTION

RECOMMENDATION 31: A comprehensive study and action program is needed to improve the quality and use of printed teaching materials and other instructional media. Such a study and action program requires the participation of both the producers and the consumers of these instructional materials and media.

INSTRUCTIONAL MEDIA

RECOMMENDATION 32: School authorities should examine the potentialities of automation for storage and retrieval of pupil personnel data and instructional materials.

AUTOMATION

RECOMMENDATION 33: New concepts of space should permit and encourage (a) varying sized groups ranging from small seminars to multiple-class; (b) independent study with visual and/or acoustic privacy as required; (c) access to a variety of instructional media; (d) multiple use.

SPACE UTILIZATION

Key considerations in planning for better utilization of space are (a) flexibility and (b) environment which respects the learner and his need for a sense of amenity if his learning is to be most efficient.

APPENDIX B | *Notes and Footnotes*

CHAPTER ONE

1. See, for examples, the following: (a) Educational Policies Commission. *The Purposes of Education in American Democracy.* Washington, D.C.: National Education Association, 1938; (b) National Association of Secondary-School Principals. "The Imperative Needs of Youth of Secondary School Age." *Bulletin of the National Association of Secondary-School Principals* 31:145; March 1947.

CHAPTER TWO

1. Moulton, Dorothy E. *The Teaching of Literature in the Senior High School: A Historical and Critical Study of Recent Trends Based upon an Analysis of Selected Professional Publications, 1911-1955.* Doctor's Thesis. Ann Arbor: University of Michigan, 1959.

2. Bruner, Jerome S. *The Process of Education.* Cambridge, Mass.: Harvard University Press, 1960. 97 pp.

3. National Education Association, Association for Supervision and Curriculum Development, Commission on Current Curriculum Developments. *Using Current Curriculum Developments.* Washington, D.C.: National Education Association, 1963.

4. Tykociner, Joseph T. *Research As a Science–Zetetics.* Urbana, Ill.: the Author (University of Illinois), 1959. p. 18.

5. Schwab, Joseph J. "Inquiry, the Science Teacher, and the Educator." *School Review* 68: 180; Summer 1960.

6. Dewey, John. *How We Think.* Revised edition. Boston: D. C. Heath & Co., 1933. 301 pp.

7. Schwab, Joseph J. Speech delivered at the National Education Association Disciplines Seminar, Washington, D.C., June 15, 1961. See the following: National Education Association, Project on the Instructional Program of the Public Schools. *The Scholars Look at the Schools: A Report of the Disciplines Seminar.* Washington, D.C.; the Association, 1962. p. 3.

8. Peterson, A. D. C. *Arts and Science Sides in the Sixth Form.* A Report to the Gulbenkian Foundation. Oxford, England: Department of Education, Oxford University, 1960.

9. See, for examples, the following: (a) Munro, B. C. "Meaning and Learning." *Alberta Journal of Educational Research* 5: 268-81; 1959; (b) Newman, S. E. "Student vs. Instructor Design of Study Method." *Journal of Educational Psychology* 48: 328-33; October 1957.

10. For a summary of pertinent research, see the following: Russell, David H. "Concepts." *Encyclopedia of Educational Research.* Third edition. (Edited by Chester W. Harris.) New York: Macmillan Co., 1960. pp. 323-29.

11. For a summary of pertinent research, see the following: Blair, Glen M., and Jones, R. Stewart. "Readiness." *Encyclopedia of Educational Research.* Third edition. (Edited by Chester W. Harris.) New York: Macmillan Co., 1960. pp. 1081-85.

12. Whitehead, Alfred North. *The Aims of Education.* New York: Macmillan Co., 1929. Chapter 2.

13. Bruner, Jerome S. *Op cit.* Chapter 3.

14. Russell, David H. *Op cit.*

15. *Ibid.* p. 323.

16. For Dewey's discussion of this point, see the following: Dewey, John. *Experience and Education.* New York: Macmillan Co., 1938. pp. 86-112.

17. For a summary discussion of research and tentative conclusions, see the following: Marx, Melvin H. "Motivation." *Encyclopedia of Educational Research.* Third edition. (Edited by Chester W. Harris.) New York: Macmillan Co., 1960. pp. 895-98.

18. For a review of research supporting this view, see the following: *Ibid.*, p. 898.

19. Overman, J. R. "An Experimental Study of the Effect of the Method of Instruction on Transfer of Training in Arithmetic." *Elementary School Journal* 31: 183-90; November 1930.

20. Two recent publications that bring together the results of research on creativity are the following: (a) Torrance, E. Paul. *Creativity.* What Research Says to the Teacher, No. 28. Prepared by the American Educational Research Association in cooperation with the Department of Classroom Teachers. Washington, D.C.: National Education Association, 1963; (b) Taylor, Calvin W. *Creativity: Resume and Outlook.* New York: McGraw-Hill Book Co., 1963.

21. See, for examples, the following references: (a) Parnes, Sidney J. *Compendium No. 2 of Research on Creative Imagination.* Buffalo, N.Y.: Creative Education Foundation, 1960; (b) Russell, David H. "Higher Mental Processes." *Encyclopedia of Educational Research.* Third edition. (Edited by Chester W. Harris.) New York: Macmillan Co., 1960. pp. 652-53.

22. Torrance, E. Paul. *Conditions for Creative Growth.* Paper prepared for presentation to elementary and secondary school faculties of Roseville, Minnesota, Public Schools, November 14, 1960. (Mimeo.)

23. See, for example, the following: Anderson, Harold H. "Creativity and Education." *College and University Bulletin* (Association for Higher Education), May 1961.

24. For further discussion of the need for introducing pupils to an interdisciplinary organization of knowledge as well as to the structures of the separate disciplines, see the following references: (a) Henry, Nelson B., editor. *The Integration of Educational Experiences.* Fifty-Seventh Yearbook, Part III, National Society for the Study of Education. Chicago: University of Chicago Press, 1958. 278 pp.; (b) Caswell, Hollis L. "Difficulties in Defining the Structure of the Curriculum." *Curriculum Crossroads.* New York: Bureau of Publications, Teachers College, Columbia University, 1962. pp. 103-11.

CHAPTER THREE

1. National Education Association. *Labels and Fingerprints.* Joint statement issued by the American Association of School Administrators, the Association for Supervision and Curriculum Development, the National Association of Secondary-School Principals, the National Education Association Department of Elementary School Principals, and the National Education Association Department of Rural Education. Washington, D.C.: National Education Association, 1960. 16 pp.

2. For a summary of recent research and an indication of the depth and range of unanswered questions, see the following references: (a) Tyler, Fred T. "Individual and Sex Differences." *Encyclopedia of Educational Research.* Third edition. (Edited by Chester W. Harris.) New York: MacMillan Co., 1960. pp. 680-88; (b) for a more extended discussion, see the following: Tyler, Fred W., editor. *Individualizing Instruction.* Sixty-First Yearbook, Part I, National Society for the Study of Education. Chicago: University of Chicago Press, 1962.

3. For discussion of this point, see the following: Wilhelms, Fred T. "The Curriculum and Individual Differences." *Individualizing Instruction.* Sixty-First Yearbook, Part I, National Society for the Study of Education. Chicago: University of Chicago Press, 1962. pp. 62-64.

4. For a summary of research on this point, see the following: Riessman, Frank. *The Culturally Deprived Child.* New York: Harper & Brothers, 1962. Chapter 6.

5. Basic studies include the following: (a) Centers, Richard. *The Psychology of Social Classes.* Princeton, N.J.: Princeton University Press, 1949. 244 pp.; (b) Davis, Allison. *Social Class Influences upon Learning.* Cambridge, Mass.: Harvard University Press, 1948. 100 pp.; (c) Davis, Allison, and Havighurst, Robert J. "Social Class and Color Differences in Child Rearing." *American Sociological Review:* 142-49; April 1953; (d) Deutsch, Martin. *Minority Groups and Class Status As Related to Social*

and Personality Factors in Scholastic Achievement. Ithaca, N.Y.: Society for Applied Anthropology, 1960; (e) Eells, Kenneth, and others. *Intelligence and Cultural Differences.* Chicago: University of Chicago Press, 1951. 388 pp.; (f) Havighurst, Robert J. *Growing Up in River City.* New York: John Wiley & Sons, 1962. 189 pp.; (g) Hollingshead, August B. *Elmstown's Youth.* New York: John Wiley & Sons, 1950; (h) Mulligan, Raymond A. "Socio-Economic Background and College Enrollment." *American Sociological Review:* 188-96; April 1951; (i) Sexton, Patricia. *Education and Income.* New York: Viking Press, 1961. 298 pp.

6. Among those most widely discussed in current educational literature are the Higher Horizons program in New York City and the Great Cities Gray Areas School Improvement Program, which is supported by the Ford Foundation and includes a variety of projects that are being conducted in 10 large cities: Buffalo, N.Y.; Chicago; Cleveland; Detroit; Milwaukee, Wis.; Philadelphia; Pittsburgh, Pa.; St. Louis; Washington, D.C.; and San Francisco, Calif. Other experimental programs are being carried on under the sponsorship of state education departments and local school systems. In New York State, for example, 16 school districts are cooperating with state educational authorities in Project ABLE, which is focused on improving education for culturally deprived children and youth.

7. National Education Association. "School Dropouts." *NEA Journal* 51: 57-58; May 1962. The program is reported by Superintendent John Prasch and Leslie Paffrath, president of the Johnson Foundation, which is helping to support the project.

8. For a more complete description, see the following: (a) New York City Public Schools. *Higher Horizons Program, First Annual Progress Report, 1959-1960.* New York: Board of Education, 1961. 73 pp. (Multilith); (b) New York City Public Schools. *Higher Horizons Bulletin,* April 1962.

9. For two expressions of this view, see the following: (a) Conant, James B. *Slums and Suburbs.* New York: McGraw-

Hill Book Co., 1961. pp. 57-60; (b) Educational Policies Commission. *Education and the Disadvantaged American.* Washington, D.C.: National Education Association, 1961. pp. 16-17.

10. *Ibid.*, pp. 17-18.

11. *Ibid.*, p. 18.

12. For elaboration of this point, see the following: Reissman, Frank. *Op cit.* Note especially Chapters 2, 4, 5, 11, and 12.

13. See, for example, the following studies: (a) Schneller, Pete. *Unwilling Learner and Drop-Out Study, Ballard High School, Seattle, Washington, 1958-1961.* Seattle, Wash.: Board of Education, 1962. (Mimeo.); (b) New York City Public Schools. *Experiment in Guidance of Potential Early School Leavers.* New York: Board of Education, 1956.

14. During the 1960's about 7.5 million boys and girls will leave school before graduation, according to U.S. Department of Labor estimates, unless present trends are radically altered. See the following: National Committee for Children and Youth. *Guidelines for Consideration of the Dropout and Unemployment Problems of Youth.* Washington, D.C.: the Committee, 1961. p. 7.

15. Schreiber, Daniel. "School Dropouts." *NEA Journal* 51: 51; May 1962. For the report of an intensive study of one group of dropouts among whom emotional disturbances proved to be a major cause of school difficulties and school leaving, see the following: Lichter, Solomon, and others. *The Drop-Outs.* Glencoe, Ill.: Free Press of Glencoe, 1962.

16. Havighurst, Robert J., and Stiles, Lindley J. "National Policy for Alienated Youth." *Phi Delta Kappan* 42: 283-91; April 1961.

17. An example of such a program which has been set up in New York City is described by the following: McBride, Julia K. "School Dropouts." *NEA Journal* 51: 55-56; May 1962. For other examples, see the following: Kvaraceus, William C., and

others. *Delinquent Behavior, Vol. 2: Principles and Practice.* Washington, D.C.: National Education Association, 1959. 350 pp.

18. Havighurst, Robert J., and Stiles, Lindley J. *Op. cit.*

19. For a description of the program, see the following: (a) New York City Public Schools. "Curriculum Programs and Materials To Meet the Dropout Problem." *Curriculum and Materials.* New York: Board of Education, Fall 1961; (b) Savitzky, Charles. "A Rehabilitation Project in Cooperative Education: Work Experience Program." *High Points* 41: 5-19; November 1959.

20. New York City Public Schools. *Curriculum Materials for Meeting School Retention and Pre-Employment Needs.* Curriculum Bulletin No. 8, 1960-1961 Series. New York: Board of Education, 1961. The units of study included in this bulletin were drawn from materials that had been developed and used in various slow-learner groups. They are (a) Our American Heritage; (b) Language Arts; (c) You As a Consumer; (d) You and Success on the Job; (e) You As a Worker in Industry; (f) How Our Government Works; (g) Your Family Membership; (h) Your Use of Leisure Time; (i) Your License As a Future Driver; (j) Personal Mathematics; (k) Using Mathematics As a Worker and Citizen; (l) Science in Daily Living; (m) Saleable Skills.

21. For a description of the program by its director, Bernard C. Greene, see the following: National Education Association. "School Dropouts." *NEA Journal* 51: 56-57; May 1962.

22. St. Louis Project Proposal, Great Cities Improvement Program. *The School and Community Work-Related Education Program.* New York: Ford Foundation, n.d. (Mimeo.)

23. Information provided by Bureau of Guidance, New York State Education Department, Albany.

24. For details reported by Superintendent Dale Parnell, see the following: National Education Association. "School Dropouts." *NEA Journal* 51: 58; May 1962.

25. For a review of major studies, see the following: Carter, Harold D. "Gifted Children." *Encyclopedia of Educational Research.* Third edition. (Edited by Chester W. Harris.) New York: Macmillan Co., 1960. pp. 583-93.

26. See, for example, the series of publications of the National Education Association Project on the Academically Talented Student and the special school programs that are described or listed in these bulletins.

27. Drews, Elizabeth M., editor. *Guidance for the Academically Talented Student.* National Education Association, Project on the Academically Talented Student, and American Personnel and Guidance Association. Washington, D.C.: National Education Association, 1961. p. 13.

28. Getzels, Jacob W., and Jackson, Philip W. *Creativity and Intelligence.* New York: John Wiley & Sons, 1962. 293 pp.

29. *Ibid.*, pp. 60-61.

30. For a review of current research on creativity and intelligence, see the following: Anderson, Kenneth E., editor. *Research on the Academically Talented Student.* Washington, D.C.: Project on the Academically Talented Student, National Education Association, 1961. pp. 36-40. Also see the following: Mackinnon, Donald W. "What Makes a Person Creative?" *Saturday Review* 45: 15ff; February 10, 1962.

31. For a fuller description, see the following: (a) New York City Public Schools. *Demonstration Guidance Project: Fourth Annual Progress Report, 1959-1960.* New York: Board of Education, 1960; (b) Schreiber, Daniel. "Raising Sights to Higher Horizons." *Strengthening Democracy.* New York: Board of Education, May 1960; (c) Hillson, Henry T., and Myers, Florence C. *The Demonstration Guidance Project, 1957-1962.* New York: Board of Education, 1963.

32. Impellizzeri, Irene H. "Nature and Scope of the Problem." *Guidance for the Underachiever with Superior Ability.* (Edited

by Leonard M. Miller.) U.S. Department of Health, Education, and Welfare, Office of Education, Bulletin 1961, No. 25. Washington, D.C.: Government Printing Office, 1961.

33. Studies have indicated that underachievement for boys often begins in the primary grades, while for girls the critical school year is grade 6. See the following for summary statement: *Ibid.*, pp. 23-24, 31.

34. Anderson, John E. "The Nature of Abilities." *Talent and Education.* (Edited by E. Paul Torrance.) Minneapolis: University of Minnesota Press, 1960. pp. 27-28.

35. For descriptions of identification programs in a number of school systems, see the following: Havighurst, Robert J.; Stivers, Eugene; and DeHaan, Robert F. *A Survey of Education of Gifted Children.* Supplementary Education Monographs, No. 83. Chicago: University of Chicago Press, 1955. Criteria for identifying talented students in the subject areas of art, English, mathematics, music, social studies, and science are presented in the series of bulletins prepared by the NEA Project on the Academically Talented Student.

36. The summary that follows represents a synthesis of recommendations made in the following: (a) the bulletin series of the NEA Project on the Academically Talented Student; (b) Havighurst, Robert J., editor. *Education for the Gifted.* Fifty-Seventh Yearbook, Part I, National Society for the Study of Education. Chicago: University of Chicago Press, 1958. 420 pp. Specific recommendations for various curriculum areas may be found in the bulletins of the NEA Project on the Academically Talented Student. Such issues as whether or not gifted children should be placed in separate classes and whether team teaching or some other type of organization should be used to provide instruction by specialists are not considered in the pages that follow, since these and similar issues are discussed in another volume of the Project report, *Planning and Organizing for Teaching.*

37. New York State Department of Education, Office of Curriculum Development. *Curriculum Adaptations for the Gifted.*

Albany: the Department, 1958. p. 34. For a selected list of publications suggesting such enrichment activities, see the following: Drews, Elizabeth M., editor. *Op cit.* Appendix A.

38. See the following for a list of such programs being conducted in various parts of the United States: *Ibid.,* Appendix B.

39. For elaboration of this point, see the following: Veatch, Jeannette. "Grouping Is the Function and Process of Content." *Educational Leadership* 18: 425-28; April 1961.

40. For a summary review of pertinent studies, see the following: Hildreth, Gertrude. "Individual Differences." *Enyclopedia of Educational Research.* Revised edition. (Edited by W. S. Monroe.) New York: Macmillan Co., 1950. p. 569.

41. For discussion of one plan for using independent study in secondary schools, see the following: Trump, J. Lloyd, and Baynham, Dorsey. *Focus on Change: A Guide to Better Schools.* Chicago: Rand McNally and Co., 1961. pp. 26-29.

42. See the following: (a) Conant, James B. *The American High School Today.* New York: McGraw-Hill Book Co., 1959. pp. 46-47, 51-55; (b) Wiles, Kimball, and Patterson, Franklin. *The High School We Need.* Association for Supervision and Curriculum Development, Commission on the Education of Adolescents. Washington, D.C.: National Education Association, 1959. pp. 8-12.

43. Conant, James B. *Op cit.* p. 47.

44. For a description of these and other practices, see the following: Ford, Edmund A. *Rural Renaissance: Revitalizing Small High Schools.* U.S. Department of Health, Education, and Welfare, Office of Education, Bulletin 1961, No. 11. Washington, D.C.: Government Printing Office, 1961.

CHAPTER FOUR

1. For discussion of various philosophies of education and the effects of social change on educational decisions, see the follow-

ing: (a) Brubacher, John S., editor. *Modern Philosophies and Education.* Fifty-Fourth Yearbook, Part I, National Society for the Study of Education. Chicago: University of Chicago Press, 1955. 374 pp.; (b) Tyler, Ralph W., editor. *Social Forces Influencing American Education.* Sixtieth Yearbook, Part II, National Society for the Study of Education. Chicago: University of Chicago Press, 1961. 252 pp.; (c) Phenix, Philip, editor. *Philosophies of Education.* New York: John Wiley & Sons, 1961. 137 pp.; (d) Smith, B. O.; Stanley, W. O.; and Shores, J. H. *Fundamentals of Curriculum Development.* Revised edition. New York: World Book Co., 1957. 685 pp.; (e) *Education in a Changing Society*, a volume of the report of the Project on Instruction.

2. For an expression of this view, which is urged by supporters of the Council for Basic Education among others, see the following: Smith, Mortimer. "Why We Disagree." *Saturday Review* 44: 80-81ff; January 21, 1961.

3. For a statement of this view, see the following: Fischer, John H. "Schools Are for Learning." *Saturday Review* 43: 72; September 17, 1960.

4. See, for example, the following: Hanna, Lavone. "Meeting the Challenge (A Statement of Beliefs)." *What Are the Sources of the Curriculum?* Washington, D.C.: Association for Supervision and Curriculum Development, National Education Association, 1962. p. 50.

5. Butts, R. Freeman, and Cremin, Lawrence A. *A History of Education in American Culture.* New York: Henry Holt & Co., 1953. p. 386. For discussion of the trend toward an expanded curriculum through the nineteenth and early twentieth centuries, see the following: *Ibid.*, pp. 379-92, 538-51.

6. See the following: U.S. Department of Health, Education, and Welfare, Office of Education. *Recommendations: Composite Report for Forum Findings, 1960 White House Conference on Children and Youth.* Washington, D.C.: Government Printing Office, 1960. pp. 18-26.

7. See, for example, the following: Fischer, John H. *Op cit.*

8. For a review of adult education programs, see the following: Hendrickson, Andrew. "Adult Education." *Encyclopedia of Educational Research.* Third edition. (Edited by Chester W. Harris.) New York: Macmillan Co., 1960. pp. 30-42.

CHAPTER FIVE

1. Alexander, William M., and Moorer, Sam H. "Balance in the Curriculum, A Working Paper." (Mimeo.) Quoted in the following: National Education Association, Association for Supervision and Curriculum Development. *Balance in the Curriculum.* 1961 Yearbook. Washington, D.C.: National Education Association, 1961. pp. 5-7.

2. These recommendations were among those selected from the total Conference report by a follow-up conference of educators as having "central importance" for elementary education, but they apply to the total program of the school from the kindergarten through grade 12. U.S. Department of Health, Education, and Welfare, Office of Education. *Implications for Elementary Education: Follow-Up on the 1960 White House Conference on Children and Youth.* Office of Education Bulletin 20033. Washington, D.C.: Government Printing Office, 1961. pp. 4-5. Numbers of the recommendations are those assigned in the original Conference report.

3. See, for example, the following: Jewett, Ann, and Knapp, Clyde, editors. *The Growing Years–Adolescence.* 1962 Yearbook, American Association for Health, Physical Education, and Recreation. Washington, D.C.: National Education Association, 1962. 320 pp.

4. American Vocational Association. *Industrial Arts in Education.* Statement by the Industrial Arts Policy and Planning Committee, American Vocational Association. Washington, D.C.: the Association, n.d.

5. For a fuller discussion of the modern industrial arts program, see the publications of the American Industrial Arts Association, National Education Association, Washington, D.C.

6. For a fuller discussion of the modern home economics program, see the publications of the American Home Economics Association, Washington, D.C., and the Department of Home Economics, National Education Association, Washington, D.C.

7. For a fuller discussion of vocational education programs, see the publications of the American Vocational Association, Washington, D.C.

8. For a summary of information about the development and current status of extraclass programs, see the following: Faunce, Roland. "Extra Curricular Activities." *Encyclopedia of Educational Research.* Third edition. (Edited by Chester W. Harris.) New York: Macmillan Co., 1960. pp. 506-11.

9. See, for example, studies summarized in the following: Trump, J. Lloyd. "Extraclass Activities and the Needs of Youth." *Adapting the Secondary-School Program to the Needs of Youth.* Fifty-Second Yearbook, Part I, National Society for the Study of Education. (Edited by William G. Brink.) Chicago: University of Chicago Press, 1953. pp. 161-62.

10. For fuller discussion of this point, see the following: *Ibid.*, pp. 164-66.

11. See, for examples of such criticisms, the following: (a) Flesch, Rudolph. *Why Johnny Can't Read.* New York: Harper & Brothers, 1955. 222 pp.; (b) Walcutt, Charles G., editor. *Tomorrow's Illiterates.* Boston: Little Brown & Co., 1961. 168 pp.

12. Gates, Arthur I. *Reading Attainment in Elementary Schools: 1957 and 1937.* New York: Bureau of Publications, Teachers College, Columbia University, 1961. p. 22.

13. Spache, George D. *Are We Teaching Reading?* Gainesville: University of Florida, 1956. Excerpts are reprinted in the follow-

ing: Harris, Albert J. *Readings on Reading Instruction.* New York: David McKay Co., 1963. pp. 25-28.

14. Clift, David H., editor. *Adult Reading.* Fifty-Fifth Yearbook, Part II, National Society for the Study of Education. Chicago: University of Chicago Press, 1956. Chapter 1.

15. See the following: Austin, Mary C., and others. *The Torch Lighters: Tomorrow's Teachers of Reading.* Cambridge, Mass.: Harvard University Press, 1961. Chapters 4 and 5.

16. Educational Testing Service. *Learning To Read: A Report of a Conference of Reading Experts.* Princeton, N.J.: the Service, 1962. pp. 16-17.

17. Harris, Albert J. *How To Increase Reading Ability.* Fourth edition. New York: Longmans, Green & Co., 1961. p. 8.

18. Robinson, Helen M. "Controversial Issues in Improving Reading Instruction." *Report of Regents Conference on the Improvement of Reading.* Albany: New York State Education Department, 1962. p. 17.

19. For a more detailed discussion, see the following: (a) *Report of the National Committee on Reading.* Twenty-Fourth Yearbook, Part I, National Society for the Study of Education. Bloomington, Ill.: Public School Publishing Co., 1925; (b) Harris, Albert J. *Op. cit.* Chapters 1-4.

20. For a review of research dealing with reading readiness, see the following: Gray, William S. "The Teaching of Reading." *Encyclopedia of Educational Research.* Third edition. (Edited by Chester W. Harris.) New York: Macmillan Co., 1960. pp. 1115-17.

21. See, for example, the following: Fries, Charles C. *Linguistics and Reading.* New York: Holt, Rinehart and Winston, 1963. Chapter 7.

22. For fuller discussion of this issue and for reviews of pertinent research, see the following: (a) Moskowitz, Sue. *When Should*

Systematic Reading Instruction Begin? Paper presented at the 1963 convention of the International Reading Association. Chicago: the Association, 1963; (b) Gray, William S. *Op. cit.;* (d) Harris, Albert J. *Op. cit.* Chapter 2; (d) Shane, Harold G., and Mulry, June Grant. *Improving Language Arts Instruction Through Research.* Washington, D.C.: Association for Supervision and Curriculum Development, National Education Association, 1963. pp. 10-15.

23. Taylor, Christian P. "The Effect of Training on Reading Readiness." *Studies in Reading.* London: University of London, 1950. pp. 64-80. Summarized in the following: Gray, William S. *Op. cit.* pp. 11-15.

24. Fries, Charles C. *Op. cit.* p. 187.

25. For a brief report of the program, see the following: Carnegie Corporation of New York. " 'Tis Time He Should Begin To Read." *Carnegie Corporation of New York Quarterly* 9: 1-8; April 1961.

26. Washburne, Carleton. "Individualized Plan of Instruction in Winnetka." *Adjusting Reading Programs to Individuals.* Supplementary Education Monographs, No. 52. Chicago: University of Chicago Press, 1941. pp. 90-95.

27. Thomson, Jennie L. "Big Gains from Postponed Reading." *Journal of Education* 117: 445-46; October 15, 1934.

28. For fuller discussion of this issue, see the following: (a) Dolch, Edward W. *Teaching Primary Reading.* Third edition. Champaign, Ill.: Garrard Press, 1960. Chapters 12 and 13; (b) Durkin, Dolores. *Phonics and the Teaching of Reading.* New York: Bureau of Publications, Teachers College, Columbia University, 1962. Chapter 6; (c) Hildreth, Gertrude. *Teaching Reading.* New York: Henry Holt & Co., 1958. Chapters 7 and 8; (d) Educational Testing Service. *Op. cit.;* (e) New York State Education Department. *Report of Regents Conference on the Improvement of Reading.* Albany, N.Y.: the Department, 1962.

29. See the following: *Ibid.*, especially papers by Helen R. Robinson, Charles E. Wingo, and Mae Carden.

30. Fries, Charles C. *Op. cit.* See also the following: Bloomfield, Leonard, and Barnhart, Clarence L. *Let's Read.* Detroit: Wayne State University Press, 1961.

31. Fries, Charles C. *Op. cit.* p. 156.

32. Wingo, Charles E. *Report of Regents Conference on Improvement of Reading.* Albany: New York State Department of Education, 1962. p. 23.

33. *Ibid.*

34. Pertinent reports include the following: (a) Agnew, Donald C. *The Effects of Varied Amounts of Phonetic Training on Primary Reading.* Durham, N.C.: Duke University Press, 1939; (b) Buswell, Guy Thomas. *Fundamental Reading Habits: A Study of Their Development.* Supplementary Educational Monographs, No. 21. Chicago: University of Chicago Press, 1922; (c) Gates, Arthur I. "Results of Teaching a System of Phonics." *Reading Teacher* 14: 248-52; March 1961; (d) McDowell, John B. "A Report on the Phonetic Method of Teaching Children To Read." *Catholic Educational Review* 51: 506-19; October 1953; (e) Sparks, Paul E., and Fay, Leo C. "An Evaluation of Two Methods of Teaching Reading." *Elementary School Journal* 57: 386-90; April 1957; (f) Sexton, Elmer K., and Herron, John S. "The Newark Phonics Experiment." *Elementary School Journal* 28: 670-701; May 1928; (g) Tate, Harry L. "The Influence of Phonics in Silent Reading in Grade I." *Elementary School Journal* 37: 752-63; June 1937; (h) Witty, Paul, and Sizemore, Robert A. "Phonics in the Reading Program: A Review and Evaluation." *Elementary English* 32: 355-70; October 1955.

35. McDowell, John B. *Op. cit.*

36. See, for example, the following: Sparks, Paul E., and Fay, Leo C. *Op. cit.*

37. For fuller descriptions of the characteristics of basal reading series and of their use in group instruction, see the following: (a) Harris, Albert J. *Op. cit.* pp. 71-77; (b) Herrick, Virgil E., and others. "Basal Instructional Materials in Reading." *Development in and Through Reading.* Sixtieth Yearbook, Part I, National Society for the Study of Education. (Edited by Paul A. Witty.) Chicago: University of Chicago Press, 1961. pp. 165-88; (c) Strickland, Ruth G. "The Language of Elementary School Children: Its Relationship to the Language of Reading Textbooks and the Quality of Reading of Selected Children." *Bulletin of the School of Education* (Indiana University, Bloomington) 38: 1-131; July 1962. The article compares the oral language patterns of children with patterns used in reading textbooks with the conclusion that in the textbooks "there appeared to be no scheme for the development of control over sentence structure which paralleled the generally accepted scheme for the development of control over vocabulary." p. 70.

38. For an example of one teacher's record keeping, see the following: Fisch, Muriel. "Record Keeping for Individualized Reading." *Grade Teacher* 76: 90-91ff; November 1958. Reprinted in the following: Harris, Albert J. *Readings on Reading Instruction.* pp. 191-94.

39. For fuller description of procedures for individualized developmental reading, see the following: Miel, Alice, editor. *Individualized Reading Practices.* New York: Bureau of Publications, Teachers College, Columbia University, 1958.

40. For a review of these studies, see the following: (a) Gray, William S. *Op. cit.* pp. 1121-22; (b) Harris, Albert J. *How To Increase Reading Ability.* pp. 118-19.

41. *Ibid.,* p. 120. See also the following: Evans, N. Dean. "Individualized Reading—Myth and Facts." *Elementary English* 39: 580-83; October 1962.

42. One recent survey of widely used reading series reported the following vocabulary ranges: preprimers and primers, from 121

to 189 different words; grades 1-3, from 1,261 to 1,810 different words; grades 4-6, from 3,894 to 4,436 different words. New words were introduced at all levels in the ratio of 1 new word to every 50 to 110 running words. Herrick, Virgil E., and others. *Op. cit.* pp. 177-78.

43. Gray, William S. *Op. cit.* p. 1120.

44. See, for examples, the following: (a) Herrick, Virgil E., and others. *Op. cit.*; (b) *Ibid.*

45. Harris, Albert J. "Ivan and Johnny—A Critical Review." *International Reading Association Conference Proceedings.* (Edited by J. Allen Figurel.) Chicago: the Association, 1962. Volume 4.

46. See, for example, the following: Trace, Arther S., Jr. "A Summary Analysis of the Reading Program in American Schools." *Report of Regents Conference on the Improvement of Reading.* Albany: New York State Department of Education, 1962. p. 41.

47. Gray, William S. *Op. cit.* pp. 1119-20.

48. See, for example, the following: Klineberg, Otto. "Life Is Fun in a Smiling, Fair-Skinned World." *Saturday Review* 46: 75-77ff; February 16, 1963.

49. New York State Department of Education. *Op. cit.* p. 64.

50. See, for example, the following: Washburn, Watson. "The Reading Crisis." *Report of Regents Conference on the Improvement of Reading.* Albany: New York State Department of Education, 1960. p. 49.

51. See, for examples, the following: (a) Gray, William S. *Op. cit.*; (b) Gates, Arthur I. "What We Know and Can Do About the Poor Reader." *Education* 77: 528-33; May 1957. Reprinted in the following: Harris, Albert J. *Readings on Reading Instruction.* pp. 434-40.

52. Bruenig, Marjorie. *Foreign Languages in the Elementary Schools of the United States, 1959-1960.* New York: Modern Language Association of America, 1961. p. 1.

53. For fuller exposition of these arguments, see the following: (a) Andersson, Theodore. "The Optimum Age for Beginning the Study of Modern Languages." *International Review of Education* 4: 209-306; 1960; (b) Modern Language Association of America. *Foreign Languages in Elementary Schools: Some Questions and Answers.* Report of work conference, 1953. New York: the Association, 1953. (Mimeo.); (c) Parker, William R. *The National Interest and Foreign Language: A Discussion Guide and Work Paper.* Revised edition. Washington, D.C.: Government Printing Office, 1962; (d) Penfield, Wilder. "The Learning of Languages." *F L Bulletin* No. 62 (Modern Language Association of America), 1960. (Mimeo.)

54. Modern Language Association of America. "Childhood and Second Language Learning." *F L Bulletin* No. 49 (Modern Language Association of America), 1960. (Mimeo.)

55. For fuller presentations of these points, see the following: (a) Carroll, John B. "Foreign Languages for Children: What Research Says." *National Elementary Principal* 39: 12-15; May 1960; (b) Parker, William R. *Op. cit.* pp. 17-24; (c) Modern Language Association of America. "When Should Second Language Learning Begin—Opinions of Neurologists and Psychiatrists." *F L Bulletin* No. 1 (Modern Language Association of America), 1957. (Mimeo.)

56. Modern Language Association of America, Foreign Language Program Research Center. *Foreign Languages in the Elementary School: A Second Statement of Policy.* Report of a conference sponsored by the Modern Language Association of America, 1961. New York: the Association, 1961. (Mimeo.)

57. For further discussion of these elements, see the following: Fraser, Dorothy M. "Improving the Educational Program for World Leadership." *Education for World Leadership.* 1960 Yearbook, National School Boards Association. Evanston, Ill.: the Association, 1960. pp. 100-10.

58. The Program for Improving the Teaching of World Affairs, carried on in Glens Falls, New York, under the joint sponsorship of the Glens Falls Board of Education and the National Council for the Social Studies. See the following for a brief description of the program: National Education Association, Project on the Instructional Program of the Public Schools. *Current Curriculum Studies in Academic Subjects.* (Prepared by Dorothy M. Fraser.) Washington, D.C.: the Association, 1961. pp. 79-82. A definitive report of the project will be pubished in the near future by the National Council for the Social Studies.

CHAPTER SIX

1. National Education Association. *Controversial Issues in the Classroom.* Washington, D.C.: the Association, 1961. p. 10. The quotation is from a policy statement of the Des Moines (Iowa) Public Schools on treatment of controversial issues, which is reproduced in this bulletin.

2. See, for examples, the following: (a) *Ibid.* (Policy statements that have been adopted by school boards in different parts of the country have been reproduced here); (b) Committee on Academic Freedom. "The Treatment of Controversial Issues in the Schools." *Social Education* 15: 232-36; May 1951, and Committee on Academic Freedom. "Freedom To Learn and Freedom To Teach." *Social Education* 17: 217-20; May 1953. (two policy statements of the National Council for the Social Studies); (c) California Teachers Association, Commission on Educational Policy. *Controversial Issues in the Public Schools.* San Francisco: the Association, 1957. (a policy statement of the California Teachers Association); (d) Gross, R. E. *How To Handle Controversial Issues.* How To Do It Series, No. 14. Revised edition. Washington, D.C.: National Council for the Social Studies, National Education Association, 1961. (a summary discussion of

widely accepted criteria for selection of issues to be studied and of methods of instruction); (e) Committee for Economic Development, National Task Force on Economic Education. *Economic Education in the Schools.* New York: the Committee, 1961. p. 73. (a strong recommendation by economists for the study of controversial economic issues in the schools). The following summary of criteria for selection and procedures in directing study of controversial issues in the classroom is based on these and similar statements.

3. California State Department of Education. *Policies on Teaching Controversial Issues Adopted by California School Districts.* Sacramento: the Department, n.d. p. 16. (Mimeo.) Quotation is from policy statement adopted by the Governing Board of the Armijo Joint Union High School District, July 18, 1960.

4. Adapted from the following: Committee on Academic Freedom. "The Treatment of Controversial Issues in the Schools." *Social Education* 15: 234-35; May 1951.

5. See, for example, the following from which much of this summary has been adapted: California Teachers Association. *Controversial Issues in the Public Schools.*

6. American Bar Association. *Instruction on Communism and Its Contrast with Liberty Under Law.* Chicago: the Association, 1962.

7. Joint Committee of the National Education Association and the American Legion. *Teaching About Communism: Guidelines for Junior and Senior High School Teachers.* Indianapolis, Ind.: American Legion, 1962.

8. American Bar Association. *Op. cit.* p. 5.

9. See, for examples, the following: (a) Myer, Alfred G. *What You Should Know About Communism.* Chicago: Science Research Associates, 1953; (b) Schlesinger, Arthur M., Jr. *What About Communism?* New York: Public Affairs Committee, 1950; (c) Williams, Chester W. *Freedom Answers Communism.* New

York: Scholastic Corporation, 1955; (d) Tufts Civic Education Center. *The Isms and You.* Revised edition. New York: Comet Press Books, 1957. Produced in cooperation with the National Council for the Social Studies.

10. See resolution as quoted in the following: Joint Committee of the National Education Association and the American Legion. *Op. cit.* p. 2.

11. Quoted in the following: American Bar Association. *Op. cit.* p. 4.

12. Wilcox, Francis O. "Education for Overseamanship." *NEA Journal* 47: 50; November 1957.

13. National Council for the Social Studies. *Social Education* 22: 1-224; April 1958.

14. American Bar Association. *Op. cit.* p. 5.

15. Joint Committee of the National Education Association and the American Legion. *Op. cit.* p. 3.

16. Hechinger, Fred M. "Calls for Courses on Communism Being Pressed on Public Schools. *New York Times,* September 24, 1961.

17. See the following for a listing of these and similar findings in a survey made by John P. Lunstrum, Indiana University: *Phi Delta Kappan* 43: 190; February 1962.

18. Miller, Richard I. "Teaching About Communism." *Saturday Review* 7:62; March 23, 1963.

19. Major sources drawn upon for this discussion are the following: (a) U.S. Department of Health, Education, and Welfare, Office of Education. *Education for Freedom and World Understanding: A Report of the Conference on the Ideals of American Freedom and the International Dimensions of Education.* Washington, D.C.: Government Printing Office, 1962; (b) Fischer, John H. "Teaching the Nature of Communism." *Social Education* 22: 187-90; April 1958; (c) Armstrong, John A. "The

USSR." *High School Social Studies Perspectives.* Boston: Houghton Mifflin Co., 1962; pp. 299-324; (d) Hartshorn, Merrill F. "Teaching About Communism." *California Social Science Review* 1: 20-21; June 1962; (e) Maryland State Board of Education, Resolution No. 1962–148; (f) McClosky, Herbert. "Political Education and Conflicting Ideologies." *California Social Science Review* 1: 6-7 ff; June 1962; (g) Miller, Richard I. "An Approach to Teaching About Communism in Public Secondary Schools." *Phi Delta Kappan* 43: 189-92; February 1962; (h) New York State Education Department. *Teaching About Communism: A Guide for Social Studies Teachers, Grades 9-12.* Albany: the Department, 1962; (i) Petrovich, Michael B. "Russia and Eastern Europe in Primary and Secondary Education." *The Social Studies and the Social Sciences.* New York: Harcourt, Brace & World, 1962. p. 241-81; (j) Ventura County Schools. *Teaching About Communism: A Resource Guide for Teachers.* Ventura County, Calif.: Board of Education, 1961.

20. See, for example, the treatment provided in the following: Lee, Baldwin. *Capitalism and Other Economic Systems.* Case Economic Literacy Series, No. 2. Washington, D.C.: Council for Advancement of Secondary Education, 1959.

21. Petrovich, Michael B. *Op. cit.*

22. Fischer, John H. *Op. cit.*

CHAPTER SEVEN

1. Cummings, Howard H., and Mackintosh, Helen K. *Curriculum Responsibilities of State Departments of Education.* Washington, D.C.: Government Printing Office, 1958.

2. Dapper, Gloria, and Carter, Barbara. "Is Education News?" *Saturday Review* 45: 84-85ff; March 17, 1962.

3. An exception to this situation is found in the learning materials that have been produced by various independent curriculum

projects. In these projects, most of which are financed by special grants from foundations or federal funds, learning materials have been developed with the explicit intention of changing the curriculum. For descriptions of such projects, see the following: National Education Association, Project on the Instructional Program of the Public Schools. *Current Curriculum Studies in Academic Subjects.*

4. For example, see the following: Dooley, M. Constance. "The Relationship Between Arithmetic Research and the Content of Arithmetic Textbooks, 1900-1957." *Arithmetic Teacher* 7: 178-83; April 1960. Recommendations in yearbooks of the National Society for the Study of Education and the National Council of Teachers of Mathematics were found to be quickly applied.

5. National Education Association, Association for Supervision and Curriculum Development, Commission on Current Curriculum Developments. *Using Current Curriculum Developments.* Washington, D.C.: National Education Association, 1963.

6. Information about the Project on Contemporary Music of the Music Educators National Conference may be obtained from Bernard Fitzgerald, director of the Project, Music Educators National Conference, National Education Association, Washington, D.C.

7. Information about the School Health Education Study may be obtained from Elena M. Sliepcevich, director of the Study, National Education Association, Washington, D.C.

8. Stiles, Lindley J. "Who Speaks for Education?" *Nation's Schools* 67: 65-69; May 1961.

9. Cummings, Howard H., and Mackintosh, Helen K. *Op. cit.* p. 33.

10. See, for example, the following: National Education Association, Department of Audiovisual Instruction. "Year II of NDEA." *Audio-Visual Instruction* 5: 1-64; January 1960.

11. Testimony given before the Subcommittee on Education, House Committee on Education and Labor, June 2, 1961, by Edgar Fuller, executive secretary of the Council of Chief State School Officers. (Mimeo.)

12. Council of Chief State School Officers. *Resolutions and Legislative Policies Adopted by the Council of Chief State School Officers, Annual Business Meeting, Miami Beach, Florida, November 23, 1962.* Washington, D.C.: the Council, 1962. p. 3. (Mimeo.)

13. Cummings, Howard H., and Mackintosh, Helen K. *Op. cit.* pp. 32-33.

14. Stiles, Lindley J. *Op. cit.*

15. *Final Report of the Citizens Advisory Commission, As Submitted to the Joint Interim Committee on Education of the California Legislature,* November 1, 1960. p. 80.

16. See the following: Gardner, John W. "National Goals in Education." *Goals for Americans: The Report of the President's Commission on National Goals.* Englewood Cliffs, N.J.: Prentice-Hall, 1960. p. 98.

APPENDIX C / *Officials of the National Education Association, the National Committee, and Others Involved in This Volume*

NEA OFFICIALS

Robert Wyatt	President*
William G. Carr	Executive Secretary
Lyle W. Ashby	Deputy Executive Secretary
Lawrence G. Derthick	Assistant Executive Secretary for Educational Services

* The NEA presidents in office during the life of the Project were: Hazel A. Blanchard, Ewald Turner, and Clarice Kline.

NATIONAL COMMITTEE

Melvin W. Barnes, *Chairman*
Superintendent of Schools
Portland, Oregon

Thomas G. Pullen, Jr., *Vice-Chairman*
State Superintendent of Schools
Baltimore, Maryland

William M. Alexander
Professor of Education
University of Florida
Gainesville, Florida

Sarah C. Caldwell
Teacher
Kent Junior High School
Akron, Ohio

Hollis L. Caswell
President Emeritus
Teachers College, Columbia University
New York, New York

Joe A. Chandler
Executive Secretary
Washington Education Assn.
Seattle, Washington

Rufus E. Clement
President
Atlanta University
Atlanta, Georgia

Marion Cranmore
Principal
Burns Park School
Ann Arbor, Michigan

Carol Douglass
College of Education
University of South Florida
Tampa, Florida

Robert J. Havighurst
Professor of Education
University of Chicago
Chicago, Illinois

James D. Logsdon
Superintendent
Thornton Township High School and Junior College
Harvey, Illinois

Philip H. Phenix
Professor of Education
Teachers College, Columbia University
New York, New York

I. James Quillen
Dean
School of Education
Stanford University
Stanford, California

G. Baker Thompson
Superintendent of Schools
Delaware County
Media, Pennsylvania

STAFF

Ole Sand, Director

Richard I. Miller, Associate Director

Margery Thompson, Program Specialist

Therese Fleishman, Margaret Overington, and Marjorie Glenton, Staff Assistants

REVIEWING COMMITTEE FOR THIS VOLUME

Mrs. Clifford N. Jenkins
President
National Congress of Parents and Teachers
Chicago, Illinois

Francis Keppel
Dean
Graduate School of Education
Harvard University
Cambridge, Massachusetts

B. Othanel Smith
Professor of Education
University of Illinois
Urbana, Illinois

Randall M. Whaley
Vice-President for Graduate Studies and Research
Wayne State University
Detroit, Michigan

Paul Woodring
Editor
Education Supplement
Saturday Review
New York, New York

OTHERS WHO COMMENTED UPON MANUSCRIPT

Harold H. Abelson
Dean
School of Education
City College, City University of New York
New York, New York

Arno Bellack
Professor of Education
Teachers College, Columbia University
New York, New York

Charles E. Bish
Director
Project on the Academically Talented Student
National Education Association
Washington, D.C.

Edgar Fuller
Executive Secretary
Council of Chief State School Officers
Washington, D.C.

Margaret Gill
Executive Secretary
Association for Supervision and Curriculum Development
National Education Association
Washington, D.C.

Merrill F. Hartshorn
Executive Secretary
National Council for the Social Studies
National Education Association
Washington, D.C.

Albert J. Harris
Professor of Education
Queens College
City University of New York
New York, New York

Dorothy Neubauer
Associate Executive Secretary
Department of Elementary School Principals
National Education Association
Washington, D.C.

Harry N. Rivlin
Dean of Teacher Education
City University of New York
New York, New York

Daniel Schreiber
Director
School Dropouts Project
National Education Association
Washington, D.C.

Ronald O. Smith
Supervisor of Social Studies
Portland Public Schools
Portland, Oregon

PARTICIPANTS IN DISCIPLINES SEMINAR

Ralph W. Tyler, *Chairman*
Director
Center for Advanced Study in the Behavioral Sciences

George B. Carson
Director
Service Center for Teachers
American Historical Association

Stanley Chapple
Director
School of Music
University of Washington

Lee J. Cronbach
Professor of Education Psychology
University of Illinois

David Easton
Professor of Political Science
University of Chicago

Gilbert C. Finlay
Professor of Education
University of Illinois

Alfred B. Garrett
Chairman
Department of Chemistry
Ohio State University

George Gerbner
Institute of Communications Research
University of Illinois

Preston E. James
Chairman
Department of Geography
Syracuse University Graduate School

Albert H. Marckwardt
Acting Director
English Language Institute
University of Michigan

William Riley Parker
Distinguished Service Professor of English
Indiana University

Philip H. Phenix
Professor of Education
Teachers College
Columbia University

G. Baley Price
Executive Secretary
Conference Board of the Mathematical Sciences
American Association for the Advancement of Science

I. James Quillen
Dean
School of Education
Stanford University

B. Othanel Smith
Professor of Education
University of Illinois

Joseph J. Schwab
Professor of Education, and
William Rainey Harper
Professor of Biology
University of Chicago

Lawrence Senesh
Professor of Economic Education
Purdue University

Gresham M. Sykes
Professor of Sociology
Dartmouth College

Frederick J. Whiteman
Associate Dean
The Art School
Pratt Institute

PARTICIPANT-OBSERVERS IN DISCIPLINES SEMINAR

Melvin W. Barnes
Arno A. Bellack
Howard R. Boozer
Sarah C. Caldwell
Philip J. Conley
Marion Cranmore
Howard H. Cummings
George W. Denemark
Dorothy M. Fraser
John I. Goodlad
Paul R. Hanna
William C. Hartshorn
Robert E. Henze
Frederick H. Jackson
J. Boyer Jarvis
Philip Lambert
Rose Lammel
John R. Mayor
Willard C. Olson
Thomas G. Pullen, Jr.
I. James Quillen
Henry W. Riecken
Robert M. Rosenzweig
Boyd C. Shafer
Robert L. Silber
Mortimer Smith
John M. Stephens
Florence Stratemeyer
Fred R. Thompson
Gordon B. Turner
Richard H. Wilson
F. L. Wormald

EXECUTIVE SECRETARIES OF NEA DEPARTMENTS

Department	Executive Secretary
American Association for Health, Physical Education, and Recreation	Carl A. Troester, Jr.
American Association of Colleges for Teacher Education	Edward C. Pomeroy
American Association of School Administrators	Finis E. Engleman
American Association of School Librarians	Dorothy A. McGinniss
American Driver and Safety Education Association	Norman Key (NEA Staff Liaison)
American Educational Research Association	J. Raymond Gerberich
American Industrial Arts Association	Kenneth E. Dawson
Association for Higher Education	G. Kerry Smith
Association for Supervision and Curriculum Development	Margaret Gill
Audiovisual Instruction	Anna L. Hyer
Classroom Teachers	Margaret Stevenson
Council for Exceptional Children	William C. Geer
Elementary-Kindergarten-Nursery Education	Ethel Thompson (NEA Staff Liaison)
Elementary School Principals	Robert W. Eaves
Foreign Languages	Frederick D. Eddy
Home Economics	N. Katherine Schlup (NEA Staff Liaison)
Music Educators National Conference	Vanett Lawler
National Art Education Association	Charles M. Dorn
National Association of Educational Secretaries	Mary Koehler
National Association of Journalism Directors	Lawrence G. Derthick (NEA Headquarters Contact)

Department	Executive Secretary
National Association of Public School Adult Educators	Robert A. Luke
National Association of Secondary-School Principals	Ellsworth Tompkins
National Association of Women Deans and Counselors	Barbara Catton
National Business Education Association	Hollis P. Guy (Executive Director)
National Council for the Social Studies	Merrill F. Hartshorn
National Council of Administrative Women in Education	Lois M. Clark (NEA Staff Liaison)
National Council of Teachers of Mathematics	James D. Gates (Acting Executive Secretary)
National Retired Teachers Association	Newell Walters (NEA Staff Liaison)
National School Public Relations Association	Roy K. Wilson (NEA Staff Liaison)
National Science Teachers Association	Robert H. Carleton
Rural Education	Robert M. Isenberg
Speech Association of America	Lawrence G. Derthick (NEA Headquarters Contact)
Vocational Education	Lawrence G. Derthick (NEA Headquarters Contact)

NEA COMMITTEES, COMMISSIONS, AND DIVISIONS RELATED TO THE PROJECT ON INSTRUCTION

NEA Journal	Mildred S. Fenner Editor
Press, Radio, and Television Relations	Roy K. Wilson Director
Publications	Sidney Dorros Director
Research	Sam M. Lambert Director

Educational Policies Commission	James E. Russell Secretary
Safety Education	Norman Key Executive Secretary
Teacher Education and Professional Standards	Don Davies Executive Secretary
Student NEA	Richard M. Carrigan Director
Future Teachers of America	Wilda Faust Director
Citizenship	Lucile Ellison Secretary
International Relations	Paul E. Smith Secretary

SPECIAL PROJECTS RELATED TO THE PROJECT ON INSTRUCTION

Academically Talented	Charles E. Bish Director
Educational Implications of Automation	Virgil M. Rogers Director
English Composition Laboratory	Arno Jewett Director
School Dropouts	Daniel Schreiber Director
Technological Development	James D. Finn Principal Investigator
Urban Project	Allan M. West Special Assistant to the NEA Executive Secretary

NEA PUBLICATIONS DIVISION PERSONNEL WHO ASSISTED IN PUBLICATION OF THIS VOLUME

Barbara Dickinson	Editor
Robert W. O'Leary	Book Designer

APPENDIX D / *Reports of the NEA Project on Instruction*

MAJOR REPORTS

Schools for the Sixties: A Report of the NEA Project on Instruction. New York: McGraw-Hill Book Co., 1963. 146 pp.

Education in a Changing Society. Washington, D.C.: National Education Association, 1963. 166 pp. $1.75.

Deciding What To Teach. Washington, D.C.: National Education Association, 1963. 264 pp. $2.25.

Planning and Organizing for Teaching. Washington, D.C.: National Education Association, 1963. 190 pp. $2.

AUXILIARY REPORTS

The Scholars Look at the Schools: A Report of the Disciplines Seminar. Washington, D.C.: National Education Association, 1962. 64 pp. $1.50.

The Principals Look at the Schools: A Status Study of Selected Instructional Practices. Washington, D.C.: the Association, 1962. 76 pp. $1.50.

Current Curriculum Studies in Academic Subjects. (Prepared by Dorothy M. Fraser.) Washington, D.C.: National Education Association, 1962. 101 pp. $2.

ARTICLES IN PERIODICALS

Alexander, William M. "Assessing Curriculum Proposals." *Teachers College Record* 63: 286-93; January 1962.

Barnes, Melvin W. "Developments in Instruction." *Educational Leadership* 20: 261-65; January 1963.

Fraser, Dorothy M. "What Content and When?" *National Elementary Principal* 42: 13-19; September 1962.

Goodlad, John I. "Toward Improved School Organization." *Elementary School Organization.* Fortieth Yearbook. Washington, D.C.: Department of Elementary School Principals, National Education Association, 1961. Chapter 4, pp. 60-127.

Hanna, Paul R. "Curriculum and Instruction." *NEA Journal* 52: 52-54; January 1963.

Havighurst, Robert J., and Alexander, William M. "Bases for Curriculum Decisions." *National Elementary Principal* 42: 8-12; September 1962.

Miller, Richard I. "Teaching About Communism in the Public Schools." *Journal of Secondary Education* 38: 198-210; April 1963.

Miller, Richard I. "Curriculum Frontiers in the 60's." *Illinois School Board Journal* 30: 17-18, 21, 25; March-April 1963.

Miller, Richard I. "Teaching About Communism." *Saturday Review* 46: 62-64, 76-78; March 23, 1963.

Miller, Richard I. "Science and Values." *Science Teacher* 29: 5; December 1962.

Miller, Richard I. "Seminar on the Disciplines." *Science Teacher* 28: 31, 32, 35-37; October 1961.

Pullen, Thomas G., and Fraser, Dorothy M. "What To Teach?" *NEA Journal* 51: 34-36; October 1962.

Rehage, Kenneth, and Goodlad, John I. "Unscrambling the Vocabulary of School Organization." *NEA Journal* 51: 34-36; November 1962.

Sand, Ole. "Six Basic Issues in Determining What To Teach." *Chicago Schools Journal* 43: 170-77; January 1962.

Sand, Ole. "The Instructional Program of the Public Schools." *Georgia Education Journal* 55: 8-10; October 1961.

Sand, Ole. "The Profession Speaks: NEA Project on Instruction." *NEA Journal* 50: 53-54; May 1961.

Sand, Ole. "Reports on Some National Studies in Education: The NEA Project on Instruction." *Bulletin of the National Association of Secondary-School Principals* 47: 163-170; April 1963.

Sand, Ole. "Can We Prepare Children for Tomorrow's World?" *Instructor* 71: 6; May 1962.

Sand, Ole. "The Instructional Program of the Public Schools." *Leadership Challenge of the 60's.* Washington, D.C.: National Association of State Teachers Associations, 1961.

Sand, Ole. "Current Trends in Curriculum Planning–Their Implications for Music and the other Arts." *Music Educators Journal* 50: September 1963.

Sand, Ole, and Miller, Richard I. "New Goals in Instruction." *California Teachers Association Journal* 59: 25-28; May 1963.

Sand, Ole, and Miller, Richard I. "Curricular Innovations." *Bulletin of the National Association of Secondary-School Principals* 47: 120-23; May 1963.

Sand, Ole, and Miller, Richard I. "Perspective on National Studies in the Disciplines." *Journal of Secondary Education* 38: 27-33; January 1963.

Tyler, Ralph W., and Miller, Richard I. "Social Forces and Trends." *NEA Journal* 51: 26-28; September 1962.